FIELDS OF PLENTY

FIELDS OF PLENTY

A FARMER'S JOURNEY IN SEARCH OF REAL FOOD
AND THE PEOPLE WHO GROW IT

Text and Photographs by

MICHAEL ABLEMAN

CHRONICLE BOOKS

SAN FRANCISCO

To my father,
for imparting to me the spirit of rural life;
in memory of David Brower,
I will miss his courage and friendship;
and to all those who practice the patient
art of agriculture.

Library of Congress Cataloging-in-Publication Data:
Ableman, Michael.
    Fields of Plenty / by Michael Ableman ;
    photographs by Michael Ableman.
        p. cm.
    ISBN 0-8118-4223-1
    1. Organic farming—United States. 2. Organic
    farming—British Columbia. 3. Farms, Small—United States.
    4. Farms, Small—British Columbia.
    5. Natural foods. 6. Cookery.
    I. title.
    S605.5.A249 2005
    631.5'84'0973—dc22

                        2004030955

Manufactured in Singapore
Design: Gretchen Scoble

Distributed in Canada by
Raincoast Books
9050 Shaughnessy Street
Vancouver, British Columbia V6P 6E5

10 9 8 7 6 5 4 3 2 1

Chronicle Books LLC
85 Second Street
San Francisco, California 94105
www.chroniclebooks.com

Contents

"Let us not forget that the cultivation of the earth is the most important labor of man. When tillage begins, other arts will follow. The farmers, therefore, are the founders of civilization."

❧

—Daniel Webster

CHAPTER I

☾

SPIRIT WRESTLERS

A FARMER'S JOURNEY IS NORMALLY TAKEN IN WINTER, WHEN FIELDS ARE at rest and orchards are bare and dormant. It's strange and awkward to be leaving now, with the year's work yet to be harvested. The rows of melons, beans, squash, and potatoes—so tidy when they were planted last spring—have merged and melded in a riot of pregnant vines and plants. Strawberry plants with leaves as large as dinner platters yield their first plump, crimson fruits. Rows of sweet-pea flowers burst with color, dominating the last of the spring vegetables that surround them; asparagus, spinach, radish, carrots, and beets are now overwhelmed by heirloom tomatoes, sweet peppers, Charentais melons, and fresh shelling beans just days away from harvest.

I walk the fields and orchards, saying goodbye, making last-minute notes of jobs that need to be done, details forgotten. I used to think it was the big ideas and grand plans that mattered. Now, I see it's all about the small things—and there are a lot of them.

Leaving in winter was always easy. The farm was battened down, the fields and orchards mulched and moist with winter rain, the market closed. I always returned before buds swelled and fields dried and warmed for planting. I could tell myself I wouldn't miss anything, because winter—while necessary—is simple. Summer is a different story. Summer is the culmination, the time when the entire year's work is manifested.

This year, for the first time in twenty years, I will see summer come to other people's land. I have set my heart on a pilgrimage—part personal, part political—to see my fellow farmers. In winter, we can only talk, about philosophies, techniques, risks, and accomplishments. In summer, the land will speak for itself. Fields everywhere will be full of food and farmers will be harvesting the accumulation of their ideas and experiences. Last winter, when I got the calling, it seemed like a good plan. Now, as my departure looms, I am not so sure.

My small farm on Salt Spring Island, in British Columbia, is blessed with a northern Mediterranean climate supported by the protection of Vancouver Island to the west and the mainland to the east. Salt Spring farmers take advantage of this phenomenon by producing a surprising array of fruits, vegetables, meats, and dairy products, a level of diversity one might expect to see in California or Italy. But with our blessings come responsibility and a dangerous temptation to plant with abandon in spring, setting in motion a busy and demanding summer. As I look around, I can see what I dare not say, that this summer will yield an abundant harvest of hard work for those I'm leaving behind.

We've had endless meetings to discuss planting and harvest schedules, compost, irrigation, and marketing. Now, as I hold the last meeting, I have an almost out-of-body experience, watching myself futilely trying to button down the unpredictable season into a to-do list. My farm helper, Anthony, looks at me earnestly and takes notes and reassures me that all will be well. My wife, Jeanne Marie, is counting on divine intervention to help her keep things going while tending our two-year-old son, Benjamin. I have faith in all of them, of course, and the kind of naive oblivion that all explorers must maintain as they turn their backs on home and sail away.

♣

IT'S 5:00 A.M., AND I'M PUTTING THE LAST ITEMS ON THE TRAILER FOR the short trip to the Ganges farmers' market, the last one I will do this season. Filet beans, salad greens, strawberries and raspberries, four types of basil and striped German tomatoes, Costata Romanesco zucchini and yellow crookneck squash share the load with 3-foot stems of leek flowers and squash blossoms and bags and tables and awnings and piles of burlap. The early morning trip to market is beautiful. There is a light mist hanging over Saint Mary's Lake; the fields along its edges are dotted with bales of field hay neatly lined up in checker formation. An easy breeze is blowing, and the first rays of sun set a small flock of black-faced sheep aglow. As I crest the hill above the village of Ganges, the harbor comes into view, dotted with sailboats and framed by Goat and Deadman and the Three Sisters Islands. The boats bring tourists and shoppers from nearby islands, from the mainland, and from across the border in the United States. Each Saturday we gauge the day's market by how many boats are tied up in the small marina.

I look forward to market day. It's the one time each week when I can visit with my fellow farmers, compare notes on how the season is progressing, share gossip and ideas, and have brief exchanges with visitors and other islanders while offering samples and weighing and bagging and making change.

As always when I arrive, Kerry is already set up, with jars of jams and pickles in rows on her table. Julia and Susan have carefully placed the photographs of Blossom, Solace, and Emma, their favorite Jersey cows, behind the samples of Baby Blue, Savory Moon, and White Grace cheeses. Ron and Margareta check their cooler stocked full of smoked tuna and salmon. Charlie arrives with hundreds of braids of Portuguese, Chinese, and Korean garlic; Heather, with her wood-fired olive, potato, and rosemary breads; Rosalie, with fresh-cut lilies, delphiniums, and dahlias; Raj, with herbs and plants; and David, with goat and sheep cheeses. We greet each other, check out products and displays, discuss pricing and the weather, and speculate on how the day will go.

I'm hesitant to tell my fellow farmers that soon my eldest son, Aaron, and I will do the unthinkable: leave at the peak of the summer season for a three-month journey. As the customers press in, we all turn to the job at hand, answering questions, making change, weighing up our wares, and handing them over to be carried away with a cheery wave and a "See you next week."

After we return from the market, I watch Aaron, now 23, carry little Benjamin through the farm, sampling strawberries and cherry tomatoes and parsley and radishes. My sons come to me, juice dripping down their chins, proud and happy with the best of the day's catch in their hands: the remains of a Santa Rosa plum half eaten by the little one, a ragged piece of reddish yellow flesh hanging from a pit, the first plum of the season presented to me as a sticky gift, just as I am carefully squeezing the last supplies into the Volkswagen van in preparation for our journey.

Aaron runs back to the house for a few last-minute items: a trumpet; a banana box full of hardcover books; several huge, blank canvases; and a box of oil paints. I look at him with disbelief, trying to picture where I'll put them and wondering whether he really understands how long we'll be sharing this tiny space.

This is our first trip together in years. When he was younger, I dragged him on every major adventure I could think of. But after some testy wilderness experiences—biking over mountain passes, kayaking for five days in the freezing rain, and almost drowning and running out of food—Aaron started hesitating before accepting my invitations. Now, as we look into the interior of our 6-by-14-foot combination bedroom/office/kitchen/car, I sense that we both are having second thoughts. As we say our final goodbyes to Jeanne Marie and Benjamin, I am wondering what the hell we're doing, leaving our comfortable world on an uncertain journey in search of something I don't quite understand myself.

❧

MY LAST VOLKSWAGEN VAN DIED IN THE EARLY EIGHTIES OF HEAT exhaustion on a steep mountain road in California. I swore I'd never have another one, having grown tired of replacing air-cooled engines like they were AA batteries and wanting more protection than a tin-can shell. But there is no home on the road quite like them, and so here I am at almost fifty, setting out in a 1989 Volkswagen packed with provisions and notebooks, cameras and film, and a wooden fife and a couple of blues harmonicas. The young man who sold it to me had his whole family present when I went to pick it up. Aunts and uncles and parents stood by like I had come for their daughter, checking me out, making sure that I was worthy.

As we turn right onto Vesuvius Bay Road, the worries start to recede, and I begin to seriously think about the odyssey ahead. I am scheduled to see twenty-five farmers spread out from British Columbia to New Mexico to Maine. They've all consented to host me at their busiest time of year, and though none have asked, they must all assume I am not really a farmer, but some kind of photographer/journalist pretender. They know as well as I do that nobody whose livelihood depends on farming would be on the road in summer.

A few have asked why I chose them, some suspiciously, others incredulously. Most farmers are not used to being photographed or interviewed. I never liked it myself, since the reporter usually got something wrong, and I always felt the urge to tell the irritated photographers how best to capture my land, grumbling when they went for dewdrops on the fence posts when they should have been noticing the manly sweep of my cornfield or the perfect rows of romaine and red leaf running between the peach trees.

As I think about the list of farmers I've assembled, I have to marvel myself at how it came together. A couple of them are well-known in foodie circles, even in the national press, but most I chose out of my own gut curiosity. I want to see and taste the products of those who are happily married to a place, growers who know instinctively, from trial and error and from careful observation, the precise moment to harvest, which soils grow the most flavorful melons or the best grain, how to ensure peak plant and animal health, which varieties are the most beautiful and flavorful, and what techniques enhance those qualities.

I want to see vegetable farmers, orchardists, dairy farmers and cheese makers, grain growers, and those who raise and butcher animals. I want to reassure myself that abundance is enhanced, not sacrificed, by humane and sustainable practices. I also want to know how my own skills stack up to other small farmers and to learn from them what I can. I want to know whether other farmers' lives are as complicated as my own, whether they think about quitting, what their best moments are. Do they feel marginalized from a world of corporate consensus, or freed from convention, or both? I have always wondered why I keep farming despite all the uncertainties. Have other people figured out a better way?

When I started traveling in the 1980s, the organic farming I practiced was only just beginning to revive in this country. If I wanted to see my peers, I thought, I had to go far from home. For ten winters, during breaks from farming, I traveled to document what traditional farmers were doing in Asia and Africa, in South America and Europe. I wanted to know how the same fields could be farmed over and over for centuries and still remain fertile and productive, and I wanted to see the remnants of a community-based agriculture that was beginning to unravel under the pressures of globalization. I'm glad I sneaked into rural China, and hoed and drank whiskey alongside Peruvian farmers, but in truth, though we shared a bond of farming that was fundamental and powerful, their culture and way of life were comfortably different from my own, the lessons abstract.

At the time in North America, traditional agriculture was all but gone, agrarian life reduced to a faceless industrial exercise. Farming had become a lowly form of drudgery, soils were depleted, waters were polluted, and the rural landscape was sliding into social, cultural, and economic decline. For many people, food itself seemed to be little more than an inconvenient necessity, something to be prepared and consumed as quickly as possible.

The farm I was running in California—where Aaron grew up—was something of a curiosity, its 12 acres packed with hundreds of varieties of fruits and vegetables gradually becoming surrounded by suburban housing developments. This change was both a threat and an opportunity as our neighbors struggled to understand the unfamiliar presence of a small farm and discovered its benefits. Over time I started finding kids in the orchard and the strawberry patch, and our neighbors started to walk the short distance to our produce stand rather than drive to the nearby super-market. We held farm events and workshops, and raised our community profile, even as the last open fields in the neighborhood became houses and Fairview Gardens became an island in suburbia.

By 1995 Fairview Gardens was employing more than twenty-five people and providing food and education to thousands every year. It was drawing national attention as a successful economic and community model of local organic-food production. At the same time, Fairview's longtime owner (and chief beekeeper), Cornelia Chapman, was starting to consider passing it on to her heirs. I knew the temptation to sell valuable acreage would be powerful. But I also knew that Fairview had earned its place in a culture that was seeing an explosion of farmers' markets, school food gardens, and chef/farmer collaborations. An intense community-wide effort produced an unusual solution: Fairview Gardens became the Center for Urban Agriculture, a nonprofit trust that would ensure the land's agricultural future.

In the process I had become more administrator than farmer, and Fairview had attracted talented people who could steward it in ways that I no longer could. I needed a change; Jeanne Marie and I wanted to try owning our own place and farming within a smaller community. I wanted to get back to what I knew best: putting my hands back to work in fields and orchards.

We chose our place on Salt Spring Island for its rich bottomland soils, east-west exposure, and early warm springs, and set about remaking it as a diverse market garden and orchard. I still did speaking engagements and participated as founder and executive director of the Center for Urban Agriculture. But gradually I became more and more absorbed by the particular needs of our local community and of the little ecosystem I was building, even as "Organic," with a capital O, began to thrive in the media and in the halls of civilization and government.

Now, as I set out on the road again, my questions are broader. How do we make sure that pure food is available to all, not just those who can afford it? How can we grow food without depending on vast amounts of energy and foreign oil? How can we reduce the distance food travels from the field to the plate? What scale is appropriate for our farms, and how do we grow with less water and fewer outside inputs? How can we protect and enhance biodiversity and the natural environment within and around our farms? How do we attract young people to our profession?

This journey will take me to see those who are trying to answer these questions, not in some philosophical vacuum, but in ways that are real and practical and visible. Are they making a difference? I don't know, but I'm eager to find out.

⚘

IT HAS JUST STARTED GETTING DARK WHEN I STEER THE VAN OFF THE last ferry from Long Harbor to the British Columbia mainland. We're headed to the interior and our first stop—the home and fruit farm of George and Anna Zebroff and their family. The two-lane road runs past the dairy farms of the Fraser Valley and winds along the Fraser River to the little town of Hope, where it begins to climb up and over the Cascade Mountains.

Like many of Canada's western provinces, British Columbia was founded on extraction; logging and fishing and mining have been the traditional economic mainstays. The majestic mountains and conifer forests, the spectacular islands and rivers, are never very far from clear-cuts and strip mines and pulp mills and overfished waters. But these industries have been struggling: U.S. lumber tariffs, depleted fish populations, and fewer significant mining reserves are forcing some in the province to rethink its direction. More than in any other place in North America, small farms are popping up here at a staggering rate, their scale informed by a geography that does not allow for the vast flat fields and orchards that are more common to the south.

We spend the night in a provincial campground along the Similkameen River. We go to bed with the whoosh of late-night trucks, rhythmic blasts of wind filtered through the giant fir trees separating us from the road.

The next morning, cool and lush changes to hot and dry as we descend into the mouth of the Okanagan Valley. In 1980, Aaron's mother, Donna, and I worked in an organic orchard just across the border from here in Malott, Washington. We had just come out of several years in an agrarian commune in Southern California and arrived penniless and desperate for work. The small orchard that employed us hired me as field foreman for the apple harvest and Donna as a picker. My job was to "swamp" (move) bins for the crew of hippie and Mexican pickers. At night we camped along the Okanagan River, bathing in water I later found out was a toxic soup fed from the runoff of hundreds of commercial fruit farms. We slept among the apple trees directly across from a native burial ground. Many evenings we would go to sleep to the sound of drumming and chanting.

The Similkameen Valley, which Aaron and I are now entering, acts as the western doorway to the Okanagan. The valley is carpeted with fruit trees, apples and cherries and peaches and apricots. As the only "desert" region in Canada, the area has an ideal climate: stone fruit loves the cool nights and hot, dry days. There is a direct relationship between British thermal units and sugar content, the dry weather prevents disease, and the cool nights accent the color of the fruit.

The road into the little town of Keremeos, at the mouth of the valley, is lined with fruit stands. Each establishment proudly advertises its wares with a particular angle: signs read "Organically grown" or "Native grown," one display is staged with antique tractors, another is part of a small café. We continue out of town and up toward the bench road that winds above the valley. The Zebroff orchard is the last on the road, perched on the side of a hill with views over miles of orchards into the mountains of the Okanagan range and the United States beyond.

I have always been fascinated by the dramatic changes in climate that can exist within short distances. At Fairview Gardens, in Southern California, the temperature could be ten degrees different between the main farm, closer to the coast, and our avocado orchard, located five minutes up the canyon. On Salt Spring Island, crops ripen weeks earlier on one side of the tiny island than on the other. Here, at the Zebroffs' farm, the microclimate is pronounced, influenced by a sage-covered hill that towers behind the land and acts like a massive solar bank, absorbing heat throughout the day and releasing it at night.

There are no signs to indicate the names of the farms here, no clearly defined separations between orchards, but it is easy to see the contrasts in philosophy and practices of each of the owners manifested by the weeds and grass under the trees, the style of pruning, the diversity of varieties and species. Piles of manure and an old dump truck sit on the road in front of the Zebroffs' place. The day is hot, and when we arrive the sky is dark and red from a forest fire just over the border in Washington state.

Anna Zebroff greets us on the porch of their farmhouse, a converted shed, and apologizes for her hands, which are covered with flour and dough. I show her my own hands, still stained with island soils, and tell her never to apologize for dirty hands. I have a bad habit of judging people by their hands. I am reassured when someone offers me a rough, callous mitt.

People come to this way of life in all kinds of ways. The Zebroffs came to this dry hillside above the Similkameen Valley by way of the writing of Rachel Carson and the siren song of the apricot. George Zebroff remembers the day in 1973 when they first visited their land. "The real-estate guy was hesitant when he saw us in this old jeep with our two babies, so he pointed to this place and said, 'Go take a look out there.' It was a balmy spring evening, the apricot blossoms were in full bloom, and it was utterly enticing and seductive. We had knowledge of the apricot as an important staple of the Hunza region of Pakistan and the people of the Caucasus— so-called primitive cultures that had tremendous longevity. I had the notion, a peasant ideology, that we were going to manipulate this piece of earth to feed my family and then sell the surplus."

But the primary driving force for establishing a farm was children and family. "Having your family is the greatest measure of sustainability," George says. "There's nothing more pleasurable than digging spuds with a guy who's now bigger than you, who happened to be your child.

"Have you ever seen two grown men sorting small dry cherries?" George asks, pointing to two of his sons towering over drying racks filled with tiny fruit. They have just finished working out, and the muscles on their 6-foot bodies are pumped up and defined as they pick out the delicate cherries one at a time.

Three generations of Zebroffs live on the farm. All the kids went off to college and to travel. All continue to return and help out. The eldest son, Yuri, earned a degree in agriculture, married his childhood sweetheart, and came back to help run the farm.

I think of Aaron and wonder whether he will keep returning as he does to help out in the summers. I consider the reality of most farms across North America, where the children have watched their parents' hard work and struggle, and escaped as soon as possible. Most urban parents encourage their kids to leave the nest, but it seems to me that pushing them out on their own is a modern concept born of a society that no longer works the land and no longer sees the value that comes from keeping multiple generations together.

George grew up in a Doukhobor community near Grand Forks, British Columbia. The Doukhobors were vegetarian pacifists who came to western Canada at the turn of the twentieth century to escape persecution in Russia. They were often referred to as "spirit wrestlers"—a fitting description for a people who were committed to living a spiritual life in very practical ways within a broader culture that was heading the other direction.

I remember visiting the remnants of Doukhobor communal farms as a young man. The clusters of well-constructed wooden buildings appeared like ghost towns through the Kootenay region of British Columbia. I, too, was living in a commune at the time, and seeing those abandoned villages reminded me that no matter how noble or idealistic our efforts are, they likely will end up the same: as relics of

history. Few Doukhobors continue to maintain a connection to the land and to the kind of intentional, simple living emblematic of their history and their life in community. The Zebroffs are an exception.

"Our Doukhobor ancestors were so dedicated to a higher principle," George says, "that they were willing to give their lives for it. It behooves us to strive to do the same." In the 1890s, Doukhobor conscripts went AWOL from the Russian army and publicly burned large caches of guns. Both of George's grandfathers were beaten and exiled to Siberia and the Caucasus for their pacifist beliefs.

Anna and George met in the crowded Prague railway station in 1970. Anna had just missed her train and was sitting with two older people George assumed were her parents. He was so attracted to her that he approached them and introduced himself, in Russian. This was not too long after the Soviet invasion of Czechoslovakia, and the Russian language was not particularly well loved. The older couple sitting with Anna immediately got up and left, but Anna stayed seated, impressed by this man's bold approach. George and Anna married, lived in England for a time, and eventually settled in the Similkameen Valley, where in time they became known to the locals as "the Russian organic hippies on the hill."

"When we were growing up, we spoke a different language and ate sandwiches made on dark bread," George's son Yuri tells me. "We kind of fit in, but we were always a little different—different language, different culture, but, most pronounced, different thinking."

The usual thinking in the area tended toward chemical farming, so the Zebroffs ran their blower spray rig through the orchard filled only with water, rather than pesticides, to show their neighbors that they were just like them. Now the sprayer sits in the orchard, rusting and settling into the ground. While an arsenal of biological and botanical sprays are available to the new organic farmer, the Zebroffs no longer spray anything. This is a great accomplishment for tree-fruit growers, who conventionally do battle with a host of pests and diseases that prey on their perennial crops.

Sustainable agriculture is usually discussed in terms of the well-being of the land or the quality of the food, but seldom in terms of the sustainability and well-being of those doing the work. On the Zebroff farm, there is an ease to the way the work takes place. No one is giving orders or instructions; everyone seems to be gliding through the various jobs in a relaxed, joyful way. It feels so different from the typical level of high-pitched activity and stress so common on many soft-fruit farms at harvest's peak, when the entire year's work is concentrated into a few weeks and farmers are faced with the pressure of selling highly perishable products. To make your living as a fruit farmer is to embrace a precarious livelihood dependent on biological and climatic forces beyond one's control.

"People often talk about the importance of freedom," Anna says, "but very few actually get to experience it the way that we do." There is a palpable feeling of independence here—from typical organic dogma, from the institutional and industrial mind-set of food and farming, and from consumption and materialism.

The cherry harvest has just finished; the last of it is spread out on drying racks or set aside in containers and bags. The Zebroffs grow seven varieties: Van, Bing, Lambert, Sam, Royal Anne, Black Tartarian, and Stella. Moorpark and a few Tilton apricots are heaped in metal buckets on the loading dock, ready for fresh packing or processing. The Blenheim apricots, one of my favorite fruit varieties of all, haven't ripened yet, nor have the Goldrich, Goldbar, or Skaha.

Like most farm kids, George seems to always have a piece of fruit in his mouth. When I ask him about his favorites, he mumbles, "The one I'm eating." He reminds me that, obvious as it might sound, the important thing is to pick ripe. Not the kind of ripe that most folks have come to expect, a little color and hard enough to ship, not even the ripe you might find at a farmers' market, and often not the ripe that is advertised as such. A farmer's idea of ripe is standing in the orchard under the tree, reaching up and grasping one that calls to you, with color that is deep and complete and has no memory of green. A farmer's ripe has a fragrance that seizes you, the fruit gives a little when you touch it and releases itself easily to your hand. It's one of the special rewards of hard work done well, a private and intimate event, reverently received in the quiet of a moment on land that is well loved and nurtured.

There will be no ripe-peach experience for us on this trip. It's too early. The Red Haven, the Glohaven, the old classics Elberta and Hale, the Globe, and the Cresthaven peaches are still green and just beginning to show the first red blush.

Having grown peaches commercially on the coast of California in a less-than-ideal climate, I have a great appreciation for fruit grown in hot interior valleys. We were always limited by lack of chill in the winter and heat in the summer, making it difficult to develop sugars and color properly. Here the conditions are perfect; the climate and water and soils come together to give the fruit its own identity.

It is strange to be standing in the Zebroffs' orchard after two years of enjoying cherries, apricots, and peaches hauled from their farm over the mountains to our coast by young people who resell it by the case. While the fruit has always been delicious, my relationship with it has been distant, like getting to know someone only from a voice on the telephone. Visiting the Zebroffs after years of eating their fruit clarifies without any doubt how people and their place so distinctly inform the food they grow.

There is a kind of healthy chaos on this farm; everything seems to get done, but nothing appears terribly well-organized. The farm activity never seems to stop, but, instead, blends and melds with time spent hanging out or in conversations. Hundreds of chickens and geese and turkeys free range under the trees and in and around stored ladders and rusty equipment. A large tom turkey who has anointed himself king of the flock charges my legs every time I turn my back. Younger fruit trees are interplanted among fifty-year-old Van cherry and Moorpark apricot trees, trunks twisted and knotted with age, demanding respect with branches that spread as much as 30 feet. The understory of the orchard is alive, as mixed grasses, burdock, mallow, and clovers provide pasture for poultry and habitat for beneficial insects.

I struggle a bit in my head with what I perceive as disorder. I like having my farm organized but probably spend too much energy swinging back and forth between chaos and cleanup. Here the physical world is not fussed over. Typical divisions of work and life and the separation of farm animals and humans seem somewhat ignored in a wonderful intermingling of fruit, animals, humans, and machinery, all held in marginal check by a loose network of fences.

George tells me he doesn't want to be part of what he calls the "empire of waste." Everything is used and recycled. Apricots are sold and eaten fresh, number twos made into jam or dried or frozen, the kernels eaten and packaged as medicine. Even the roads in front of the main packing shed are paved with cherry pits from the pitting machine.

George takes two visiting children and me into the little barn where he does his milking. A handmade cedar-bark canoe hangs incongruously from the rafters of the barn. George hugs Dobra, his Jersey cow, tells me how much he loves her, and without any stanchion or holding device squats down to milk her. He stops to visit with his milk goat, Minda, and tells me that she's his "fountain of youth." I discover why later.

The fundamental Doukhobor principle of nonviolence is still exhibited in the way the land is treated and in how food is coaxed from it without the incredible harm so often done to agricultural land. So much industrial agriculture has violence at its heart; the cutting of forests, the draining of wetlands, the massive machines ripping ground open, the fumigants and soil sterilants, the fertilizers and fungicides and herbicides and pesticides, the arrogant manipulation of genes, the treatment of animals and the loss of biodiversity. "It's pretty hard to wrestle with feeding ourselves while still respecting all creatures," George tells me, "but wrestle one should."

Viewed from a broader ecological time frame, most farming ecosystems are very immature, held down by constant disruption; the tilling and mowing, and constant emphasis of the domesticated over the wild. The Zebroffs' farm is also an imposed ecosystem, but there seems to be a semblance of ecological stability and self-sufficiency, requiring less human interference and input to thrive and produce. This idea of a steady state, where soil fertility is self-sustaining and the farm is viewed as a living organism, replenishing its fertility with its own waste, is the ideal for many of us who are trying to shift the agriculture paradigm.

I try to buy some fruit from George, but it's difficult to get him to come up with a price. It's not that he doesn't put value on the labor and the foods he and his family produce, but he seems uncomfortable every time dollars come into the equation. He is much more interested in taking measure in other ways. Although the farm supports the family and on some level acts like a business, you would be hard-pressed to get George or Anna to use the word business to describe what they do. For them it is a way of life, made available to others through the food they produce and through a level of old-world hospitality that seems to extend to every passerby.

Without anyone's asking, boxes of apricots, greengage and crabapple and mulberry jams, baskets of cherries, and a free-range chicken are all mysteriously piled into our van. A young man who has been visiting with his wife and two children comes running up to our vehicle with a case of apple juice. "George said to tell you that if you can't drink all of this to bathe in it," he says breathlessly.

As we are preparing to leave, George pulls me aside. "You have eaten our apricots fresh and dried, you drank our apricot nectar and even tried the kernels, but there is one thing left." There is a slightly mischievous tone in his voice as he guides me to the front of the house. There, on the stump of a cherry tree now used as a table, are a bucket of fresh goat's milk; a container of amber honey; and a tall, slender glass bottle filled with a clear liquid. This, he tells me, is apricot elixir.

There is ritual to all of this. In Russian he asks his young grandson to demonstrate. With a spoonful of honey in one hand and a glass of warm milk in the other, the young boy alternates back and forth. Then comes the elixir. George mixes it with goat's milk, and we toast. It is a powerful drink, but it goes down easy. He pours another, and we drink again. I protest when he offers me a shot without the milk. It is hot, we have a long drive, and I haven't had much to eat. He insists, and we drink again. Grapevines and cherry and apricot and apple and plum trees swirl beneath us in a carpet of green, grandchildren roll and giggle in a nearby hammock, piles of multicolored potatoes and greens and meats are being prepared for Sunday dinner, and I am back as a child with my own Russian-descended grandparents, sitting at their table, drinking and eating and sharing.

♣

Apricot Cobbler with Cornmeal Biscuits

SERVES 8

Although apricots will grow in many regions, George and Anna Zebroff picked the perfect place to grow one of their favorite fruits: a dry climate with plenty of heat during ripening. It's surprisingly difficult to find really good apricots; the best 'cots are grown with little, if any, water, so ask your grower whether he or she irrigates the trees, and, if so, how close to harvest.

My favorite variety of all time is one that George and Anna produce and that we grow at Fairview Gardens: Royal Blenheim. It's an old variety, and it often matures small and not so perfect-looking, but the flavor is as rich as that of any you'll find.

This is a charming, old-fashioned dessert—the kind your grandmother made (or should have made). The buttery yellow cornmeal biscuits give the cobbler a rough, craggy top, and the fruit juices spill over the sides. The cornmeal gives the biscuits a little extra crunch, and goes well with the tart apricots.

2½ pounds apricots, halved, pitted, and cut into ½-inch-thick wedges

¾ cup plus 2 tablespoons sugar

CORNMEAL BISCUITS

1½ cups all-purpose flour

½ cup cornmeal

3 tablespoons sugar, plus 2 to 3 tablespoons for sprinkling

1 tablespoon baking powder

½ teaspoon baking soda

1 teaspoon kosher salt

¼ cup cold unsalted butter, cut into ½-inch pieces, plus 2 tablespoons, melted

1½ cups heavy cream

Heavy cream or vanilla ice cream for serving (optional)

Preheat the oven to 425 degrees F.

Put the apricots and sugar in a large bowl and toss well to combine. Transfer to a 10-inch deep-dish pie pan. Place the pie pan on a baking sheet lined with aluminum foil and bake until the fruit begins to bubble, 25 to 30 minutes.

MEANWHILE, MAKE THE BISCUITS: Combine the flour, cornmeal, 3 tablespoons sugar, baking powder, baking soda, and salt in a large bowl. Add the cold butter pieces. Using your hands, toss the butter around to coat each piece with the flour mixture—this helps the butter to cut in evenly. Using a pastry cutter or 2 knives, cut the butter into the flour mixture until there are no large lumps and the mixture is the texture of coarse oatmeal. Make a well in the center of the dough and add the cream. Stir, gradually pulling in the dry ingredients from the sides of the bowl, to make a soft, moist dough.

When the fruit begins to bubble, remove the pie pan from the oven and spoon biscuit-size mounds of the dough on top—don't worry if the fruit is covered unevenly. Brush the dough with the melted butter and sprinkle to taste with the 2 to 3 tablespoons sugar. Return the cobbler to the baking sheet in the oven and bake until the biscuits are golden brown, 12 to 14 minutes. Transfer to a wire rack and let cool for about 15 minutes. Serve warm or at room temperature, in a puddle of heavy cream or with a scoop of vanilla ice cream, if desired.

Roasted Apricots

This is a great way to serve apricots in a savory—as opposed to sweet—way. They're delicious with grilled bread and a soft, runny cheese.

SERVES 4 TO 6

1 pound apricots, halved, pitted, and cut into ½-inch-thick wedges
¼ teaspoon kosher salt
Freshly cracked black pepper to taste
1 tablespoon sugar
1 tablespoon olive oil
Toasted baguette slices and soft cheese such as Brie for serving

Position a rack in the upper third of the oven and preheat to 450 degrees F.

Place the apricots, skin side down, in a shallow baking dish large enough to accommodate the fruit in a single layer without overlapping. Season the apricots with the salt and a few twists of pepper. Sprinkle the sugar on top and drizzle with the olive oil. Roast until the apricots are tender when pierced with a small, sharp knife, 15 to 20 minutes. Adjust the oven to broil, and broil just until the apricots are nicely browned with a few charred tips, about 2 minutes. Serve warm or at room temperature with the toasts and soft cheese.

Brandied Cherries

MAKES 2 PINTS

George Zebroff blew away my longtime stereotype image of cherry growers as either having nerves of steel or being totally crazy. One of the earliest of spring deciduous fruit crops, cherrys are susceptible to all kinds of mishaps from rain and bird damage to blossom freeze. Any cherry lover has probably wondered why there is so much fluctuation in availability and price from year to year.

This simple recipe extends the normally too short cherry season. Brandied cherries keep for several months, so this is a great recipe when there is the rare surplus. Dark red cherries are the best choice—the lighter varieties don't keep as well and look a little anemic. The cherries can also be pitted, but unpitted cherries with the stems on have the best flavor.

You can fold the cherries with a splash of their syrup into vanilla ice cream or serve them with panna cotta or biscotti. They're also good roasted in a hot oven and served with fowl—especially duck.

1 pound crisp, dark, organic sweet cherries such as Bing

2 cups good-quality, inexpensive brandy

¾ cup sugar

3 tablespoons water

Trim the cherry stems with kitchen scissors—you can clip the stems short or just trim the very ends. Rinse the cherries in cold water and let dry on paper towels. Combine the brandy, sugar, and 3 tablespoons water in a small bowl and stir to dissolve. Gently pack the cherries into 2 sterilized pint-size jars with tight-fitting lids. Pour the brandy mixture over the cherries to cover. (Remove a cherry or two if the fruit is not completely submerged in the liquid.) Seal the jars and store in a cool, dark place for 3 weeks to allow the cherry and brandy flavors to mingle, then refrigerate. The cherries will keep for several months in the refrigerator.

Cherry Compote with Balsamic Vinegar

This is simple to make and delicious with vanilla ice cream or panna cotta. The balsamic adds a little kick and balances the cherries nicely.

SERVES 4 TO 6

1 pound crisp, dark, organic sweet cherries such as Bing, pitted and halved

¼ cup sugar

½ cup water

1 teaspoon kirsch

Pinch of kosher salt

1 to 2 teaspoons rich, high quality balsamic vinegar

Vanilla ice cream or Panna Cotta (page 184) for serving

Combine the cherries, sugar, water, kirsch, and salt in a heavy-bottomed, medium saucepan. Cook the mixture over medium-high heat until the sugar dissolves and the liquid thickens slightly, about 4 minutes. Remove from the heat and add the vinegar to taste.

Serve the cherries warm or chilled over vanilla ice cream; or chill and serve with Panna Cotta.

CHAPTER 2

☾

MILITANCE

WE'VE BEEN ON THE ROAD FOR ABOUT TWENTY-FOUR HOURS, BUT IT feels like several weeks. It's hot, and the world outside our island feels angry and crowded. I miss Jeanne Marie and Benjamin and the farm, and I can't stop wondering what the hell I'm doing on a long journey in the middle of the summer with my fields full of food.

The 150 miles from Bellingham, Washington, to Olympia is a continuous ribbon of bumper-to-bumper cars and trucks. We've got the windows cranked wide open, and the air blowing in is anything but fresh. The exhaust system on the van has self-destructed, and it sounds like we're driving an eighteen-wheeler with the Jake Brake going all the time. We're a day off schedule already, and I'm feeling pretty cranky.

We're holding out, stomachs rumbling, for Portland, Oregon, and Higgins's restaurant. I'm torturing myself with images of the peak-season Oregon tomatoes, local berries, and regional cheeses and fish that we'll surely find on Higgins's menu.

I can tell a lot about a restaurant's principles and philosophy (if it has any) by reading its menu. When I find a restaurant that tells me where the ingredients come from and whose land and labor are behind them, if I can tell how far things have traveled from the field to the plate, I know I am being served by people who understand that the best food begins on a good farm. Settling into the booth at Higgins's and reading the menu filled with farmers' names, I feel a sense of anticipation. The wild salmon is troll-caught Oregon Chinook, and the heirloom tomatoes ripened just down the road in Canby, at Sheldon and Carol's place. The potatoes are Gene Thiel's, pulled from silt soils on the banks of Wallowa Lake, near Joseph, Oregon. Though I love knowing the history and source of every ingredient, I have a self-imposed code that usually prevents me from ordering anything that needs more than a three-word description. I make an exception and decide on risotto with Oregon chanterelles, sweet corn, peppers, and citrus-onion vinaigrette. Aaron orders fettuccini with grilled summer vegetables, local feta, and a basil-walnut pesto.

In this former go-go dance club turned restaurant, Greg Higgins and crew cure and smoke their own meats, make jams and pickles, and prepare lunch and dinner seven days a week, all out of a kitchen the size of a single-wide mobile home. Greg tells me the only time no one is working in the kitchen is between 1 and 4 A.M. When I mention that we are headed out to Anthony Boutard's farm, his face lights up. He says the first time he opened a box of Boutard's melons, they were still warm from the sun and the fragrance bowled him over. As if summoned by the memory, one of the chefs comes out of the tiny kitchen and over to our table, bearing a package of the house prosciutto.

"I hear you're going to Anthony and Carol Boutard's place," he says as he offers us the meticulously wrapped package. "Would you bring this to them?" Then, as if I need any encouragement, he turns toward us, wagging his finger, and adds, "You must try Boutard's melons. They are the best."

It's only 29 miles from downtown Portland to the Boutard farm, but it takes us close to an hour and a half along the winding road that dumps abruptly from a wooded trail into the Wapato Valley. I am directionally impaired, and the van speaks only in kilometers (all our directions are in miles), so trying to find anything at night is a real challenge. It doesn't help that I'm exhausted from driving all day and the only light for miles around seems to be the one inside the van.

Eventually we stumble onto the farm, move our way cautiously up the drive, and find Anthony waiting with flashlight in hand to guide us to a camping spot among a grove of giant Gary oaks.

The next morning, while Aaron sleeps in, Anthony picks me up at dawn on his John Deere Gator. The early morning air is cool as we blast off in a cloud of dewy dust—a stark contrast from the heat of the last couple days.

A New Englander trained in forestry, Anthony came to Oregon to take a job with a conservation organization and was soon consumed with agricultural-policy issues. As a result, he says, he became "besotted with farmland." Lured into Portland's well-established community-gardening movement, he and Carol grew their first beans and melons on a small downtown plot alongside fiercely competitive gardeners who fought to produce the first tomatoes, the best yield, or the finest compost. The Boutards' passion for land and growing food translated into a five-year search for a farm of their own that led to this out-of-the-way valley cradled within the larger Willamette agricultural region.

Nothing is totally flat here; in any direction, the land either lifts up or falls away. Out of the farm's 144 acres, 120 are under cultivation; the remainder is a small canyon and an oak savanna that provides habitat for wildlife and a refuge from the heat and exposure of the rolling, open fields. A 20-acre knoll of thornless black-berries—more blackberries than I've ever seen in one place—is bordered with tidy, undulating rows of melons, beans, and other crops. Buckwheat fills in between the cultivated rows, and cover crops or pasture carpet all the open fields. Anthony navigates down along the edge of a small valley into an overgrown field and pulls up to a young tree—the proud beginnings of his new chestnut orchard. My mind runs through the same kind of calculation I did when my baby son was born two years ago: how old will I be when he enters his teens? These trees will not produce for another twelve years, growing up to 80 feet high over a life span of hundreds of years.

Near the center of the property, the farm staff and their families are relaxing in an open, grassy commons next to housing that looks clean and well organized. Housing for birds is everywhere. There are spacious homes for barn owls constructed out of 55-gallon plastic drums, small wooden kestrel boxes, and fifty-three houses for swallows and wrens made out of scrap wood. The invitation is clear: if you've got two wings and an appetite for gophers, rats, moles, voles, or mosquitoes, this is definitely the place to land.

Anthony and Carol's own house is still conspicuously under construction and looks more like it belongs in New England than in the Oregon hills. Built with natural cooling like the fruit barns I used to visit back East, the entire structure is one story, designed to accommodate Anthony's bad knees and the possibility that he could "roll the tractor and end up in a wheelchair." The kitchen walls are lined nearly floor to ceiling with well-used cookbooks. Wren boxes hang just outside the big picture window that overlooks the fields into the distant Chehalem Valley. On the walls, Anthony's black-and-white panoramic photographs capture the abundance of European farmers' markets, where the overflowing piles of melons, leeks, lettuces, and summer squashes echo the piles of beans, tomatoes, and melons spread across the Boutards' countertops. It's clear that, at least in summer and fall, this room is where it all happens—canning and freezing, packing berries, and experimenting with new bean recipes.

I remember Anthony telling me over the phone that he and Carol are "militant about flavor." It sounded more like the dramatic rant of some French chef than an Oregon farmer. But I would soon discover that the Boutard beans, melons, and berries have been pushed and finessed to the point that a wise chef would be best to stay out of the way and let each of the items speak for itself.

As Anthony, Aaron, and I gather at the big kitchen table for lunch, Carol serves cool zucchini soup, a simple white sulfur bean cooked in sage with summer savory and shallot, and some local cheese and bread. The meal is closed with an almost communion-style offering of thin wafers of the much-revered Charentais melon—my first glimpse of the Boutard's chief passion.

When I ask about the cream-colored Zolfino beans we've just eaten, Anthony takes a deep, portentous breath and goes into an almost encyclopedic treatise on the subject. The farm produces twenty to twenty-five varieties of fresh shelling and dry beans on 4 acres. Anthony scours obscure seed catalogues and European markets with the resolve of a rare-coin collector. He's determined to capture the full culinary range of bean characteristics—nutty, vegetable-like, sweet, floury, creamy, buttery. He cooks some, like Maine yellow eye, to take on the flavor of their accompanists; others, like Vermont cranberry or the red-streaked borlotto, he allows to dominate with their own flavor. He seeks out varieties with thin skins, believing that the skins harbor the chemistry that causes digestive problems.

At the farmers' market, he presses his customers to decide what the beans are for before they buy. If they're planning minestrone, it will need to be a cannellini or a Soldier; if they're accenting lamb, he might push the flageolets. He encourages customers to explore the larger, meatier shell beans over the slim filets, which he says have become a little too "precious."

When the Boutards' daughter, Caroline, first returned home from her studies at Cornell, she reported how fanatical New Englanders are about their beans and seemed relieved. "Now I know you're not so crazy, Dad," she told him. I am reminded of dozens of similar conversations between my son and his crazy dad. I'm secretly pleased that Aaron is hearing this story, that he knows it isn't just me.

After lunch I ask to take a look at the farm equipment. It's one of those bonding things farmers do. Anthony eagerly ushers us out to see the homemade bed shaper and chisel plow that sit along the side of one of the buildings.

In one of the barns, a row of old Citroën cars is gathering dust. Somewhat apologetically, Anthony tells me he likes to collect them. He shows me the 1972 Citroën DS21 Safari that until recently was his sole delivery vehicle. He tells me the backseat holds between sixty and eighty flats of berries, and the front can be filled with fresh shell beans and melons. He points out the Citroën 2CV, the classic

French farmer's vehicle, designed with a hydraulic suspension system to carry eggs on bumpy rural roads without any breakage.

I am especially excited to see the Fiat-designed crawler inside a huge metal barn. Anthony tells me he never uses a wheel tractor on his fields. I test Aaron by asking if he knows why. He answers with one word, "compaction," and I can almost hear him thinking, "Obviously." He's grown up hearing my own compaction lectures to the crew and seen me drive visitors crazy by restricting where they can drive and park and walk. Anthony nods approvingly. He is in love with the crawler and relays how it leaves no impact on the land except at the row ends when turning; he tells me how his footsteps leave a far greater imprint. He's one of the few farmers I've heard be so conscious of this important aspect of stewardship.

The Boutards next take us into a side room and show off their pea and bean sheller. It is a beautiful handmade machine, its wood frame painted green, with the manufacturer's name hand-burned into the side. A wooden drum with rotating rubber fingers breaks the beans out of the pods and deposits them into a vibrating chute below that separates out the chaff.

As we emerge from the dim light of the bean-shelling temple into the heat of the midafternoon Oregon sun, my thoughts shift to the blackberry puzzle that has been germinating in my brain since morning. I'm used to seeing these thorny, independent-minded plants growing wild along every fence line and every abandoned field. I'm trying to adjust to seeing them lined up so cooperatively here in vast straight, thornless rows, laden with amazingly large fruit.

Covering the crown of the highest point of the Boutard land, the blackberries are a dominant force. There are sixty-five rows of them, each extending up to 450 feet in two blocks. It takes 150 pickers a month and a half to harvest this field. Most of the crop is under contract to Cascadian Farms, to be resold in 12-ounce frozen packages and jars of jam.

Anthony hands me a copy of Oregon State University's *Caneberry Newsletter.* "It reads like a war manual," he cautions as I scan the warnings about redberry mites, purple blotch, and septoria leaf spot. An in-depth discussion about drenching the crops with insecticide baths of diazinon or Guthion shares the same paragraph with the "hopeful" news about approval by the school-lunch program to purchase excess berries.

The more I read, the more I feel like there's a disease or insect waiting around every corner. An article on chemical cane burning reveals how the contact herbicide labeled Aim (carfentrazone-ethyl) gives a "good burn." I learn about the new liquid formation of bifenthrin, or Brigade, and about Goal and Galigan 2E and Sniper. I thought that university-extension agents had moved beyond being salespeople for the chemical companies, but here's the pitch, presented matter-of-factly with a

"Dear Friends" greeting at the beginning. I'm experiencing a major disconnect here. I can't find one lousy bottle of Brigade or Sniper on the whole Boutard place, yet the plants are healthy and vigorous and loaded with fruit.

"Berries are every bit as complex as wine grapes, with none of the baggage," Anthony tells me. "I can talk about a blackberry with the same language as you hear people waxing about wine." People are often surprised to discover how much control farmers have over the complex flavor and characteristics of the foods we produce. The sugar and acid of the fruit, and a range of textural qualities, are often tied to irrigation, soil fertility, harvesting times, storage—even the pickers' skill. Every summer, visitors to our farm in British Columbia harvest the wild black-berries that surround the property. Even after thorough instructions, they inevitably return with buckets full of shiny, unripe ones, equating black with ripe. Harvesting blackberries is subtle: a half day too early, and the fruit is tart and acid; too late, and it falls apart, doesn't keep, and loses some of the complexity of its flavor.

I wander down the 450-foot rows of Chester, Triple Crown, and Loch Ness blackberries, seeking out the dull, black fruit that comes to me easy. I taste one, then another, then another. I can't believe it, but, nine berries later, each one has provided a different experience: some implode in my mouth, others slowly melt, others are sweet and silky, some are warm and smoky. It's amazing that such a small package can produce such a powerful experience.

I try to get Anthony to expound on what makes these so good. I want to hear about technique, some secret that I can take with me. Instead, he says, "If you want good fruit, you have to treat your pickers well, good trellising for ease of picking, good outhouses, hot coffee at the right times."

Hot coffee! Good outhouses! I was expecting him to tell me about pruning or a particular blend of compost or special irrigation techniques. And yet, if you believe as I do that food embodies the energy of the people who grow and harvest it, then coffee and outhouses and the well-being of those doing the work are as important as any technique.

Just before sunset I wander off, ostensibly to take photographs. All day I haven't been able to get the taste of those blackberries out of my mind. The temptation is too much. I drive out to the field, and, somehow, out of sixty-five rows, I find the Triple Crowns we tasted earlier in the day. I park the vehicle and walk up and down each side of the row, gorging myself.

I have never allowed anyone to do this on my own farm. I've always joked that we have closed-circuit cameras, that a hidden scale at the entrance to the farm weighs you when you come in and when you leave, and that we send you a bill for the difference. My farm is tiny, with thousands of visitors, I tell myself, trying to assuage my guilt. This place is huge by comparison, acres of rows loaded with 200,000 pounds of fruit. At dinner I confess, present my purple-stained hands, stick out my tongue, and provide a lame estimate of how much I think I ate, offering to pay. They laugh and accuse me of being fickle, arriving with an obsession about melons and leaving with a new love.

Earlier in the day, before the heat settled in, we watched as Anthony, Carol, Zenon, and his brother-in-law, Abel, performed the harvest ritual for the next day's Sunday market. Zenon and Abel carefully select blackberries one at a time and place them into paper baskets in flats. Carol and Anthony reserve the bean picking for themselves. In matching white shirts and khaki pants, they move down the rows with buckets, collecting Valentine and Sophia and flageolet shell beans. The white shirt is part of Anthony's regular uniform; he tells me he likes to be visible in the fields. With his towering 6-foot-plus frame, I don't think that is a problem.

I once walked into a radio interview in San Francisco uncharacteristically dressed in a nice shirt and pants. The interviewer made some comment to the effect that I didn't "look like a farmer." I realize most people have a picture in their minds of someone in overalls and holding a pitchfork. Now, in this field, I find myself having the same response: in his clean white shirt, Anthony looks more like food explorer than farmer.

The Charentais melons are reserved for last. Alleys of flowering buckwheat separate the melon rows. As a summer cover crop, buckwheat is ideal for loosening up soils and providing some cover from the sun and a food source and habitat for bees and other beneficial insects. The fruit itself is covered with a scattering of straw to prevent sunburn. Anthony screeches with excitement when a frog hops out of the planting onto a nearby leaf.

The smell around the field is so distinctive, so rich, sweet, and musky, that I could be blindfolded and led through this farm, acre after acre, and know with certainty when I had come within 100 feet of the Charentais. Of all the senses, smell has the most amazing ability to transport one across years and miles and life experiences. Now it takes me to my own melon fields on our small farm just a few hundred miles north of here. This year, my neighbors will not have the pleasure and amusement of watching me as I crawl on all fours through my own small Charentais field with my nose to the ground, smelling and picking. I will miss the pride of delivering the fruit to local restaurants and displaying it at the farmers' market. This year, someone else will get to watch brain cells exploding with new taste information in the minds of those who are lucky enough to have their first sample. This melon does not even need to be eaten; I am satisfied—as I used to be with my Babcock peaches—to just hold one and smell.

Now I watch as Anthony and Carol bend over to smell, carefully checking for the telltale yellowing of the long-stemmed leaf nearest to the fruit. The melons are the Boutards' calling card, melding this farm into the minds of local chefs and eaters at the farmers' markets.

Anthony compares them to thoroughbred horses and then corrects himself, saying they are more like opera singers. "They need to be pampered, pampered, pampered," he tells me.

Carol adds that they are like children: "You have to treat them right from the beginning. From the time they start, you don't want a moment of discomfort." She shows me a choice specimen oozing a rust-colored liquid from near the stem. Anthony says the French value melons that bleed like this, comparing the nectar to the blood of Christ or the menstrual cycle.

People try to compare Charentais with what they know as a Western cantaloupe, or muskmelon, but they are completely different in smell and in taste and in texture. I ask Anthony to differentiate, and he uses language like "more fruitlike," "evokes apricots and plums," "a sweet, delicate fruit flavor with a strong perfume and distinct texture, not as musky."

"I tell customers at the farmers' market to smell and select the melon that fits them," he says. "Each one is an individual; each smells and tastes different." While there is nothing New Agey about this, it still reminds me of the people who carry pendulums at the farmers' markets, divining whether the energy in our food is right for them. I imagine a future in which food sophisticates can access a special adviser who has the ability to help them find just the right melon or winter squash that fits their personality and makeup.

Anthony says they expect only two or three really great fruits per plant, and Carol reminds me that you "can't be greedy if you want to grow the absolute best," an approach they can live with on a farm this large. "It's too emotional," Anthony adds as the day's harvest winds down. "We nurture these plants through the season, and then, all of a sudden, you have to cut them off and watch them die. I have to turn them under as soon as possible. I can't stand to see dying plants in the field."

The next morning, the Boutards get into their van, loaded with beans and melons and flats of blackberries for the farmers' market in Portland. We are left behind to take photographs and record some final impressions. I walk down and explore some of the wild areas near our van and wander over to take a portrait of the row of old Citroëns. Then, out of nowhere, I get this longing, like one of those lustful thoughts that grabs hold of you and won't let go. It's the damn blackberries. I give in, head for the field, and gorge myself one last time before getting in our vehicle and heading south.

♣

We stop south of Gaston to photograph a broken-down home on an old farmstead. There is moss on the bits of roof that still remain, and sunflowers grow where the kitchen once was. As we drive away, I think about who lived in that house, how many children they conceived and raised there, how many meals they harvested and served, and wonder if their dream has fallen down along this road or if life just moved them on to something else. I try to imagine what that could be, and I can't. I have farmed since I was nineteen, and I know I will never willingly stop, so every dilapidated farmhouse feels like it had to be a loss. As we drive away, I still feel it in my chest.

On Highway 47, we whir past the Psalm 1 nursery, wheat fields dotted with huge oaks, and fields of hops and boysenberries. Machine-stacked hay bakes in the sun, rundown trailers and center-pivot water cannons pressure-blast columns of water onto fields of everything. School buses collect dust in storage, yielding the summertime road to the Winnebagos and Jet Skis that ride on trailers behind every truck and RV. Acres and acres of blacktop parking are full, servicing row after row of outlet stores, where the summer harvest is in full swing.

Outside Salem, the huge Oregon Garden packinghouses lie dormant and ready to process fall apples. But apples no longer truly mark a season—the fruit will be graded and packed and placed in controlled-atmosphere storage where the oxygen is replaced with nitrogen gas, suspending all life processes, so that apples can be sent to market anywhere, anytime. Somehow, as I think about the marvels of modern food storage and distribution, another bit of summer drains out of the day, as if the logic of one season following another has been upended. Now, on this Oregon road, seasons are marked by RVs and school buses, and tied to turtle-necks and tank tops rotating through fields that have been paved over and planted with outlet malls.

Near Roseburg, the first rain in months has turned the road into a slip slide, creating the conditions for a massive wreck involving a big rig. Passing the remains of these people's lives strewn across the highway, transformed by a momentary nod or swerve, reminds me how fragile our existence really is. I drive with awareness and caution.

Just south of Ashland, we pass over Siskiyou Pass, at 4,000-plus feet above sea level. Just as we reach the pass, the oil-pressure light comes on, beeping its warning of impending engine doom. I freak out and wrench the van over into the brake-check area along with the big rigs that are preparing themselves for the long grade down into California. There is plenty of coolant in the reservoir, and all the belts look good, so I allow it to cool down and then start the engine. All seems well, but, with years of Volkswagen experience, I'm feeling uneasy. As we come down the grade and cross the border into California, we see the warning signs for the U.S. Department of Agriculture's checkpoint.

The van is laden with vine-ripe tomatoes, blackberries, and garlic. I decide that I can relinquish the insipid organic pluots from an Ashland natural-foods market but will have to smuggle the blackberries and tomatoes. Aaron scrambles to stash the produce, but, instead of humans standing at the checkpoint, there are signs reading "No Inspection Today." I guess it's the budget cuts. It's hard for me to understand how funneling four lanes of interstate traffic into this checkpoint can do anything to keep out mad cows and gypsy moths. As the low concrete-block buildings of the checkpoint fall behind us, I settle into the arid expanse of the California landscape just as Mount Shasta appears in all of its glory, snowy peaks rising, dominating the world for miles around.

Based on the area's natural ecology, the floor of the Scott Valley, just south of Yreka, should be blanketed with golden grasses of summer. Instead, it's an electric green that just doesn't seem possible from these native soils and stands in dramatic contrast to the understated dry hills of pine, oak, and chaparral that envelop it. This is hay country, carpeted wall to wall with alfalfa supported by wells that suck millions of gallons of water from deep within the earth into miles of giant wheel lines that shoot it into the hot, dry, evaporating air.

We're on our way to see Jennifer Greene's grain farm, and I bet Aaron I can pick out her place without looking at the numbers on the mailboxes. In the distance, in a world of monochrome green, I spot an area of interlocking brown, red, and gold. The lines, shapes, and scale are different, not flat or straight or perfect like everything else around it. As we get closer, it appears like a quilt, multicolor patches with shapes and heights that change every 40 or 50 feet.

We turn in and drive up the lane that leads to the house. An Allis-Chalmers All-Crop combine sits beside the barn, a black chow chow patrols the driveway, and piles of garbanzo beans are drying on top of tarps and barrels and multicolored cotton bedsheets.

I'm not sure what to expect. Most of the farmers we contacted over the last few months were thrilled to have us visit, but Jennifer was cautious, wanting to make sure that we would take the time to get to know her and the place, that we would work together for a while before I began photographing or taking notes.

As we greet each other, seeing a face seems enough to dissolve any reservations. Jennifer tells me not to worry, that she won't smash my camera if I take it out, and immediately launches into a high-energy tour of the farm. This is new territory for me—aside from a 15-acre planting of barley and oats I did when I was about twenty, I don't have much experience with grains and cereals. Jennifer moves fast and is throwing so much information at me that I'm having trouble keeping up.

Jennifer's 30-acre canvas is filled with one-third- to one-half-acre plots of amaranth, barley, millet, teff, heirloom wheats, blue and yellow popcorns, garbanzos, lentils and fava beans, pumpkin, sunflower, and poppy seeds, all merging and mingling together. There are ten families of crops and fifty-six cereals in a breathtaking rotation of pastures, grains, spring legumes, and dried beans.

Picture agriculture in America and you see amber fields of wheat, soy, or corn, fields that extend for as far as your eye can see with one variety of a single cereal or pulse. The sight before me blows all that away. This looks more like the grain production I saw in parts of Africa, Asia, and South America. The fields look like they were planted by a vegetable farmer turned grain producer.

In fact, Jennifer started her farming career apprenticing and working on various vegetable farms. "Vegetable farming sucks," she tells me now. "I don't know how you people do it!" She tells me she doesn't like the "hustle" of vegetable farming, that she prefers "the slowness of grains."

In December 2002, eighty-five-year-old Floyd Evans handed Jennifer the keys to the house and drove off, having sold her the land he had lived on and farmed for thirty years. Before leaving, the old man apologized that he hadn't sprayed the alfalfa field that dominated the property. Jennifer had been farming grain on leased land 250 miles south in Yolo County. She was thrilled to find a place she could afford, with the water and climate that would support her chosen crops, and left behind the easy climate and politics of Yolo for the unknown.

There is an American flag flying at the entrance to every farm in this valley. Jennifer tells me that many of her old friends would be hesitant to move to an area like this, seeing it as too redneck and right-wing. She tells me that she, too, is conservative and that her politics are "not that different from my neighbors'." Being conservative in the literal sense of the word is about knowing the limitations of one's resources, conserving and caring for them with an eye toward the future, a timeless concept that has somehow gotten a radical reputation.

Jennifer recites a point-by-point list of her guiding principles, in which life and work are one enterprise: the farmer should actually be hands-on, the working environment should empower people and welcome children, the work should scale to the environment and an appropriate aesthetic. If it seems dogmatic, I can't help but notice that Jennifer pursues these values in an atmosphere that is alternately fierce and deliberate, spontaneous and casual. Even basic. The house seems little more than a place to crash at night; all the important parts of life, including the cooking, are lived outdoors. Even with all her self-reliance, Jennifer seems to attract a parade of visitors—kids, neighbors who come to lend a hand, or folks who stop by to learn or just to hang out.

Jennifer introduces her two dogs as mutts. The third "dog," a Toggenburg milk goat named Toggy, has the run of the whole place. I catch Toggy feeding on a pile of dry beans and start to chase her away. Julia, who lives and works here, tells me to leave her be. "The goats on this farm are like the cows in India," she says, "free to go where they want."

We spend part of the afternoon harvesting poppy-seed heads and tossing them into buckets. Jennifer breaks a seed head off, turns it upside down and pours it out into her palm like pepper from a shaker with large holes. She eats the small pile of black seeds and invites us to do the same.

The seed heads will become part of a monthly share for each of the one hundred member families of her CSA program. CSA stands for Community Supported Agriculture, a program in which families pay at the beginning of the season for a weekly share of the year's harvest. Jennifer's San Francisco families will receive her grains along with fruits, vegetables, meats, and dairy from several other farms.

Jennifer's contribution includes freshly milled flours, polenta, cornmeal, pancake mix, beans, and seeds. Every share arrives in a handmade cloth bag with the family's name sewn on and recipes for graham crackers, and sprouted-wheat bread; it includes a newsletter with homegrown philosophy, farm stories, and current farm activities presented in an organic layout that mixes typefaces, handwritten messages, and pasted-in photos and stories. The newsletter feels like the farm itself.

I photograph Jennifer at sunset standing in her wheat field. She complains about the location, reminding me that she is trying to get away from wheat domination and move folks toward some of the less known, less popular grains. "The wheat people have convinced everyone that there is only grain: wheat." We move into the millet and buckwheat.

Later, as I head toward an old tractor sitting at the back of one of her fields, Jennifer stops me, telling me not to take pictures of the tractor. This is a horse-powered farm, and she doesn't want people to get the wrong idea. The tractor was brought over by a concerned neighbor to take some pressure off spring field preparation. Here, a pair of six-year-old Norwegian Fjord horses provide the traction, pulling an offset disc for soil prep and to cover seed, and powering a single-row cultivator through the rows of new plants in the spring and summer.

When it comes time for dinner, Jennifer kneads Len hard red wheat sourdough into flat breads and slides them into a wood-fired oven that sits against the side of the barn next to a brick firebox covered with steel grate and griddle. She walks out to the field and returns with green beans, squash, and onions, which she rough slices along with a few potatoes. All this is thrown onto the griddle with a little sesame oil. Several ears of Painted Mountain corn, picked late at roasting stage, are placed alongside the vegetable mix, where they form a wall, keeping the veggies from falling off the edge.

I find Aaron out in the grain fields covered in oil paint and soil, looking like a kid. He has been out here all afternoon recording his impressions of the place, mixing seeds and soil into the paint for texture. The light is almost gone, and I drag him back to the practical reality of dinner. We sit with Jennifer and Julia on bales of straw, eating warm, puffy flat breads, homemade hummus, and grilled vegetables by candlelight with a sliver of new moon hanging overhead, the dogs asleep underfoot and grain ripening over the fence.

I ask Jennifer about her choice to farm alone. "Even among the organic-farming crowd, the women end up in the office or the house, with the men driven by the need to produce a cash crop," she explains. "It's really sad because that's not what many of them want to do.

"I'm lucky—I'm on my own," she says with no trace of irony. I marvel at the magnitude of what she has taken on so independently. Later she tells me that if she were to get together with someone, it would have to be a nonfarmer, someone who would not try to take over the work that she loves. "Maybe a lawyer," she says.

Early on our second morning, I find Jennifer milking the goats. I offer a cheery good morning, which she ignores. As I walk away I hear her mutter, "I love you, Toggy" to the goat, whose head and horns are buried in the grain bucket.

I understand. I used to love to go out in the quiet and the cold of a winter morning, animals leaning into me warm and heavy as I squatted and milked. Milking was my quiet time, jets of milk rhythmically hitting stainless steel, buckets filling with milk and foam. It was one of the first farm chores I taught Aaron to do, and one of the gifts I could give him. I leave Jennifer's private goat space and head out and into the fields, camera in hand.

There is heavy dew on everything, and, by the time I am called in for breakfast, I am soaked. I try to politely refuse, not wanting to be taken care of, but she insists, telling me that she's a big breakfast person and that we should come and join her. My hesitation ends when she tells me that she is making waffles.

I go off to change into dry clothes, and when I return I find Jennifer in the grinding room, stones whirling as she selects from buckets and bags of whole grains, pouring a handful of Canadian hull-less barley, amaranth, and teff into the hopper. As the flour comes out, she runs her hands through it, delighted by its smooth texture and cream color.

The resulting waffles are golden and light. I hold back from burying them in maple syrup and am pleased that I can still taste each individual grain variety. It is rare for most people to experience this. We often agonize over the quality of our vegetables or fruit, wax eloquently over cheese or wine, but accept flours, edible seeds, and cereals that are rarely fresh and come from a very limited diversity of plants. There is a remarkable difference in taste when seeds are grown well and served fresh and when flours are ground immediately prior to being used.

After breakfast, Jennifer introduces us to eighty-three-year-old Howard Berry, who lives nearby. He and Jennifer co-own a plow. "She owns the handles," Howard says. "I own the blade." He keeps suggesting different men that Jennifer should marry, most of whom she says are too young.

More to the point, Howard and Jennifer share an old, broken-down combine that had once seemed to be beyond repair. Jennifer and a friend spent several weeks restoring its beauty and usefulness, taking the old machine apart, feeding it gallons of grease, and putting it back together. These graceful, community-scaled machines were the norm fifty years ago, allowing a farmer to grow a wide range of seed and grain crops and providing freedom from hand cutting and threshing. Now, too many of these perfectly sized tools of self-sufficiency rust and decay along the fence lines of farms all across America.

For Jennifer, it remains the right tool for her scale and diversity. But it also seems to be a symbol of restoration and preservation, an acknowledgment of a smaller-scale agriculture that once dominated this country and her desire to bring pieces of it back. With its functional beauty, it's one more element of what I'm coming to understand as Jennifer's personal aesthetic.

I used to think I was one of the few individuals who came to farming more as an artist than as a farmer. I was a little shy about this, worried that my approach to the land as a canvas would somehow limit my ability to produce good food. Since that time, I have met many farmers who also go to great lengths to consider the artistic along with the agricultural. Although Jennifer comes off as being chop-chop practical, the fields and arrangement of crops reveal a great appreciation for the visual.

In fact, having started off less than enthusiastic about being photographed, she now art directs my picture taking: "Why don't you try getting it from that angle?" or "You really should photograph the amaranth—it would be so beautiful against

the mountains." I normally would bristle at being directed like this, but there is a playfulness in her manner, and I'm having fun accommodating.

I approached this farm with some misgiving, and I have now become caught up in a series of fresh and unfamiliar experiences both in the field and at the table. Last night's dinner—tortillas made with finely ground Oaxaca green-corn flour on the open fire grill, lentils, homemade feta cheese, and a frittata made with eggs from Jennifer's chickens—came late, when it was too dark to see, so each bite was a surprise.

I realize I am used to being able to almost taste a connection between the vegetables, fruit, dairy, eggs, and even the meats we eat at home, and their source. I have not had that same relationship with grains. Although we buy oats, wheat, barley, and millet from organic sources, they come in 50-pound bags from large-scale producers growing on hundreds and thousands of acres someplace out there in the great middle of the country. It has always been the anonymous piece in our diet, and, for some reason, we have accepted that this is the way it has to be. And yet, grain is nutritionally so fundamental, so basic and necessary to our diet and to the diet of the animals we depend on for meat, milk, and eggs. We probably could survive without another carrot or tomato, but could we survive without rice or wheat or quinoa or corn?

These last couple days have demystified all of this, placed the possibility of regional small-scale grain production into my vision. I have played with the idea of growing some grain over the years, have tried to grow just about everything else, but now I am scheming in my mind: What fields, and where would they be? What equipment might be around my region, and how might I access it and resurrect it? Where are the seed sources, and what varieties will perform well on our island in the north?

On my last morning, I look back and forth across the fence line that divides Jennifer's grain fields from her neighbors' alfalfa. In Jennifer's fields, hundreds of birds land atop the newly formed corn tassels, flitting from one to the next. As I walk through the millet and buckwheat and teff, a mouse scurries through, dodging the stalks. Where only alfalfa thrived just last year, new life is beginning to move in, supported by a greater diversity of plants and the dense cover and seeds that now exist here.

Just across the fence, perfectly parallel rows of newly turned alfalfa lie fluffy above the vast mowed green. In its own way, alfalfa, too, is beautiful; the cut grass smells rich in my cultural memory. But even though alfalfa is a good neighbor—with its 30-foot root system reaching deep into the hardpans, bringing up nutrients and fixing nitrogen in leguminous nodes—it's like having only one neighbor with one face, and no place for any of the wild things to be. The contrast is both subtle and dramatic, and I would love to see how Jennifer's Windborne Farm evolves, how the explosion of variety and diversity that comes from one woman's militancy will mature.

♣

Fresh Shell Bean Gratin

Anthony Boutard is a bean fanatic. He inspired me to grow fresh shelling beans by providing the seed from some of his favorite varieties.

Shelling beans is one of the real pleasures of summer. Most people shy away from them because of the extra work, but eaten at the fresh stage they are melt-in-your-mouth wonderful. If you can, seek out someone who is growing a range of European and American shelling beans, and experiment with different types.

This recipe was adapted from Chez Panisse Vegetables *and it's a real crowd-pleaser. This one is made with marjoram, but you can also use sage, oregano, basil, or rosemary (sparingly). This version doesn't call for any spice, but try adding a good pinch of hot pepper, or get out the preserved peppers and pass them at the table.*

2½ to 3 pounds fresh shell beans (about 3 cups shelled)
6 tablespoons extra-virgin olive oil
Kosher salt to taste
1 small onion, cut into ¼-inch dice
4 cloves garlic, finely chopped
2 teaspoons chopped fresh marjoram
¼ cup chopped flat-leaf parsley
2 medium tomatoes, peeled, seeded, and roughly chopped
1 cup fresh bread crumbs

Shell the beans and discard any discolored or shriveled beans. You should end up with about 3 cups shelled beans. (The yield will vary depending on the variety.) Rinse the beans in cold water and put them in a medium saucepan with water to cover by about 1 inch. Bring the water to a boil, skimming off any foam that floats to the surface, and add 2 tablespoons of the olive oil. Reduce the heat and gently simmer the beans, stirring occasionally, until tender, 15 to 30 minutes, depending on the variety and maturity. If the beans start to peek through the liquid during the cooking process, add a splash more water. Remove from the heat and season the bean liquid with salt—the beans will absorb the salt gradually. Set the beans aside to cool slowly in the cooking liquid.

Meanwhile, preheat the oven to 350 degrees F. Heat a medium sauté pan over medium heat and add 2 tablespoons of the olive oil and the onion. Season with salt and cook until the onion is tender, about 6 minutes. Add the garlic, marjoram, and parsley and sauté just until the garlic is fragrant, about 1 minute. Add the tomatoes, season again with salt, and cook for 1 to 2 more minutes, until the tomatoes are softened.

Strain the cooled beans, reserving the liquid. Combine the beans in a gratin dish with the onion and tomato mixture and stir to combine. Add enough of the bean-cooking water to almost cover. Taste and adjust the seasoning with salt, if necessary. Combine the bread crumbs with the remaining 2 tablespoons olive oil and sprinkle them over the beans in an even layer. Bake until the juices are bubbling at the edges and the bread crumbs are evenly browned, about 45 minutes. Serve warm.

Charentais Melon Soup

I was surprised to hear Anthony and Carol Boutard suggest doing anything but slicing (or smelling) these special melons. A good French melon needs to be appreciated unadulterated, but this simple recipe really enhances the melon lover's experience.

Choosing a Charentais at the market is the first and most important step, done best with a well-tuned nose. The rest is easy. This recipe is light and refreshing—perfect for a hot day. The basil and tarragon complement the melon without overpowering it, and the radish coins on top are a surprisingly nice touch. If you can, leave one or two of these melons on the counter in the kitchen for a couple days; the fragrance will fill the house.

4 ripe, fragrant Charentais melons

2 teaspoons finely chopped fresh tarragon

2 teaspoons finely chopped fresh basil

Pinch of kosher salt

1 to 2 tablespoons fruity olive oil

1 to 2 radishes, cut into very thin, round slices, for garnish

Put 4 shallow soup bowls in the refrigerator to chill.

Halve the melons and scoop out the seeds. Using a large knife, shave off the rind—be sure to remove the thin layer of green flesh just beneath the rind as well. Cut the flesh into small chunks and puree until smooth in a blender. Add the tarragon, basil, and salt, and blend again to incorporate. Transfer the melon puree to a medium bowl and stir in the olive oil to taste. Chill the soup in the refrigerator for at least 15 minutes but no more than 2 hours. Ladle the soup into the chilled bowls, garnish with the radish slices, and serve immediately.

Charentais Melon with Sweet Wine

SERVES 4

Anthony tells us that when he wants to get a little adventurous he simply halves one of these melons, removes the seeds, and fills the seed cavity with sweet wine. This recipe is a little more involved, but it's still a nice, simple treatment for a good melon.

2 ripe, fragrant Charentais melons

2 to 3 tablespoons sweet wine, such as Muscat or Beaumes-de-Venise, chilled

1 tablespoon finely chopped fresh mint

Freshly cracked black pepper to taste

Halve the melons and scoop out the seeds. Using a large knife, shave off the rind—be sure to remove the thin layer of green flesh just beneath the rind as well. Cut the flesh into slices about ½ inch thick and arrange neatly on a platter. Sprinkle with the wine to taste and the mint. Finish with a few twists of pepper and serve immediately.

NOTE: For a simple alternative, halve the melons, remove the seeds, and fill the seed cavity with chilled sweet wine.

Blackberry Sherbet

Although I've grown just about every type of berry, my visit to the Boutards was my first experience with cultivated thornless blackberrys. Wow! I love the "wild" ones, but Boutard's cultivated fruit was large and juicy with the most diverse range of complex flavors, as if every berry was different from the last.

MAKES 1 QUART

Of course dead-ripe blackberries are a must for this simple recipe. If you can, go out and harvest your own, or seek out a grower who grows the thornless ones. Remember a blackberry needs to be more than black to be ripe. Look for ones that have lost their shine and taste for ripeness until you've got it down.

8 cups blackberries
1½ cups sugar
¾ cup water
2 tablespoons fresh lemon juice
1 tablespoon kirsch

Combine the blackberries, sugar, and water in a nonreactive, medium saucepan. Gently heat over medium heat just until the sugar dissolves and the berries begin to soften and release some of their juice, 3 to 4 minutes. Puree the berry mixture 1 cup at a time in a food processor, and then pass the puree through a medium-mesh sieve into a bowl, pressing on the contents with the back of a wooden spoon to extract all of the juice. Discard the seeds. Add the lemon juice and kirsch and stir to combine. Cover and refrigerate until chilled, about 2 hours. Freeze in an ice-cream maker according to the manufacturer's instructions.

Pita Bread

MAKES 16
PITA BREADS

Pulling puffed pitas hot out of Jennifer Greene's wood-fired oven on a clear, warm August night was one of the real sublime moments of our journey.

You don't have to have the wood-fired oven or the grain growing across the fence, or even a new moon rising, to get pitas to puff. This recipe will get them going right in your own kitchen oven, though high-quality flour and a pizza stone make all the difference. The pitas are wonderful warm out of the oven, or lightly toasted when they start to go stale.

2½ cups lukewarm water

2 teaspoons active dry yeast

3 cups whole-wheat flour

1 tablespoon kosher salt

1 tablespoon olive oil, plus extra for coating the bowl

2 to 3 cups all-purpose flour, plus extra for dusting

Combine the water and yeast in a large bowl and stir to dissolve. Add the whole-wheat flour and stir, in one direction only, to activate the gluten, about 1 minute. Drape a kitchen towel over the bowl or cover with plastic wrap and let rest the sponge for at least 10 minutes or up to 2 hours.

Sprinkle the salt over the sponge, add the 1 tablespoon olive oil, and mix well. Mix in the all-purpose flour, about 1 cup at a time, until the dough is too difficult to stir. Turn out the dough onto a lightly floured work surface and knead, adding more of the remaining flour as necessary, until the dough is smooth and elastic, about 5 minutes. Form the dough into a ball and let rest while you wash, dry, and lightly oil the bowl. Place the dough in the bowl, cover with a kitchen towel or plastic wrap, and let rise in a warm place until doubled in volume, about 1 1/2 hours.

Meanwhile, position a rack in the lower third of the oven and place a pizza stone or baking sheet on top. Preheat the oven to 450 degrees F.

Gently punch down the dough, remove from the bowl, and divide it in half. Cut each half into 8 equal pieces and roll each piece into a small, tight ball. Place the dough balls about 2 inches apart on a lightly floured work surface or baking sheet, sprinkle with additional flour, and cover with a kitchen towel or plastic wrap. Let the dough rest for about 20 minutes.

Working with 2 dough balls at a time, roll out each ball on a lightly floured work surface into an 8- to 9-inch circle. Place the pitas, one at a time, on a lightly floured peel, and slide onto the hot pizza stone. Bake until the bottoms are lightly golden and the pitas have puffed up into a full balloon, 3 to 4 minutes. Repeat the process with the remaining dough, stacking the pitas in a kitchen towel and covering to keep warm and soft as they come out of the oven.

Multigrain Buttermilk Waffles with Poppy Seeds

As with most things, Jennifer Greene is particular about her waffles. I know, I watched her go through the carefully prescribed regime of selecting from her stash of homegrown whole grains, grinding them and preparing the mix. Most of the preparation took place in her outdoor summer kitchen while she shooed away the goats and the occasional fly.

Jennifer talked us through some grain options readily available to the home cook, and we incorporated them into a classic waffle recipe. Barley flour, in particular, is a great substitute for all-purpose flour. Store-bought poppy seeds don't compare to fresh seeds; eating the fresh ones right out of the field was a wonderful surprise. Jennifer recommends soaking store-bought seeds overnight in the buttermilk to soften them before making the waffles.

You might think these whole-grain waffles will taste like hippie food, but they are far from it; they're surprisingly light and delicious. If you can, buy the grains whole and grind your own. Most flours are not that fresh, and it's amazing what a difference it makes.

MAKES ABOUT
6 WAFFLES

1 ½ tablespoons poppy seeds

1¾ cups buttermilk

1½ cups barley flour

¼ cup oat flour

¼ cup corn flour

¼ teaspoon baking soda

1½ teaspoons baking powder

1 tablespoon sugar

½ teaspoon kosher salt

2 eggs, separated

6 tablespoons unsalted butter, melted and slightly cooled

Yogurt and fresh fruit such as berries, or sliced peaches or nectarines, for serving

Combine the poppy seeds and buttermilk in a small bowl and let soak for 1 to 2 hours in the refrigerator, or overnight if possible.

Preheat a waffle iron. Sift together the flours, baking soda, baking powder, sugar, and salt into a bowl. Whisk the egg yolks lightly in a large bowl and stir in the melted butter and poppy seed mixture. Add the dry ingredients and stir just until combined. In a medium bowl, beat the egg whites until stiff but not dry and quickly fold them into the batter.

When the waffle iron is hot, pour some batter over the grid, easing it toward but not all the way to the edges with a wooden spoon. Close the iron and cook until the exterior of the waffle is crisp and golden, about 5 minutes. Transfer the waffle to a platter and keep warm in a low oven while you cook the remaining waffles. Serve hot with yogurt and fresh fruit.

CHAPTER 3

☾

OUTLAWS

CALIFORNIA'S INTERSTATE 5 RUNS FAST ON A NORTH-SOUTH AXIS through the hot, windy Central Valley. Once, not too long ago, the valley's massive oaks rose out of dry golden grasslands in the summer and vast marshland in winter in a wild spectacle so dramatic it was compared with Africa's Serengeti Plain. In just two generations, the oaks and wetlands have all but disappeared— and with them has gone one of the world's most significant winter habitats for migrating ducks, geese, cranes, pelicans, and the millions of silver and Chinook salmon that spawned in the vanished rivers and creeks.

Now, the vast agricultural fields that dominate this valley are greened year-round by deep wells and miles of aqueducts, artificially introduced water in what was once a natural wetland.

Nothing here has been left untouched; everything is channeled and leveled, removed and replaced, conquered and resigned. Huge, blinding silver grain eleva-tors, immaculately clean and flat-as-a-tabletop orchards, and giant tractors trailed by plumes of soil give this once-lush valley a joyless sense of purpose as it moves toward eventual exhaustion. In order to fulfill society's most fundamental need for food, we are destroying the very elements that food production depends on: soil and water. As we speed along, I consider how much has unraveled and what can never be restored.

We join the caravan of tractor trailers and cars heading south. The wind on the van is so severe that at times I have to lean into the steering wheel to keep it on the road. It's a metaphor for this place, where conventional thinking barrels on against all natural logic. I think about the farmers I'm visiting and realize that they are moving with the wind, not against it, like sailors using nature as an ally. How odd that the industrial agriculture of the last fifty years is considered conventional, while those who are rediscovering natural systems are now called alternative.

We cut west onto the relative calm of Highway 505 and connect with Interstate 80 toward the Napa Valley and Bob Cannard's farm near the town of Sonoma. I remember Sonoma County from twenty years ago, with its Gravenstein apple orchards and funky towns. Now, immaculate vineyards are planted everywhere, and I wonder who will drink all this wine.

Fifteen years ago, everyone told me that I needed to meet Bob Cannard, see his fields, and hear about his "radical" approach to the land and growing food. I remember arriving for my first visit, getting out of the car, and thinking I was lost in an abandoned field of weeds. Just as I was preparing to leave, I saw someone coming toward me carrying bucketfuls of beautiful red peppers. I walked to the edge of the field, got down on my knees, and parted the weeds. There, just beneath the cover of mustard, mallow, and amaranth, were long rows of delicate pepper plants, not as upright and sturdy as I was used to seeing, but loaded with beautiful fruit. Now, I'm wondering whether Bob will have continued his unconventional system, whether his commitment to balancing nature's crop (the weeds) with humanity's crop (the vegetables) will have waned under the force of the marketplace or just from society's pressure to conform. Not so. Aside from a few uncharacteristically well-groomed plantings near the buildings, things look more or less the same. There appears to be more abundance, the weeds and the crops seem larger and more robust, and there are more fruit trees planted everywhere.

I greet Bob by telling him that his fields look a bit weedy, a comment that would place most folks in this part of the world firmly on the defensive. He smiles and shakes my hand.

Cannard started working this land in 1976, when he was twenty-two. It had previously been home to one of the nation's premier turkey farms, where the standard broad-breasted white turkey was first bred. Forty thousand turkeys patrolled this land for almost thirty years as the topsoil washed away down its sloping surface with every rain. "There was a mind-set here of cleanliness and order," Bob recalls, explaining that the ground had been compacted and saturated in turkey shit and that even the creeks had been "straightened" with bulldozers. He was invited to do some landscape renewal, so he traded the labor for his first year's rent.

He tells me that he deliberately chose a damaged place so he could learn nature's processes. He grew up in the nursery industry, where everything is forced and pushed and manipulated. He attended agriculture school and eventually dropped out when his most fundamental questions were not answered: Why are wild places naturally healthy, while the fields and orchards of commercial agriculture are a continual battleground? There had to be a way to build a truly healthy food-production ecosystem, one that somehow blends the will of the farmer with the will and wisdom of nature.

Bob's first planting was a small patch of broccoli. "Everything died," he says, probably from the low level of soil life and nutrition after years of clean cultivation and heavy-handed control. "The land was compacted and anaerobic and had been sprayed to death with weed killers," he remembers. "There were no weeds or small birds—the mammal life was reduced to scavengers like ground squirrels, possums, and rats."

Bob started in, using mechanical cultivation and cover crops to open the soil up. He introduced raw crushed rock and oyster shell for mineral nutrients and biological teas to inoculate the soil with beneficial microorganisms, slowly coaxing it back to life. Gradually it yielded hardy calendula, amaranth, and grasses, then clover and wild oats, and eventually some of the most sought-after salad greens in California. Now, there are turtles, salamanders, and fish in the creek, and wild turkeys and songbirds living on the land. And lots of weeds.

Bob's fundamental less-is-more philosophy is based on the idea that the less you do, the less you will have to do. He likes to let nature take some responsibility. "I used to have to do many regular feedings for the plants, like light snacks. Now I only have to provide a bit of crushed rock or biological inocula occasionally. Now the energy is held in the soil, it's a steady-state food supply, and the soils are more wild than cultivated. "My dream is not to have to plant anything, and just wander around gathering," he says. When I see the rows of Florence fennel and radicchio that have been self-seeding and managing on their own for years, I can imagine that possibility.

At first the restaurants didn't want Bob's radicchio. "It's too bitter," they told him; they were accustomed to the more pampered, watered, heavily protected brand of other growers. "But this stuff has suffered," Bob counters. "It has to rely on the rocks and the minerals and the more difficult conditions." Now, people want that full rich taste; bitter is okay, it's "in." It's another note in the evolving American palette.

The majority of Bob's harvest goes to Chez Panisse restaurant in Berkeley, the celebrated mecca for foodies worldwide, the temple of the field-to-the-plate revival.

Every Monday and Thursday, an unmarked white van pulls up the long drive into Bob's farm and winds its way down by the creek to a cluster of bay trees where small stackable white boxes of produce sit in the shade.

The boxes are meticulously filled with squash blossoms, rosemary, thyme, savory, green beans, spring onions, red and white potatoes, red and yellow cherry tomatoes, and wild strawberries, all lined up on top of wooden benches. The driver, Dhondup Karpo, has worked at Chez Panisse since arriving from Tibet twelve years ago. When I finish stealing the spirits of the vegetables with my camera, Dhondup takes a stack of crisp, white linen cloths from the van and carefully covers and tucks in each of the fifty boxes of food. There is a preciousness about this, and I can imagine his rural relatives in Tibet chuckling to see him coddling these baby vegetables. He loads them in the van for the trip back to Berkeley, where they will be blended into the day's menu of roasted beet salad; wild nettle pizza; and turnip, sage, and cranberry-bean sauté. "I want the people who eat my food to have vegetable dreams," Bob says.

Bob's relationship to this piece of land is similar to the relationship I had with Fairview Gardens, the farm I ran for over twenty years in Southern California for the Chapman family, who in many ways except title let it be mine. Bob, too, has spent most of his adult life on land he doesn't own, renting it from the owners, who live on-site. "Ownership," he tells me, "is a manifestation of insecurity." I must be insecure. After more than twenty years nurturing someone else's land, after having been critical of private ownership, I purchased my farm in British

Columbia. Owning land or having some sense of long-term security on it does allow one to think about it and care for it in ways that are deeper and more thoughtful. But I still wonder whether we ever really own a piece of land. I do know that, for better or for worse, we all leave our mark on the places where we live and grow.

"If humans are as evolved as they think they are, then the land under their control should be better than nature's soil," Bob tells me. I reflect on the period of time in the late eighties when I looked into buying something of my own near the farm in California. Most of the places we looked at had a home and some land. Without exception, the homes were well cared for and maintained, but the land always seemed to be under some sort of assault, either through erosion, overgrazing, compaction, use of poisons, cutting of native brush and trees, or accumulation of junk or trash. I realized then that most people understand how to take care of a building but have never been mentored or taught how to nurture a piece of land, soil, trees, or the wild things and the watershed. Many folks hold title to land but are completely disconnected from it and seldom leave it better for their tenure. I wonder out loud if all private ownership should come with a contract or commitment to the land, requiring that the owner take a class, pass an exam, and fulfill certain stewardship responsibilities.

Bob's own sense of responsibility to this piece of land started with three years of restoration. He and his crew tore down dilapidated buildings; cleaned up old wire, posts, and fences; and filled in a pervasive crop of gaping ditches to claim 25 acres of the 170-acre property for growing food. In a little valley surrounded by hillsides of mixed oak forest, he now cultivates orchards of peach, apricot, lemon, mandarin, cherry, plum, and walnut trees. Many, I come to find out, are ungrafted seedlings. When I question the wisdom of planting unpredictable seedlings, he jumps at the chance to set me straight: his two hundred peach trees, all planted from seeds, ripen at different times over a very long season, unlike those in a commercial orchard, where the fruit ripens simultaneously in large blocks of single varieties.

"The fruit from each tree has individual characteristics," he continues. "Some have coarse textures, some are finer in texture and more aromatic, and one wild seedling produces small, fuzzy fruits with intense flavor." For the longest time, no one wanted that fruit. Then a local chef returned from Italy, where he had encountered a similar variety and people who were thrilled to use it. "Now," he says, "my most undesirable peach tree has become my most popular."

Bob lives in a former egg-packing house built in 1880 that at one time was scheduled for demolition. The building contains storage, a bedroom, and a kitchen and dining area. A 20-foot-long handmade wooden plank table dominates the dining area. Above it, a family of barn swallows fly in and out of a nest attached to the ceiling, their droppings accumulating on one of the oriental rugs that cover the floors.

There is no refrigerator that I can find, and I'm reminded of all the visitors at Fairview Gardens who were surprised to find our refrigerator empty. All the food was stored where it should be, safe and fresh in the fields. For me, most meals are planned on the fly in the fields, harvested right before a meal. Whenever I go out into the world, I am reminded of how lucky farmers and their families are to be able to eat so well. Even the foods we offer at the farmers' market, picked the day before, do not have the same energy and context they do when picked minutes before a meal.

The first evening, Bob cooks dinner for us. Using leftovers from the day's farmers' market, he puts together a rapid succession of small plates of food. The first course is grated kohlrabi with a little parsley, a small amount of carrot, and a dash of apple-cider vinegar. He sautés potatoes, basil, and garlic in a little of his own olive oil and does a zucchini-and-green-bean stir-fry. Then he pulls out a piece of organic Angus beef, slices it paper thin, and smiles slyly as he explains that he just spent several days eating only vegetables with some Taiwanese Buddhists. He positions himself between a cutting board and a 1950s Wedgwood Monterey stove, moving back and forth, rapid knife strokes mixing with conversation, as he chops and stirs and tastes the contents of the cast-iron pan. We all eat from the same plate using our fingers. As Aaron and I eat ravenously, it becomes clear that Bob's vegetables have thrived in their weedy surroundings.

When people talk about Bob, they always bring up the weed thing; it's the best-known and most controversial aspect about him. We are all culturally programmed to believe a farm or garden should be made up of straight rows consisting of only what we put in them, that the farmer is lording over his or her land like a general on the battlefield. This attitude has created enormous heartache, resource depletion, and pollution, and it has fueled an industry that provides every imaginable machine and chemical to give us that ultimate sense of control and mastery over our farms and gardens.

For the last fifteen years, Bob has passionately followed another vision. Rows of vegetables alternate with rows of weeds, or weeds and vegetables share the same field space. The weeds are kept in check until the planted crops dominate, and then the system is left to itself.

As with cultivation, Bob also has his own version of soil chemistry. Each plant receives a top dressing of pulverized mineral-rock dust and compost. Every irrigation originates in a 10,000-gallon redwood tank in which his home-brew compost tea is added; the composts are generated in wooden barrels that flank one side of the brewing area. Bob takes a handful of compost, a few pinches of crushed rock, some sea salt, oats with molasses, and a bit of alfalfa and throws it into a bubbling, gurgling tank; he tells me he adds everything from beer to burnt ketchup. I turn for a second to look at the field, and when I turn back, I find Bob standing on the edge, peeing into the tank.

When the tea is finished brewing, Bob adds it to an open tank that looks like an algae-covered pond. He tells me that this soup is no different than what people make for their families out of the refrigerator each day. "You feed your kids with what you have on hand," he says, explaining that this material provides the "digestive support" for the plants. As with people, he says, most physical disorders in plants are associated with nutritional deficiencies, and, "if your digestion isn't working, you have a bad attitude." Bob hits his stride and channels on like some sort of plant rights advocate. "I don't like telling the plants what to eat. It's better to give them a choice."

He prides himself on being the ultimate contrary farmer. Bring up any subject and he'll have a well-crafted thesis, normally one that flies in the face of conventional thinking. It's difficult at times to separate which parts of his rap are based on real experience and which are part of some musing expressed out loud.

I like to think of myself as fairly experimental, willing to implement even the most out-there ideas. The principles represented on Bob's farm make sense on an intellectual level, but when I see the fields, "weedy" and "unkempt," I find myself questioning, making judgments, even as Aaron seems to be grooving to Bob's philosophical beat. This is exactly the stereotype that people used to have of organic farmers—on the edge, rebellious, weird—especially if they're from California.

Bob answers my doubts as he would anyone's—with food: potatoes and beets full of character, well shaped, colors bright and consistent, greens dark and turgid, onions and berries with a sheen, herbs and flowers fragrant and strong. I ask him whether fruit size suffers from this system, and he tells me that some crops adapt better than others. "Eggplants," he says, "don't like the competition."

During our second morning, Bob throws an overnight bag in his truck and unexpectedly announces he's leaving us on our own. He tells us to make ourselves at home and stay as long as we'd like. In a strange way, I'm happy to have time to explore on my own. I wander as late-afternoon shafts of light stream over the hills that surround the farm, spotlighting the orchards and the fields of weeds and vegetables. A wind moves down the canyon in sharp blasts, making the leaves and the branches of the trees and the plants dance in the dying light.

I remember Bob telling me that some evenings he takes a glass of wine and a scythe and goes out to irrigate and to cut weeds. I'm reminded of those moments on my own farm when the crew and visitors are gone for the day and I go out alone to cultivate or graze in the fields. Those are the times when our farms speak to us, when all the conscious planning and scheming quiets down and is replaced with a knowledge that keeps us inspired and informs our best work. In those moments we merge with our land, assured that even though the world may view us as outsiders, on our land we truly belong.

"I hope I survive long enough to see my soils so rich that I won't have to plant anymore—I'll just be able to go out and harvest," Bob told us before he drove away. "Wild potatoes and Swiss chards and kales and lettuces have already become weeds here. If I am lucky and get to be an old fart, I'm going to just go out and pick what I need."

⚜

Two days later and about 50 miles southeast, I'm sitting downwind from a California-redwood hot tub filled with 300 pounds of fermenting prime grade Santa Rosa plums, 2 gallons of molasses, 10 pounds of volcanic rock dust, 2 handfuls of oyster shell, and the remains of the last batch of microbial wine. This wine will not be served in any fancy restaurants or sold in any stores, nor will anyone wax eloquently over its complex flavors. It's for the enjoyment of tomato, rosemary, and arugula plants, and apricot, plum, apple, and fig trees.

The winemaker, Rick Knoll, is a 6-foot-tall, long-haired Vietnam vet with a Ph.D. in organic chemistry and an almost-second Ph.D. in agricultural ecology who was once a member of a cold war top-security research and development project for the Lawrence Livermore Laboratories. He describes how the brew will go through many stages of decomposition, bubbling and frothing over and settling down and frothing again until it comes to a rest as a fine green liquid. At that stage he will add it in minute homeopathic amounts to the irrigation water that pumps throughout his 10-acre farm.

Rick and his wife, Christy, started farming here in 1979. They were vegetarians and had been growing their own food in their backyard in Santa Ana, California. Seeking a more rural lifestyle, they found a 10-acre alfalfa field for sale 60 miles east of San Francisco, near the town of Brentwood.

The first thing they did was plant six hundred fruit trees, haphazardly selecting a wide range of fruits from catalogues. "We liked Fig Newtons," Rick tells me, "so of the six hundred fruit trees we ordered, sixty of them were figs. When the trees came into production, we discovered that two vegetarians couldn't eat the fruit from sixty trees." So the Knolls started bringing their fruit to the farmers' market in San Rafael, twenty minutes north of San Francisco, where they garnered an instant following. "We became the fig people," Rick says.

The Knolls now sell at the Ferry Plaza farmers' market in San Francisco, a market I know well. For years, each spring we would make the six-hour trek from Fairview Gardens to San Francisco loaded with white asparagus, strawberries, cherimoyas, and mandarin oranges. A pilgrimage site for Bay Area foodies, Ferry Plaza was started by Sibella Kraus in 1993. Originally, farmers took part by invitation only. Chefs, food writers, and gourmands flocked to the ingredients that fueled their passion, a bounty hauled in by equally passionate farmers who had gone to great extremes to pick squash blossoms, berries, asparagus, salad greens— in the middle of the night by the light of the moon, with scissors designed to cut at just the right angle—then chilled at the right moment and raced to the market like a body part for some emergency organ transplant.

Earlier in the day, when I visited the Knolls at the market, all the figs were already gone. Rick tells me we should have seen people going crazy over them. He refers to them as "the sexiest of fruits" and tells me that his customers are "completely horny" for them. Figs he insists, not apples, were the forbidden fruit that tempted Adam and Eve: "Apples don't even grow in that region of the world."

The Knolls' figs are planted close together in 350-foot hedgerows that run north-south. In between the rows, buckwheat and horseradish, amaranth and lamb's-quarters and fava beans flourish. The farm also is planted in Blenheim apricots, Fuji apples, Santa Rosa plums, and a wide range of seasonal vegetables. This particular Eden is bordered with eucalyptus trees planted as windbreaks and to keep out highway dust and spray drift. Beyond the Knolls' borders are corn and hay fields; industrial, laser-perfect orchards of peaches and plums and apricots; and the current boom crop, the one that is spreading faster than Bermuda grass or bindweed and is forming one of the largest monocultures in California's long tradition of large monocultures: housing developments.

Here, the new developments sprouting on the outskirts of Brentwood are euphemistically called the Legends, Wildflower, and the Vineyards, the new streets named after long-dead groves of nut or fruit trees. The business of selling off and building on land is taking place at a staggering rate, as a new generation of farmers' kids weigh the economic return on farming their land versus developing it and choose the guaranteed cash.

It's hard to ignore the temptation of cashing in on land, especially when that land requires the level of work and commitment of a farm. But if you consider the huge demand for high-quality food, add in the jobs (twenty-seven people work on Fairview Gardens' 12.25 acres), factor in the environmental and social and health benefits, and remember that creative farmers like Rick and Christy have found a way to make a decent living, the economics of agricultural-land conversion don't look so inevitable after all.

The Knolls gross $450,000 from their 10 acres, and they paid off their mortgage out of farm income. Rick tells me that "farms can be perpetual money machines" if they are managed well. I know that to be true; in a good year at Fairview Gardens, we gross over $700,000 on 12.25 acres. I know firsthand that a small piece of land can feed a large number of people, so why shouldn't all housing developments include small farms? Why wouldn't they be at least as important as a community pool? Shouldn't developers consider food as part of a broad range of basic needs that every housing development should have, no less important than water, electricity, and sewers?

When I started at Fairview Gardens, around the same time the Knolls began working their farm, the Goleta Valley was still primarily agricultural. With its perfect Mediterranean climate and 30-foot-deep topsoils, I felt as if I had landed in an agricultural paradise. When Aaron was four, the real-estate boom began, turning many local farms into statistics; by the time he was fourteen, 46 acres of agricultural land were disappearing every hour from the country and our own home was completely surrounded with housing and commercial development. Our battles to preserve one small piece of farmland consumed vast amounts of my life and energy and nearly two decades. I was threatened with jail time over the crow of our roosters and our rich piles of compost made from recycling local waste, and challenged over the colorful roadside signs advertising our fresh products. Eventually, the land itself was threatened with development, and in one year we raised the $1 million needed to purchase the land and place it under an active agricultural conservation easement that gives the land a voice and protects it forever.

Similar dramas of threatened farms are playing out over and over, and they do not always end with the farm being spared. Driving through miles of new "communities" thrown down onto these interior deserts reminds me that it is probably only a matter of time before Rick and Christy Knoll are fielding complaints over the crow of roosters and the sweet, earthy smell of well-made compost.

Rick snaps me back to the present with a request that Aaron and I remove our shoes. "I don't understand how any farmer can feel the land with shoes on," he says. Barefoot, he takes me to see some of the "mother" fig trees, trunks almost two feet in diameter, branches large and spreading. We eat Adriatics with pale yellow skins tinged with burgundy that break open to reveal a strawberry-pink flesh. The figs are meaty here, and after feeding on a few, I'm feeling quite full and satisfied, like I've just eaten a complete meal.

The pickers wear surgical gloves and carry broomsticks with hooks on the ends to pull branches down and closer for picking. Metal picking buckets lined with white butcher paper are filled only a third of the way up to prevent bruising. At the farm's packing station, the meticulously layered stems all point in the same direction.

With complete abandonment, Christy describes her relationship with figs: "I love eating them, playing with them, telling folks about them. Figs are a happy thing." At the farmers' markets, she describes how to choose a fig and helps folks determine which ripeness they like, tries to describe the many stages of "figness."

"I make them put one in their hand and feel it," she says. "Each one is different; it's more than just soft or hard."

At the farmers' market, people seldom ask about texture or complex flavors. I always get the same question: "Is it sweet?"—as if sweet is the only quality food has. People often assume that fresh off the tree or plant is always best, but that's not always true. Our Clementine mandarins need a couple days to mellow after being harvested before they manifest their complex blend of sweet and tart. Our ever-bearing strawberries need half a day after picking to progress from sharp to almost musky. Rick talks about the personality traits of several fig varieties—which ones like to age in the cooler, which are soft and syrupy, which can be eaten more firm and fresh off the tree.

He and Christy have started putting pictures of their farm and the stages of their crops on the Internet along with ripening times. "I can tell people to get ready, and not to plan their vacation when the figs are about to come in," Rick says.

This kind of relationship with their customers helped Rick and Christy decide, after eighteen years, to drop out of organic certification. The new regulations and government rules have become so onerous, with so many new fees and inspections and so much paperwork, coupled with a watering down of the definition of organic, that many farmers who worked for years to give the word its meaning and credibility no longer use it. When Rick finally made the decision, he bought a surfboard, thinking he would be so ostracized that he'd end up spending more time surfing than farming.

The surfboard hasn't been used much. By providing extensive educational materials to their customers and using the word Tairwa, a play on the French term *terroir* ("essence of place"), to label their products, the Knolls have seen their sales actually increase. This acceptance from their customers doesn't take away the fact that they remain outsiders surrounded by industrial farming and the encroachment of development. The highway noise seems to penetrate every part of this land. Although you can get used to any noise and eventually tune it out, the road noise here is a constant reminder of the vulnerability of this place.

On our new farm in British Columbia, we are blessed with a different kind of noise. The spring sound of thousands of frogs having sex in our two ponds is deafening; starlings, quail, ravens, and geese move through in great flocks announced by insistent chirping, tweeting, and honking; carpenter and mason and bumblebees hover over every plant, seeming to pollinate them with buzzing alone. Spiders of every kind are everywhere, and there are so many snakes that in the spring I have to continually reset the mower higher and higher to keep the whirling blades from hurting them. My challenge is not so much creating the space and providing the invitation but protecting and encouraging the habitat that already exists. It's an aspect of good farming I am slowly learning: how to stay out of the way.

I used to put all my thought and creative energy into my own impositions on the land: what crops we could grow and how best to maintain control over the workings of the farm. Then I realized that, in spite of myself, there was a whole other world growing and thriving, less tamed and controlled, a bit of wildness that our fertile soils and planted trees and cover crops had inadvertently helped support.

As I did at Fairview, the Knolls started with a more or less empty canvas. They themselves were the pioneer species laying an imposed groundwork of trees and plants that allowed wildness to move in. When Rick proudly tells me that there are "night crawlers fucking in the orchard," I understand. To know that numerous creatures have settled in and are comfortable enough to reproduce themselves provides as much a sense of accomplishment and satisfaction as high yields and tasty crops. Once again, I'm reminded that farmers who are outlaws by conventional terms are actually lured by a sense of being part of something much bigger than themselves.

I think about Rick and Christy, with a will to be different, farming as I did on an island in the path of development. I sense that they are not just holding out or holding on, but, rather, moving forward with new ideas, breaking the boundaries of convention, hoping future generations will do the same.

☘

KLEIN'S TRUCK STOP, NORTH OF FRESNO, COULD BE ITS OWN CITY, with a motel, grocery store, restaurant, rows of diesel pumps and pay phones, and lines of coin-operated showers for the body and car washes for the machines. This outpost services the thousands of truckers who ply the valley's roads, delivering boxes and pallets and equipment and picking up bins and boxes and bags and piles and stacks of produce that are transported an average of 1,400 miles from the field to the plate.

We pass huge equipment yards with rows of tractors and steel implements. Stacks of aluminum and PVC pipe are everywhere, a reminder of how dependent this valley is on imported irrigation. A sign along the road reminds us that "Agriculture is our bread and butter." A few miles later: "Water is our future." Wars have been fought over oil; they may one day be fought over water as populations increase and aquifers decrease. Eighty percent of the world's fresh water is used in agriculture, but, due to inefficient transportation and application methods, only a fraction of it actually reaches the intended plants or animals.

This is ground zero for California's industrial agriculture, where almost half of all the fruits and vegetables consumed in America are grown. The bustle of tractors and semis, the immense scale, the sheer desolation are almost unbearable. The fields are empty except for endless rows of food and inconspicuous clusters of workers, few of whom live in the ubiquitous housing developments or shop in the enormous car dealerships that are now sprouting up around them faster than lettuce and carrots and beans. Here, in the unremarkable suburb of Madera, is the home of Tom and Denesse Willey of T&D Willey Farms.

I first met Tom and Denesse years ago at California's annual ecological-farming conference. In those early days of the movement, it was unusual for an organic farmer to set up shop in the belly of the beast, the Central Valley, so Tom and Denesse were something of an enigma. The only thing about their appearance that suggested a connection with this "alternative" movement was Tom's beard, which extended midway down his chest. He reminded me of the pictures I had seen of John Muir, but with tweed jacket and suspenders and an awkward limp. I didn't realize until years later that he has only one leg.

Tom studied for the priesthood, quit and became a parole officer, and went into farming after failing a physical and being turned down for a job at a juvenile facility. "Because I had a peg leg, they didn't think I could chase the kids," he says. Denesse is heavyset, with a presence simultaneously tough and warm. They met at Fresno State University, where Denesse was studying to be a nurse. Like many of the new agriculturists, neither one grew up on a farm.

They still don't live on a farm. Their simple three-bedroom tract home is 8 miles east of their 75-acre farm, which, like many in this valley, no longer has a

farmer-occupied house on the property. The farmhouses that still exist cling to their tiny footprint, crops growing right up to the doorstep, as if the home and its human inhabitants were in the way.

Denesse greets me at the door and leads me into the kitchen, where she has put together a multicourse meal of pasta and rapini; a salad of mixed lettuces, arugula, and gorgonzola cheese; stir-fried broccoli with garlic; roasted potatoes and carrots; and roast beef. All but the beef came from their farm.

I wonder how many of the Willeys' neighbors are eating like this tonight, or if their dinner came from the nearby Raley's supermarket or from the In-N-Out drive-through. How many folks living in the heart of the nation's breadbasket are eating anything grown here? Results of a 2001 California health interview study show that the Central Valley has the highest rates of food insecurity in the entire state of California. How sad and ironic that the very people who plant, hoe, and harvest the food that many Americans eat cannot afford to feed their own families while surrounded by millions of acres of food. Everything in this valley is displaced. The water comes from deep wells or through hundreds of miles of pipes and aqueducts; the farmworkers come hundreds of miles from Mexico; the rash of new housing developments are built for people who work somewhere else. Even the food leaves these fields and travels to distribution centers in San Francisco and Los Angeles before it can return to the shelves of local supermarkets.

The Willeys' first farm was in Fresno, where they leased land for twelve years until the property was sold out from under them to the local school district. Their current farm became available after its corporate owner went bankrupt. Vast regiments of almonds, peaches, and grapes and a nursery for dairy cows border the land. The only thing alive in the neighboring orchards is the fruit trees. I am fascinated by the pruning; every tree is absolutely identical. Tom tells me that his neighbor's peach orchard is famously productive, and though I'm sure I could learn a lot from their technique, it feels a little creepy, less like an orchard and more like a peach assembly line.

In many rural areas, the Willeys' 75 acres of mixed vegetables would not appear particularly unusual or outstanding. Here, the farm sticks out like a green thumb. When the Willeys started farming here, folks would stop on the road to gawk, trying to figure out what they were doing, growing so many different things on such a "small" acreage. One guy was so distracted by their unique operation that he crashed his car into a telephone pole.

The Willeys' farm is a practical place, geared for maximum production and sales. There are no shade trees taking up valuable planting space, no flowers along the road. The buildings are all function and no frill, and the land is flat, very flat.

As we walk together around the edges of the fields, I remember how it is when I show visiting farmers around my place. The first thing they always do is grab a handful of soil and smell and feel it, or just kick it around with their shoes. It's almost as if, away from their land, farmers can't settle down or feel comfortable until they've made contact with the soil. I crouch down to scoop a handful and

look up to see Tom's face light up. He clearly appreciates the gesture; my instinctive action creates a certain acceptance. This is the foundation of their work, and he's pleased I can recognize it. Their predecessors weren't exactly focused on the biological or microbial life in the soil. The Willeys describe the panic in their first year, when all of their early plantings succumbed to the weeds, how they thought they had made a big mistake in buying the place. "Tom was mostly challenged by the fact that so much of what you know is related to a specific place," Denesse says, "so even though we felt confident that we had the knowledge and tools, we were essentially starting over."

Although the majority of the Willeys' harvest is destined for wholesalers in San Francisco or Portland, or Los Angeles, or New York, 350 families, as members of the farm's CSA, now gather each week at twelve distribution sites around the valley to pick up their share of the abundance.

Denesse talks about the decision to start the CSA and attract local customers. I am amazed to hear her say that the consolidation in the organic market is pushing farms of her size out. It wasn't very long ago that a 100-acre organic-vegetable farm was considered large. I remember when one of the country's largest organic wholesalers consolidated produce from several local growers at our little farm in California, loading it onto a rented U-Haul truck. At the time, organic-vegetable farms were few and the products from our tiny 12 acres were still taken seriously. It didn't take long, however, before the wholesalers abandoned us in favor of folks with 50–100 acres. Now, even the Willeys are apparently too small to satisfy the volume demand from chains such as Whole Foods and Wild Oats. The farms that now supply those stores must play to the tune that dominates the rest of the agricultural world.

"We were trying to see five, ten years down the road," Tom says. "We were feeling like being closer to our customers, having a more direct relationship. Our own community really needed this, and we've used it as a way to raise local food consciousness. We need a local food system because of the huge disconnect between the farms and the growing urban community here."

I watch as Tom calls a midday meeting to adjust the afternoon schedule. The meeting covers specific tasks, but it also covers strategy, and what's behind the decisions. It's not like Tom couldn't just give instructions, but the approach is more inclusive, and I can see how it creates a sense of teamwork and mutual responsibility. Most farms do not include farmworkers in decisions. They are not often respected for their history and knowledge, and all they have to offer to the management of a farm.

As the seventy-five-person crew fans out, I recognize the familiar ease and dynamic that develop when people have worked together for a number of years. It becomes almost nonverbal, a dance, a knowing of what needs to be done. Tom tells me that one of his crew has been with him for thirty years, another one for twenty. "When we came to Madera, we were blessed by being introduced to these people from Oaxaca," Denesse says. "We just never could have accomplished what we accomplished without them."

I watch the finesse that goes into preparing and packing the products. Carrots are individually and meticulously sized, red-topped turnips hand-washed, greens carefully sorted. Every box contains a message, a recipe, a piece of farm philosophy, a quote, a political commentary.

"We must consider it a scientific fact that you are what you eat," writes Tom in one of their box inserts. "The same molecules that make up the food we consume become the molecules of our minds and bodies. So, unless you are your own farmer, you should choose one as carefully as you would choose your doctor or your pastor. Therefore, it is fitting that farmers, like doctors, lawyers, professors, and pastors, should command a high level of respect and income, commensurate with this level of responsibility. I consider it an honor and a privilege that you have chosen me to be your farmer."

I ride around the farm with Tom and Denesse in one of their fleet of converted golf carts, listening to them haggle over plantings and harvest times and second-guess each other's decisions. They stop at a field that has been mowed and is ready to be turned under, and Tom discovers a number of marketable beets. He and Denesse disagree on whether to save these stragglers or to move on and get the field replanted. I, too, am a gleaner; on our tiny acreage, every beet counts. It's a different story here, and I watch this delicate balance played out.

Most days, Denesse sits in a tiny office wearing a headset, fielding calls for orders, booking trucks, negotiating prices. She is tough and unyielding and insists on getting paid well for their products.

"Paying a high price for food does not guarantee that the farmer is receiving a fair return," she reminds me, "but paying a low price is pure thievery. It is a theft of the farm, the farmer, and the farmworker."

Outside the office, in the packing shed, bins of freshly harvested products are being frantically washed and sorted. Everything is packed in recycled wood boxes lined with white paper.

"I cannot tell you how many times I have argued that using wax cartons in our pack would make us more price competitive in the marketplace," Denesse tells me. "But Tom reminds me that waxed cartons merely shift the cost of packaging disposal to the community where our products end up. That's why we stick with reused and reusable packaging."

The Willeys and I both started farming in the early seventies. At the time, the organic movement was still a local, community-based effort that focused on the importance of building and sustaining living soils. Now you can see the shrink-wrapped products of corporate "organic" farms on supermarket shelves next to the Cheetos. And although some of Tom and Denesse's products may end up on those same supermarket shelves, their philosophy and the quality of their products provide an important model in a valley that is straining under agricultural pollution, water issues, development pressures, and economic hardship. They employ up to one hundred people during the peak season and gross $2 million a year while maintaining the values that sparked this movement. "How many husbands and wives can support themselves solely off their land?" Denesse asks.

Annual gross sales of $2 million may sound like a lot, but at the end of the season, when they pay all the bills and buy the seed for the next year, there usually isn't a whole lot left over. Blending economics with biology can be a challenge. Each year, the weather is different, the demand for products shifts, prices move up and down, crops and soil ebb and flow.

These issues affect the Willeys and their neighbors with equal force, but Tom and Denesse have a different way of fighting for their land and their lives. Everything is a collaboration, a give-and-take with the soil, their crew, their customers, and each other. In this beleaguered valley, surrounded to the horizon by farms that run on a different set of rules, this is not sentimentality, but the kind of stubborn belief it takes to be different.

It's hard for me to picture the Willeys as radicals or outlaws. I wonder how something as basic and necessary as growing food became so extraordinary, how farmers are being viewed like some sort of rare animals. When the district attorney was preparing charges against my roosters and compost, I found myself appealing to the community's sense of tradition and our collective agrarian memory. I discovered that what we now provide to society is more than just food—it's a simple reminder of something even more fundamental.

"To plant a seed and believe that it will germinate, outcompete weeds, bloom, set fruit, and be harvested and sold at a fair price is a great leap of faith," Denesse says. "This is why I have always said that farmers are the most faithful people on earth. Next to spiders, faith is the farmer's best friend."

❧

Tisane with Lemon Verbena

SERVES 4 TO 6

Bob Cannard has a beautiful hedge of lemon verbena that runs along one of the old turkey brooder houses at his farm. Tisane is one of the best ways to appreciate lemon verbena's lovely fragrance. This works well with both mint and lemon verbena, but you can also use them individually.

4 cups boiling water
3 leafy sprigs fresh lemon verbena, each about 6 inches in length
3 leafy sprigs fresh mint, each about 6 inches in length

Combine the boiling water, lemon verbena, and mint in a glass or ceramic teapot and let the mixture steep for 4 to 5 minutes. Strain into a pitcher and discard the herbs. Serve immediately in small, clear glasses.

Rocket Blossom Ravioli

Leave it to Bob Cannard to offer a use for rocket that's gone to seed—unless we're saving seed, most of us hack it down when it starts flowering. This recipe is a rocket revelation: the blossoms have a nice, pungent quality that stands up well to cooking, and it makes for a simple, delicious ravioli. Bob reccomends adding a little sautéed pancetta as well.

MAKES ABOUT
40 RAVIOLI
SERVES 6

PASTA DOUGH
3 whole eggs
3 egg yolks
1 tablespoon olive oil
2½ cups all-purpose flour
1 teaspoon kosher salt

RAVIOLI FILLING
1 tablespoon olive oil
1 tablespoon unsalted butter
1 medium yellow onion, cut into ¼-inch dice
Kosher salt to taste
½ pound organic rocket (arugula) blossoms, roughly chopped
1 cup good-quality, whole-milk, fresh ricotta cheese, drained if necessary
Freshly cracked black pepper to taste

All-purpose flour for dusting, if necessary
Rice or semolina flour for dusting
Kosher salt to taste
Extra-virgin olive oil for drizzling
½ lemon
Freshly grated Parmesan cheese, preferably Parmigiano-Reggiano, for sprinkling
Fresh rocket (arugula) leaves for garnish

TO MAKE THE PASTA DOUGH: Whisk together the whole eggs, egg yolks, and olive oil in a small bowl. Set aside. Combine the all-purpose flour and salt in the bowl of an electric stand mixer fitted with the paddle attachment. With the mixer on low speed, add the egg mixture in a slow and steady stream, pausing every now and then to let the egg thoroughly mix into the flour. Once you have added about two-thirds of the egg mixture, stop the mixer occasionally and check the moisture of the dough by gently squeezing a small amount in the palm of your hand. Continue to slowly add the remaining egg mixture until the dough easily holds together when gently squeezed—it may not be necessary to add all of the egg. If you've added all of the egg mixture and the dough is still too dry, add water 1 teaspoon at a time until the dough is moist enough to pass the squeeze test.

continued >

Gather the dough and divide it into 2 balls. Wrap each ball tightly in plastic, and then flatten each into a disk. Let the dough rest at room temperature for 45 minutes.

MEANWHILE, MAKE THE RAVIOLI FILLING: Heat a large sauté pan over medium-high heat and add the olive oil and butter. When the butter has melted, add the diced onion and a pinch of salt and sauté until the onion is tender, about 6 minutes. Add the rocket blossoms and another pinch of salt and sauté until the greens begin to wilt, about 2 minutes. Transfer the mixture to a medium bowl and set aside to cool. Stir in the ricotta. Season to taste with salt and several twists of pepper.

After the pasta dough has rested, use a pasta machine to knead the dough. Working with 1 disk of dough at a time, flatten the dough with a rolling pin and pass it through the rollers of the pasta machine at the widest setting. If the dough sticks to the rollers, add a sprinkle of all-purpose flour. Fold the sheet of dough into thirds, press it down with your fingertips (or run the rolling pin over it again if necessary), and pass it through the rollers again. Repeat the rolling and folding process with the rollers set at the widest setting until the dough is very smooth, about 3 times. Wrap the dough in plastic and repeat the process with the other disk of dough.

Adjust the rollers on the pasta machine to the next setting. Unwrap 1 piece of dough and pass it through the rollers. Gradually stretch the dough to the thinnest setting, passing the dough through successively narrower settings, and sprinkling very lightly with all-purpose flour as necessary to prevent sticking. (Wait until you have assembled the first batch of ravioli before you stretch the second piece of dough.)

Cut the stretched dough into 2-foot lengths and cover with a kitchen towel to prevent it from drying out. (If the dough is especially dry, mist the towel lightly with water.) Working with 1 sheet of dough at a time, lay the dough horizontally on a lightly floured work surface. Beginning about 1 inch from a short edge of the dough sheet, put 1 tablespoon of filling just below the horizontal center of the dough. Continue to put tablespoons of filling in a row along the length of the dough sheet, spacing them about 2 inches apart, leaving at least 1 inch at the other end of the dough sheet as well. Mist the dough with water and fold the top half of dough lengthwise over the filling. Working from left to right, use your fingertips to gently seal the dough around the mounds of filling. Using a ravioli cutter, trim the bottom edge of the dough, and then cut the ravioli perpendicularly into individual squares. (Leave the fold over the filling at the top of the ravioli intact.) Put the ravioli on a baking sheet lined with parchment paper and dusted with rice flour—be sure the ravioli don't overlap or they will stick together. Sprinkle the rice flour on top of the ravioli as well and set aside. Repeat the entire process with the remaining dough and filling.

Bring a large pot of water to a boil. Season the boiling water with a generous amount of salt—it should taste almost like seawater. Drop the ravioli into the water and cook until the pasta is tender, 3 to 4 minutes. Gently remove the ravioli with a flat wire-mesh strainer and place on individual serving plates. Drizzle with extra-virgin olive oil and squeeze 3 or 4 drops of fresh lemon juice on top. Sprinkle with Parmesan and garnish with a few leaves of rocket. Serve immediately, passing the peppermill at the table.

NOTE: Ravioli can easily be prepared in advance, but be sure to line the baking sheet (or sheets) with parchment paper and be extra generous with the rice flour—they tend to stick to the pan when stored for longer periods of time. Cover the ravioli with another layer of parchment and store in the refrigerator for up to 2 days. Or, wrap the baking sheet tightly in plastic and put the ravioli in the freezer. Once frozen solid, transfer the ravioli to a plastic freezer bag and freeze for up to 1 month.

Fig and Herb Salad with Goat Cheese

SERVES 4

While visiting the Knolls, I ate figs all day long, every variety at every stage of ripeness, served in many forms. One evening, Christy halved the strawberry-fleshed Adriatics lengthwise, spooned a little soft goat cheese on top of each one, garnished them with a leaf of fresh basil, and served them presented on the platter like a mandala.

The combination of pungent herbs, sweet figs, and creamy goat cheese in this recipe works well.

1 shallot, finely diced

2 tablespoons sherry vinegar

Kosher salt to taste

8 ripe figs such as Black Mission or Brown Turkey

½ cup extra-virgin olive oil

2 handfuls fresh arugula leaves (about 2 cups)

¾ cup fresh flat-leaf parsley

½ cup small fresh basil leaves

¼ cup small fresh mint leaves

1 handful young, tender frisée (about 1 cup)

Freshly cracked black pepper to taste

2 ounces goat cheese, chilled

Combine the shallot and vinegar in a small bowl with a pinch of salt and let stand for 10 to 15 minutes.

Meanwhile, trim the fig stems, cutting off just enough to remove anything tough and fibrous—you want to preserve the teardrop shape of the figs. Quarter the figs lengthwise and set aside.

Whisk the olive oil into the vinegar and shallot mixture, and taste the vinaigrette with an arugula leaf; you may want to add a little more olive oil or an extra drop or two of vinegar. Combine the arugula, herbs, and frisée in a large bowl and season with salt and pepper. Gently toss with just enough vinaigrette to lightly coat the greens. Place the greens on a serving platter or individual plates. Nestle the fig quarters around the greens and crumble the goat cheese on top. If you have any vinaigrette left over, drizzle a little on the figs and around the plate. Serve immediately.

Wild Salmon Grilled in a Fig Leaf

The first time I ate salmon in a fig leaf, I could have sworn that generous portions of fresh coconut had been heaped on prior to cooking. The fig leaf (which itself is not edible) keeps the fish moist and gives it a wonderful, sweet coconut flavor. If you're lucky enough to have your own fig tree, the best thing is to collect the leaves immediately before cooking. Sometimes we really get into it and grill the wrapped fish over coals of peach or apricot wood. In addition to the amazing flavors of this recipe, the tropical smell that perfumes the air once the fig leaf hits the grill is intoxicating.

Fig leaves can also be used to bake shrimp or goat cheese. The edge of the leaf chars and curls around whatever you bake on it, making a simple but impressive presentation.

SERVES 6

> Six 5½-ounce wild salmon fillets, skinned and boned
> Kosher salt to taste
> Freshly cracked black pepper to taste
> 6 large fig leaves
> Extra-virgin olive oil for serving (optional)

Prepare a fire in a charcoal grill or preheat a gas grill.

Season the salmon on both sides with salt and pepper. Wrap each fillet in a fig leaf. (It's OK if the fish isn't completely enclosed.)

Place the salmon packages on the grill over medium heat with the seam side of the fig leaves down—this helps to seal the leaf around the fish. Grill the salmon, turning once, until just cooked through, about 3 minutes per side. The fish should be light pink inside—it will continue to cook for a bit once you've removed it from the grill. Transfer the packages to a platter or individual plates and peel back the fig leaves. Drizzle with extra-virgin olive oil (if desired) and serve immediately.

Fig Tart with Almonds and Honey

This tart is delicious right out of the oven. The figs are glazed with honey after the tart is baked, and then the tart is put under the broiler for a few minutes. The figs come out shiny and with a few charred tips here and there, and the crust is dark mahogany brown, with little bits of caramelized sugar.

> All-purpose flour for dusting
> 10 ounces Tart Dough (recipe follows)
> 15 ripe Black Mission figs
> 6 tablespoons sugar
> 3 tablespoons ground almonds
> 1 tablespoon unsalted butter, melted
> 1½ tablespoons honey, warmed
> Whipped cream or vanilla ice cream for serving (optional)

Position one rack in the lower third of the oven and a second rack just beneath the broiler. Place a pizza stone, if available, on the lower rack, and preheat the oven to 400 degrees F.

On a lightly floured work surface, roll out the tart dough into a 13-inch circle. Brush off any excess flour on both sides with a dry pastry brush. Transfer the dough to a baking sheet lined with parchment paper and refrigerate for 15 to 20 minutes.

Meanwhile, trim the fig stems. Cut off just enough of the stem to remove anything tough and fibrous—you want to preserve the teardrop shape of the figs. Quarter the figs lengthwise and set aside.

In a small bowl, mix together 1 tablespoon of the sugar with the almonds. Remove the dough round from the refrigerator and sprinkle the sugar mixture over it in an even layer, leaving a 1½-inch border.

Neatly arrange the fig quarters in concentric circles over the nut layer on the dough, again leaving the 1½-inch border. Sprinkle with 3 tablespoons of the remaining sugar. Roll the exposed border over on itself to make a narrow pastry rim, then crimp the edge in a decorative fashion. Brush the rim of the tart with the melted butter and sprinkle the remaining 2 tablespoons sugar along the rim. (This step is critical; the sugar bubbles and caramelizes as it cooks, producing a deliciously crispy crust.)

Bake the tart in the lower third of the oven for 15 minutes. Rotate and bake for about 15 more minutes, until the crust is golden. Remove the tart from the oven and adjust the oven to broil. Using a pastry brush, gently paint the figs—not the crust—with the warm honey. Place the tart on the top rack of the oven and rotate under the broiler until the figs are golden brown with a few charred tips, 2 to 3 minutes—don't walk away from the oven. Serve the tart warm or at room temperature, with whipped cream or vanilla ice cream, if desired.

NOTE: To grind the almonds without overprocessing, carefully pulse the almonds in a food processor until very finely chopped—not perfectly smooth.

tart dough

MAKES TWO 10-OUNCE
PORTIONS OF DOUGH,
ENOUGH FOR 2 TARTS

2 cups all-purpose flour
1 tablespoon sugar
1 teaspoon salt
¾ cup cold unsalted butter, cut into small pieces
About ½ cup ice water

Combine the flour, sugar, and salt in a large bowl. Add half of the butter. Using your hands, gently toss the butter around to coat each piece with the flour mixture—this helps the butter to cut in evenly. Using a pastry cutter or 2 knives, cut the butter into the flour mixture until it is the texture of coarse oatmeal. Add the remaining butter, gently toss again to coat each piece with the flour mixture, and quickly cut again until the larger pieces are about the size of lima beans. Sprinkle the ice water into the bowl in 2 or 3 additions, using your hands to lightly toss the mixture between your fingers to moisten it evenly. Stop adding water when the dough looks raggedy and rough but holds together when you gently squeeze a small amount in the palm of your hand. Form the dough into a brick shape—be careful not to knead it, just squeeze it gently into one solid mass. Cut the brick in half crosswise. Wrap each half tightly in plastic and press each package into a flat disk. Refrigerate for several hours to relax the gluten and chill before using.

NOTE: The dough can be frozen for up to 1 month.

Pasta with Broccoli Rabe, Hot Pepper, and Garlic

SERVES 4 TO 6

On arrival at Denesse and Tom Willey's place, we were treated to a fantastic farm-grown feast, including this pasta with broccoli rabe. I don't know why broccoli rabe (also called rapini) never gets its due; it has a wonderful bitter and nutty flavor, and it's easy to grow.

This is the perfect quick-and-easy dinner. The sauté can be done in just about the amount of time it takes to cook the pasta. For those who avoid wheat, it can be made with spelt-flour pasta; buckwheat-flour pasta is another good, earthy option.

1 cup fresh bread crumbs from country bread

6 tablespoons extra-virgin olive oil, plus extra for drizzling

Kosher salt to taste

1½ pounds broccoli rabe

1 medium red onion, thinly sliced

4 cloves garlic, finely chopped

Hot Peppers Preserved in Vinegar (page 249) or hot red pepper flakes to taste

Red wine vinegar to taste

1 pound penne pasta

Grated pecorino romano cheese for sprinkling

Preheat oven to 350 degrees F. Combine the bread crumbs and 2 tablespoons of the olive oil in a bowl and stir to evenly coat the bread crumbs with the oil. Transfer the bread crumbs to a baking sheet and bake until golden brown, about 10 minutes, stirring occasionally. Set aside.

Bring a large pot of water to a boil. Season the boiling water with a generous amount of salt—it should taste almost like seawater. Trim and discard the tough and fibrous portion of the broccoli rabe stems (about ¹/₂ inch). Roughly chop the remaining stems, leaves, and florets and set aside.

Heat a large sauté pan over high heat. Add the remaining 4 tablespoons olive oil and the onion and season with a generous pinch of salt. Sauté until the onion is tender and lightly caramelized, about 5 minutes. Add the garlic and hot peppers and continue to sauté until the garlic is fragrant, about 1 minute. Add the broccoli rabe in large handfuls, adding more after each batch has wilted, then add a splash of water and cook, stirring frequently, until the broccoli rabe is tender, about 7 minutes. (Add another splash or two of water if the pan dries out before the broccoli rabe is tender.) Add the vinegar to taste (about 2 teaspoons) and adjust the seasoning with salt, if necessary.

Meanwhile, cook the pasta in the boiling water until al dente and drain, reserving a small amount of the pasta water. Add the pasta to the broccoli rabe mixture, drizzle with a generous amount of olive oil, and toss well to combine. If the pasta is a little dry, add a splash of the pasta water. Transfer to a warm platter or individual serving bowls. Sprinkle the toasted bread crumbs and pecorino romano on top and serve.

Leek and Chard Frittata

Denesse Willey suggested this recipe, telling me that they serve it at events to showcase their produce. It's a simple use of fresh leeks and chard that gives them a leading role, not burying them beneath an avalanche of other ingredients or overwrought preparations.

A frittata is the perfect healthful food to make in advance and enjoy later. It's easy to make as long as you have a good nonstick pan; there's nothing more frustrating than having half the frittata cling to the pan when you turn it onto a plate. This version is made with Parmesan cheese, but it would also be delicious with chunks of soft goat cheese.

1½ pounds leeks

2 tablespoons olive oil

4 tablespoons unsalted butter

Kosher salt to taste

2 bunches chard, stemmed and roughly chopped

6 eggs

Freshly cracked black pepper to taste

⅓ cup freshly grated Parmesan cheese, preferably Parmigiano Reggiano

Position a rack in the upper third of the oven and preheat the broiler.

To prepare the leeks, cut off the roots, trim the tough, dark green tops, and peel off an outer layer or two. Halve the leeks lengthwise and then cut each leek crosswise into thin half-moon slices. Wash the leeks in a large basin of cold water, agitating to remove all of the dirt. When the dirt has settled, scoop the leeks out of the water with a strainer. (It's not necessary for the leeks to drain thoroughly.)

Heat a medium sauté pan over high heat and add 1 tablespoon of the olive oil and 2 tablespoons of the butter. When the butter has melted, add the leeks and a generous pinch of salt and sauté until the leeks are tender and lightly caramelized, about 4 minutes. Add the chard in large handfuls, adding more after each batch has wilted, and cook, stirring frequently, until all of the greens have collapsed and wilted. Adjust the seasoning with salt, if necessary, and set aside to cool.

Beat the eggs in a large bowl and season with salt (about 1 teaspoon) and several twists of pepper. Add the chard mixture and Parmesan and stir well to combine. Heat an 8-inch nonstick sauté pan over medium heat and add the remaining 1 tablespoon olive oil and 2 tablespoons butter. When the butter has melted, add the egg mixture and cook until the frittata begins to set around the edges and turn golden brown, about 5 minutes. Gently shake the pan to be sure that the frittata isn't sticking (it should move freely in the pan). Place the frittata under the broiler until it is golden brown and set in the middle, about 4 minutes. Remove from the oven and let stand for about 2 minutes. Carefully invert the frittata onto a serving plate. Cut the frittata into wedges and serve warm or at room temperature.

CHAPTER 4

FIRE AND MOLD

We planned our departure from the Central Valley so we'd hit the Mojave Desert in the evening, after things had cooled down. But as the sun goes down, it seems to get hotter. Aaron and I argue about whether to open or close the windows of the van. At 11 P.M., we stop for gas in Baker, California, where the 134-foot-high neon thermometer (the world's largest) registers the temperature at 103.

Above the gas station doors, misters spray into the air, cooling the entrance. I ask the cashier whether the giant phallus is accurate, and he silently nods his head. Baker is appropriately named. When I enter the men's bathroom, it's as if I've crashed a party; the women's bathroom is closed, and I find men and women sharing sinks and urinals, and young children playing on the floor. The road moves up and out of Baker to Halloran Summit, at 4,200 feet. As the elevation increases, the temperature drops. At the top of the pass, we breathe deeply before heading down the other side and back into the heat. By the time we see the blinding lights of Whiskey Pete's casino and the Nevada border, we've descended into the inferno.

It's nearly 1 A.M. in Las Vegas when we get out of the car to stretch our legs. The hot, bright streets are crowded with dazed-looking people, like zombies walking through a nighttime neon fantasy landscape. We walk a half block before hurrying back to the safety and relative sanity of our home on wheels. In the Central Valley, I understood what I was seeing; I was oriented by my own opposition. Now, I just feel addled by heat, fatigue, and the unfamiliar. I can hardly bear to think of my cool, distant farm while I'm miles away on this questionable adventure.

We drive on to Boulder City, Nevada, check into the Sands Motel, crank up the air conditioner, and go to sleep. The next morning, the message light is blinking on the motel phone. I push the button and listen: "Hey, dude. I got the stuff. I'll meet you down the street."

We reemerge into the sweltering daylight and head toward Hoover Dam. There are green lawns in front of every house—a surreal sight in this desert environment—and I flash back to another desert town in California where I saw pop-up sprinklers watering a patch of green cement. In this dry place, displaced water is everywhere. Water towers crown nearly every mountain peak and power lines crisscross the sky, carrying the captured energy of a once-wild river. At the dam, security checkpoints frame the entrance to the mother lode. Without a word, a guard in dark glasses gives us a heavy nod and lets us pass.

The dam is an engineering marvel, the ultimate in human cleverness. Placing a huge cement thumb into the midst of the mighty Colorado is right up there with sticking pig genes into spinach. As I stand on the edge of this massive hunk of concrete that holds back an entire river, I don't know whether I'm awestruck by the power it represents or by the vulnerability that makes it necessary.

Controlling water has been the fundamental task of civilization—whether for agriculture or electricity, or for the dozens of other reasons we need and want so much of it. Our quest is always based on how to get more, but it was not always so in this desert. For generations, a day's drive from here, the Hopi farmed and lived on the absolute minimum in an environment that requires miracles of farmers. They overcame the brutal demands of their traditional homeland in ways that would seem feeble to us now, even though their methods allowed them to persevere for thousands of years. It remains to be seen whether our own, more aggressive style of innovation will last as long, and at what cost.

I wonder what new adaptation will follow when the current plan doesn't work anymore. As the West is locked in year 5 of a historic drought, as farmers come under constant pressure to cede their water to fast-growing housing developments, we may soon have the chance to find out.

Highway 40 east out of Kingman, Arizona, provides some relief from the unbearable heat and traffic, and the moisture and green of the high desert and mountains west of Flagstaff are a reprieve. Eventually, the landscape levels out into a high plateau revealing a twilight horizon with a rubber-pink tinge. The momentary peace competes with the roar of semitrucks that flank the van, heading to deliver their goods to Albuquerque and points east. A Tyson Foods eighteen-wheeler blows by; giant letters boast "Feeding Your Family" as the wake nearly blows us off the road.

In Flagstaff, we stop to ask where to get fresh, local food. With no trace of irony, the woman in the beauty shop directs us an hour farther east. At the entrance to the historic La Posada Hotel restaurant, in Winslow, we're greeted with a display of traditional blue-corn Hopi flat bread and some ears of corn. The sign says "Piki bread made by Verlie Tawahongva from Hotevilla, Third Mesa" and "Hopi sweet corn grown in the gardens of El Gran Garage across the street on Route 66 by our friend and neighbor John and his dog Buster."

The walls of the adobe dining room are painted turquoise, and big windows look out onto the railway stop. We order squash blossom quesadillas, arugula, and vine-ripe tomatoes, cream of sweet corn and black-bean soup, a piece of buffalo steak rubbed in chili paste, and some cilantro-and-black-bean raviolis. After days of foraging in mini-marts, it's a relief to sit with fresh food and familiar flavors, some of them stirring long-ago memories of my visits to Hopiland. I wonder out loud if we should risk the ten-hour detour to Third Mesa and arrive unannounced.

While I was working on my first book, I made several trips with Aaron—who was seven then—to visit our friend Caroline, one of the Hopi elders living in Hotevilla. She had one of the great Hopi bean collections, and we worked with her, shelling and threshing black pintos, grease beans, and pink, red, and yellow Hopi beans. Each of the dozens of bean varieties had a story, and she lorded over that collection like it was the Ark, as if each small can of seed was the source of the world's survival. Beans are one of the most perfect foods, providing fundamental nutrition to both land and people. Nitrogen for plants is like protein for humans, a primary building block for energy and growth; beans can pull nitrogen literally out of thin air and in return give back more protein than a cow. Beans can survive on nothing, and we could survive on nothing but beans.

After the workday, we sat in the evenings in Caroline's home, eating lamb stew and pinto beans with Piki bread as we listened to stories and absorbed what we could of life in a Hopi village. Aaron says he remembers the kachina doll Caroline gave him—the Clown—masterfully carved and painted by her brother, Dan. She patiently instructed Aaron in its care, how to keep it fed with cornmeal from a pottery bowl. He talks about her gentle tone of voice and how safe he felt with her. He still keeps one of the rare photographs of that time, a picture of him and Caroline standing amid piles of beans drying in the desert sun. At the time, she was about seventy-five, and at seven years old, he stood almost as tall as she did.

As we get back in the van, I'm still caught in the spell of a long-ago time. It's been almost fifteen years since our last visit. Caroline is dead, but I would like to see her bean fields and find out whether anyone has preserved her ancient seed collection and continued to propagate the tradition. I'd like to drive to Titus's or Little Dan's cornfields and see whether some young person has continued their work. I vividly remember walking in that vast desert landscape and the surprise of discovering a lush field of corn and beans with an understory of melons and squash. There was not a pipe or tank or hose in sight. Although the Hopi I knew used tractors to prepare the fields, they still planted their corn with traditional planting sticks. Multiple seeds were placed deep in the ground, where young plants might root down and find moisture. As those seeds germinated, clusters of plants emerged, each like a small family standing together against the harsh desert climate.

Like most farmers, I've had only a few role models, and the experience in Hopiland has always stayed with me—not so much the farmers' methods as their ability to observe and work with their environment in such an intimate and respectful way.

I don't know whether it was the memory of the passerby's cautions or our tight schedule—or whether I'm afraid Hopiland would be too different and too lonely without my friends—but I let it go, and we whir past the exit at 70 miles an hour.

❧

We plunge into New Mexico's purple, red, and gold landscape, past elaborate rock towers, palaces, and pagodas that jut up into the horizon. Eventually, a beautiful agricultural valley opens up as we cross back to the Rio Grande. We drive along the river until the turnoff for the Dixon farmers' market. We're due to meet Eremita Campos there before venturing on to the farm where she lives with her daughter, Margaret, and her two grandchildren. I had heard about the Campos's farm and traditional slow-oven cooking school, and I'm eager to see how they blend the two.

We turn off the main road and follow a narrow valley lined with miniature homesteads supporting peach, apricot, and apple orchards; tiny fields of grain; pastures; and the occasional milk cow or herd of goats. It's a little oasis, kept alive and green by the waters of the Rio Grande. From the air it would be a striking sight, the cultivated land winding like a green river across the sand-colored landscape. Some of the farmers here draw directly from the river; others are served by ancient systems of irrigation ditches called *acequias,* dug hundreds of years ago and communally maintained. Every living thing seems to gravitate to the banks of the Rio Grande, the wild things competing with the farmers' crops, all jostling for their chance to suckle from the breast of the long-suffering river.

The Dixon farmers' market is a ragtag affair, about twenty farmers and backyard gardeners set up in front of the Embudo Valley Library in a rough circle, displaying small piles of green and red chiles, eggplants, heirloom tomatoes, peaches, lemonade, and roasted corn. The road into the little town is lined with pickups and old cars, and the small crowd seems to have gathered more for the conversation than for the food.

Aaron and I play "guess which farmer" and light on a thin, older, Indian-looking woman conversing with a group of well-dressed young white folks who have crowded around her stand. We wait for the group to finish before we approach. As they disperse, baskets of Ichiban and Rosa Bianca eggplants ringed by New Mexico green and poblano chiles are revealed.

We introduce ourselves, and there is an awkward pause. Then Eremita tells us that her daughter has forgotten that we are coming and that the whole family is off to the mountains to go camping. We're a little surprised, considering the planning and communications that preceded our arrival, but we move into flex mode. We agree to meet Eremita and Margaret in a couple days when they have returned. I head for the nearest pay phone and arrange to visit another farm nearby.

We drive off, following Rick Gaudet's directions to his One Straw Farm, the name drawn from Masanobu Fukuoka's seminal book *One Straw Revolution.* We follow the gravel road for 6 miles until we come to a little adobe chapel. Just past the chapel is gringo alley, a series of properties owned and occupied by white folk.

Rick and his wife, Heather, have gone to dinner in Espanola, and we are greeted by one of their interns, Ann LeFevre. She gives us a brief tour of the place, and it's immediately clear that the Gaudets are struggling a bit. The proliferating weeds are not part of an intentional system like we saw at Bob Cannard's place. The native soil looks weak and rocky.

The fields are tightly planted with an ambitious range of flowers and vegetables—tomatoes, peppers, gourmet potatoes, green garlic, tender arugula, and water-loving mâche—grown in a classic market-garden style that seems out of place in this dry desert climate. Growing arugula, salad greens, and other gourmet vegetables seems like an act of courage here, especially in this drought.

When I first came to New Mexico in the late seventies, late-afternoon rains arrived each day to quench the land and cool everything down. Now, native piñon trees are dying by the thousands from drought stress and the bark beetles that go with it. Each afternoon as we are here, the clouds come, but not the rain. Ann says they've been getting about fourteen drops every six days.

The next morning, Aaron and I go inside for tea, toast, and granola. Rick tells us that he came to New Mexico to study Western classics at St. John's College, in Santa Fe. Heather came to study Eastern classics. Together, they decided to start their own personal rebellion against society on this leased farm. Rick describes how they expanded every year, how they started out digging beds by hand and how the weeds just started coming. He describes things as "out of control," and Heather breaks in to tell me that "Rick is overwhelmed right now." They both talk about discovering their limits. "No matter how much you plant, it doesn't seem like you can keep up," Rick says.

The Gaudets' 3.5 acres supply a few restaurants with which they trade for meals, a seventy-five-member CSA, and the farmers' market in Santa Fe. For a number of years, theirs was the largest offering at the market; this year, they have four interns and one full-time paid helper.

They describe how they started off simply wanting to feed themselves and that the market gardening evolved out of that. Now the need for cash drives their operation.

"I'm on the phone either trying to get people to buy food or to pay for what they've already bought," Rick says, somewhat exasperated. "Now we want to return to self-sufficiency and get away from focusing on cash crops."

I cautiously suggest a little bit of both, moving away from so many annuals and selecting a few well-chosen perennials that can provide some cash without requiring so much labor. They listen attentively, but I'm feeling a bit awkward. I didn't come on this journey to offer opinions, especially in places where I'm just passing through. Sharing experiences and techniques is fine, but advice is a danger-ous thing. I've never taken a word of it myself.

In the morning, we walk their land, discussing irrigation systems, plant spacings, cover-crop choices, and weeds. The conversation seems to always come back to weeds. Rick shows me a series of ten 4-foot-wide beds, all completely consumed by bindweed. A friend once told me that there is only one bindweed plant in the world, that everyone's bindweed is connected by a common root system. There are rows of small carrot plants beneath the weeds and five people uncovering them one weed at a time, all by hand. It feels like everything got a few days behind sometime in the spring and never got caught up.

I know the feeling of being overwhelmed, the sense that you have just arrived at a major accident with multiple victims and you can't decide whom to treat first. It is a symptom, I remind myself, of doing too much, the result of that dangerous time in midwinter when the land is at rest and your mind starts scheming and dreaming and making big summer plans.

It's amazing how we can be so completely exhausted by the time winter arrives, but thoroughly excited each spring to begin anew. The traumas of the previous season are so easily forgotten, replaced by a more powerful instinct—to create, reproduce, grow, and feed. With seed catalogues full of enticing language, it's easy to overorder and overplant. After all, seeds are so small in late winter and take up so little space when carefully placed in flats. How easy it is to forget that those tiny seeds will grow, each one demanding our time and attention.

As we walk the land, giant cumulus clouds dance enticingly around the sky, rumbling and broiling and threatening. Cicadas chirp an incessant electric rhythm. I can feel and hear every form of life hoping and praying. The sky gets dark and loud, but no rain comes. I ask Ann as she walks by whether it's going to rain; she shakes her head and walks on. Ten minutes later, it's pouring, but no one seems to be that excited, and I sense that expectations of any significant accumulation are low.

Fridays here are just like Fridays on every farm of this scale everywhere; everyone is harvesting and preparing for Saturday-morning market. At 6:00 A.M., containers are brought out for salad mix. Five silhouettes move through the soft early light, cutting fine baby romaine, butter, Lolla Rosa, red and green oak-leaf, and Merlot lettuces. Then it's on to rainbow chard and Italian parsley, cipollini and Walla Walla onions, royal burgundy and yellow wax beans, carrots and beets, and snapdragons, fire cosmos, giant zinnias, and feverfew flowers.

I feel like I'm in some sort of time warp, standing on someone else's farm in the summer, seeing the hope and the goals of spring manifested in a bountiful harvest and a million things undone. My mind wanders home to my own fields, where my family is also preparing for the weekend ritual. Then I flash on all the times when my grand plans either worked or didn't, and circumstances told me it was time to change course and try again.

♣

THE DIRT ROAD INTO EREMITA AND MARGARET CAMPOS'S FARM TWISTS and turns as it follows the Rio Grande. It's difficult to imagine a farm out here. The land on either side of the road is rock and sandstone, and the only green things are juniper, cottonwood, and sage. But like everything else we've experienced in this region, nothing exposes itself easily.

Just when we think we're lost and are about to give up, the road opens up into a large, flat piece of land bordered by the river and cradled on three sides by towering sandstone and rock hills. We park the van alongside rows of chiles and sweet peppers and make our way through the outdoor classroom and kitchen. The crisp, white tile counters and a sleek mirror that hangs from the ceiling for class viewing seem out of place in this open-air kitchen, which is dominated by a traditional, egg-shaped *horno,* or adobe oven.

We knock on several doors and try to calm the two frenzied dogs fenced in at the back of the building. We drive to a building on the other side of the field; Aaron hops out and knocks, and, when the door opens, he is greeted less than enthusiastically. From the van window, I can see his expression change from its normal openness and warmth to dismay. I get out and go to the door and meet Margaret. She seems very busy and tells us to camp in the orchard and to join her for coffee in the morning. We're not sure we're welcome, but since it's already late afternoon, we decide to stay and see what happens the next day.

The Campos farm is made up of small fields dominated by peppers and eggplants. There is an old apple orchard, a struggling raspberry planting, and a ⅓-acre plot that contains about six wilting tomato plants spread out erratically in a field that looks as if it was flood irrigated. The scene seems to be the remains of some tomato catastrophe. I'm certain it wasn't intentionally planted this sparsely; the land is too valuable, and to flood irrigate a whole field for a handful of plants doesn't make sense.

Over coffee the next morning, Margaret apologizes for not being more hospitable, and the conversation moves immediately to tomatoes. "I thought people were going to cry after we lost the crop to wilt," Eremita says. She talks about an older couple, addicted to the farm's tomatoes, who took the failure as if it were some personal tragedy. The tomato-crop loss emerges throughout our visit like an ongoing dull ache that won't go away.

Eremita's father, Fidelino, moved to this part of New Mexico because there was water. They had a fruit stand along Highway 68 on the other side of the river. They would take their produce in wheelbarrows across a flimsy wooden footbridge.

Now, twice a week, Eremita continues the tradition in a rusting blue 1985 Dodge van with 230,999 miles on it, selling at the markets in Santa Fe and Dixon. They also tried the market in Espanola but soon stopped. Eremita explains, "We'd bring twenty-two varieties of eggplants, spend all day explaining what each one was and how to use it, and then come home with $40."

I watch through the window as eight-year-old Joaquin and six-year-old Analisa pick corn and eggplants. "Sometimes we think that we're too busy for the kids," Eremita says. "But they're getting more than most—they're getting something else." She proudly tells the story of Joaquin providing detailed cooking instructions to customers at the farmers' market, advising them on the proper way to prepare beans.

As she talks, the kids come storming in and conversation changes to lunch and watermelon and stuffed animals. "No one even makes their own tortillas anymore!" Margaret exclaims with great dismay as she carefully lays out her own homemade tortillas and begins filling them with a stir-fry of beet greens, carrots, onion, and broccoli combined with Jack cheese and fresh tomato salsa. Eremita reminisces about some of the varieties of vegetables they've grown, discussing the strengths and weaknesses of each one as if gossiping about old friends.

"Most people have no choice in their food—it's chosen for them," Margaret says. "Taste and beauty have given way to the needs of the industrial system for foods that are durable, easy to process, and large and uniform. Most people only eat what has been marketed to them. My mom's gardens and my cooking classes are opening up a whole new world."

"People ask me when I started what was in my head," Eremita puts in. "But I didn't really think about it. It's the same for my grandson, Joaquin, as it was for me. We'd be out there as kids while our parents worked in the fields. We'd go in the wagon; we'd make a bed for my little sister in the field while we hoed. Dad would do the plowing and then go off to the mines to work. I would take over the planting and the harvesting."

"All of our grandfathers were migrant workers," Margaret adds. "They would do the heavy work in the fields and then split to the mines, or herd sheep in Montana, or pick potatoes in Colorado. The women would stay behind and do all of the hoeing and harvesting. We farm because it's who we are. It's our way of life. We can no more not plant in the spring then we can stop breathing."

But, as with many things, this farming tradition did not progress in a straight line. Margaret tells us that her mom "was behind bars for thirty years," working for the state Department of Corrections handling payroll and inmates' financial accounts. Eventually, she was promoted to a guard position in one of the high-security facilities.

After Margaret's then-husband insisted that she needed a real job, she worked at the Los Alamos National Nuclear Laboratories off and on for many years. When Eremita retired in 1987, Margaret left the nuclear facility to work with her in their grandfathers' profession, as if gathering up the pieces of tradition and family to start again. The two women constructed their adobe house by themselves with their own hands. They built their cooking school out of relationships with local chefs and a desire to preserve their rediscovered culture.

The timing, as it turned out, was trendy. Traditional food and cooking were enjoying a renaissance. Inevitably, the foodies found the Campos farm, and the clash of image and reality was probably inevitable. Margaret and Eremita trade off telling the story of a Slow Food event held at their farm. A photographer and an accompanying food stylist continuously interrupted Margaret's cooking by arranging and rearranging every dish at every step. Just after the outdoor tables had been set with specially ordered hand-sewn tablecloths and multicolored china, dark rain clouds moved in. Margaret says that she silently prayed for rain, partially for the land, but more to allow nature to throw some reality into this forced perfection. And rain it did, so hard that the arroyo that crossed the dirt road into the farm became an impassable torrent. A neighbor's propane tanks floated away, and hazmat officials were called in. Water flooded into the clean and empty plates and floated on the soaked tablecloths while the guests huddled inside, close to the wine and food, which they ate right off the counter. "For a Slow Food crowd, I never saw people eat so much so fast," Margaret says.

"I learned about food from my grandfather," she tells us. "He taught me how to love food. My grandma didn't use spices, so my grandfather used to sneak in a few rows of garlic and slip garlic into the house. Grandma would tear up his garlic plants. He would make spicy chorizo, and Grandma would be upset that he stunk up the house. Because he was a migrant worker, Grandpa learned to cook on the road—quick gravies, stews, and biscuits. He would cook me breakfast, everything with fried onions. He'd take a little yellow pepper and big chunks of onions and cook them with eggs, which he'd place on a fresh tortilla. This is how I was raised."

Eremita chuckles when she tells me that Margaret actually "grew up on instant TV dinners" for a lot of her childhood. Now, the two women have circled back around to the kind of traditional meals Margaret remembers. Their lives now revolve around the intricate logistics of when to start the fire in the clay *horno* for meat and corn that won't be served for twenty-four hours and what to prepare for the cooking class that will take place in a couple days.

There is a collision of cultures and flavors on the Campos farm, just as there is a contradictory ebb and flow between traditional values and the modern demands of jobs and single parenthood. Spanish, Mexican, and Native American foods merge and mingle together in the fields and in the kitchen. Tortillas and corn *chicos* share the table with French filet and fava beans, artichokes, eggplants, and Green Zebra tomatoes. And of course there are chiles.

Margaret tells me that there are chile wars going on between the northern and southern parts of the state. "Here, we grow them to eat," she says. "In the south, they grow them to sell. Here, we grow them for flavor; down there, it's all about processing. We live and breathe for our chiles. Of course, everyone says that theirs are the best."

That afternoon I watch as the Campos's helper, Isaac, chops fruitwood for the *horno* in preparation for the next day's cooking class. The wood is placed inside the clay dome, and at about three o'clock in the afternoon, the fire is lit. By about six o'clock, only coals are left, along with an intense radiating heat from the gaping mouth of the oven. It reminds me of a fire glowing in a prehistoric cave, like the kind of fire Prometheus must have carried—not the blazing, destructive flame of a torch, but the rich, life-giving burn of embers for cooking. Like water, fire is nearly inseparable from survival, and there is something elemental and reassuring about the red-and-orange glow.

The whole family gathers around the stove to load it. They take a dozen ears of sweet corn, soak them in water, and literally toss them into the back of the *horno*. Then they take a piece of fresh pork, salt it, wrap it in foil, and cover the whole package in wet burlap. It, too, goes into the *horno*. Margaret places a piece of plywood over the opening and throws mud mixed with straw around the edges of the makeshift door.

That night, while we're sleeping in the orchard, a major thunderstorm moves in. The thin metal-and-canvas Volkswagen shell separating us from the storm makes every flash of lightning and clap of thunder feel like it's so close that it's inside our heads. With each bolt of lightning, the interior of the van illuminates as if someone were firing off flash photos. Our home on wheels shakes and rocks and rolls.

The next morning, the world outside is washed and clean and sharp. Dewdrops of silver-gold form on emerald-green leaves. The harsh explosions of the night before have been replaced with freshly scented mountain air, and a chocolate-brown Rio Grande carries logs and branches and debris wrenched from somewhere upstream. We take photographs and then eat our oats with raspberries picked a few feet from our door.

When we emerge, final preparations are under way for the morning's cooking class. When the participants arrive, they are taken on a free-form tour of the farm. Eremita describes her successes and failures, and Margaret pipes in with some of the family's history and the culinary uses of certain crops.

When the time comes to open up the sealed *horno*, there is a hushed excitement. It has been more than twenty hours since the food was put in, and everyone gathers around as Margaret begins chipping away at the hardened adobe that has sealed the door.

She lifts the plywood away from the opening and removes the burlap-wrapped package of meat and the ears of corn. We watch with anticipation as the burlap is removed, and then the foil. The meat is placed on a plate. It's so tender, it falls apart. We eat with our fingers. Virtually nothing has been done to this meat—no marinades, no seasonings, nothing. The flavor is unbelievable, permeated by twenty hours of locked-in smoke and *horno*-clay essence. The smoky flavor of the steaming, lightly browned corn is reminiscent of apple, with a slight hint of the meat that shared its space overnight.

In the midst of the feast, Joaquin comes running up to his grandmother, eyes tortilla-wide, grabs her arm, and tells her to come quick. We all look at each other, wondering what has happened. A few minutes later they return, carrying a small stick with a 2-inch-long, fat, green caterpillar. "There are no tomatoes," Eremita tells us, chuckling, "so the tomato hornworms have moved into the grapes."

Although we had planned to stay for the whole meal, slow food takes time, and we are expected a long ways east. We say good-bye and prepare to drive off. When I try to start the van, I discover that the battery has died after two days sitting in the orchard. We roll start it and continue up the dirt road that leads out of the farm.

No sooner have we gotten under way than I hear yelling from behind us. I look in the rearview mirror, and there, behind the van, is sixty-eight-year-old Eremita, running at a full sprint and waving her arms. Directly behind her is one of the class participants, loaded down with hot rolls just out of the *horno*. We open the window to accept this gift for the road.

❦

OUT OF THE ARUGULA-AND-CHILE BELT, INTO THE LAND OF CORN AND cows and silos. In Wisconsin, just over the river from Minnesota, I'm not sure which there are more of, lakes or cows. It's certainly not people. The proprietor at the Trade Lake store and single-pump gas station asks us where we're from. When we say British Columbia, Canada, he assumes that we're lost, completely incredulous that we could be here to visit a family just down the road. "There's nothing here," he tells us and turns back to the air-conditioned comfort of the store.

The temperature during these few days in late August is in the nineties, and the humidity is at least as high. The rain that preceded us has triggered a massive fly hatch. Everything with any moisture, odor, or food value is covered, including us.

County Road Z is a well-maintained two-laner lined with somewhat shabby farmsteads right out of a Norman Rockwell painting. Mary and David Falk's place would be a little difficult to find if it weren't for the sheep-crossing signs on the road.

The Falks are celebrated cheese producers who have built a national reputation with virtually no funds, a flock of sheep of their own chance breeding, a 1950 Allis-Chalmers tractor, and a milking barn built for stabling horses.

Like many of the farmers we visit, Mary Falk has already apologized in advance, saying over the phone that they've run out of time to do any mowing around the buildings and that we should have seen the place in June. In a note sent prior to our journey, she had written, somewhat officially, "In order for you to feel comfortable here, you will need to be able to tolerate:

Lots of testosterone (I am the only female besides the dogs and the sheep)
Dogs and sheep
Llama
The smell of mold in a cheese cave
The smell of mold in a wet basement
The smell of a farm
Popcorn
Cheese
Eating late at night
Puppies
A cat
A few birds

When we finally pull up to the farm, all the warnings seem to be accurate, but the sum total is pleasant and welcoming, and we're immediately charmed by Mary's openness about the life she and David have built here over the last eight years.

In 1985, newly divorced and living in California, Mary decided to visit her parents in Wisconsin for the Christmas holidays. While she was there, she went out to look at real estate. "It was thirty below zero, and everything was encased in ice," she says. "As I was driving down the road, I felt this strange heat on my neck and suddenly had this vision of green hills covered with sheep. I thought I was having some sort of acid-trip flashback. I pulled into the driveway of this place, and a voice said, 'You will buy this farm.' I looked in the backseat of the car and checked to see if the radio was on. I was certain that I had heard a real voice. Everything was glittering with ice crystals. The land was in bankruptcy; the woman who owned the place had six kids and was struggling. It was a gut thing—I knew that if I didn't move here, maybe my life wasn't going to work. So I made an offer of $55,000 contingent on the sale of my house in California. We settled at $65,000."

After she moved in, friends dragged her away from an evening she had planned to spend alone watching creature films and steam cleaning the sofa. On the dance floor at a local dive, beneath the stuffed heads of elk and deer and cougar, amid the spinning dots of light from the hanging mirror balls, Mary met David Falk. David was living 2 miles away but spending most of his time on the road building silos.

"I was riding past his house every day on my horse without knowing it," Mary says. "My friend had been trying to put us together for a while. He was away during the week and only home on weekends, so she sent him a note. He called me immediately, and we talked for four hours. Our first date was a croquet party where one of the balls went through a plate-glass window. Soon after, David lost the lease on his place, so I asked him to move in. A year later, he asked me to marry him.

"Dave didn't want to buy into the slavery of cow milking," Mary continues. "He grew up around here and considered it a one-way ticket to hell." So they bought someone's flock of sheep, sight unseen—all they knew about them was that they were white. As it turned out, the sheep were a mix of breeds: Dorsets, Finns, and Romneys. All of them were pregnant, and each one averaged twins and triplets. "We began culling the weak ones," David adds. "We knew we needed sheep that were thrifty and could survive in an organic operation. We were selecting for excellent maternal ewes without even knowing it. People always told us that you couldn't raise sheep organically because of the parasites, but here they are."

Even though organic standards allow it, the sheep here have never had any worming medication. "We're more purist than organic," David says.

Ask anyone around here what to farm and they'll likely tell you corn or milk cows. No one would ever suggest sheep, and if they did, it certainly would not be for milk or cheese. So, when Mary and David launched their sheep-dairy operation, their families and neighbors thought they'd lost their minds.

A friend in the area was raising sheep and having a tough time making a living selling milk with no value added. So Mary and David decided to get into cheese. Faced with life-threatening chronic asthma, and told she wouldn't live past thirty-five, Mary decided it was all or nothing. She took a brief cheese-making internship and jumped in on her own.

At the time, no one in the state was making cave-aged sheep cheese. In the beginning, she used the fireplace in the 1897 farmhouse to do the aging and experimented on the back porch with cheeses in bamboo baskets. Eventually, she and David built their own caves in a wild section of their property. "I had this flavor stuck in my head like some song," Mary says. "I needed to find it."

The cheese is truly adventurous, wrapped in vodka-soaked nettles and aged on cedar boughs. If you've been raised in white-bread America, eating individually wrapped sliced Swiss or orange Cheddar singles, you'd probably think twice if you saw the Falks' cheese. Brown and crusty with ruts and holes, blue and white with brown streaks covered in leaves, they look like some bad experiment gone awry. Mary's own mother told her they look like "moldy horse turds." But their customers at the St. Paul farmers' market seek out their classic homely and ugly look, and cheese experts from around the country have bestowed them with praise.

Mary's cheese making is a strange blend of alchemy, herbology, and chemistry, with a few Hail Marys thrown in from her Catholic roots. Her willingness to experiment has brought them major accolades. *Bon Appétit* magazine awarded them the Food Artisan of the Year award in 2002, they won Best of Show from the American Cheese Society in 1998, and their cheese has been written about in the *New York Times, Chicago Tribune,* and *Wine Spectator.*

I spent most of my adult life keeping milk goats. I only dabbled in making soft cheese and never got serious enough to get good at it. But one thing I did discover is that the cheese is only as good as the quality of the milk that goes into it. Mary is an inspired cheese maker, but it's David who produces the milk. I can see that the couple are well matched. Both Mary and David are fanatics, obsessed with their work and with producing the best. David tells me that "while most wives wake up their husbands in the middle of the night for a 'booty call,' Mary wakes me up to talk about cheese."

David says, "Mary is the brains of the operation—I'm just the labor," but the management of the land and the pastures and the sheep is equally experimental. This is not your standard, by-the-book, intensive rotational grazing scheme with well-scheduled moves from one pasture to the next. There is a lot of watching going on here, an intense amount of observation and an unflinching desire to push beyond standard practice.

"At the beginning of the season, when the grass is growing fast, Dave turns them loose and lets them free range," Mary tells us. "When the summer gets hot and the grass slows down, he tightens up the grazing and confines them more, kind of drifts them along, lets them pick the choice stuff out; then, what's left behind becomes hay. You want them to keep moving and not stay in one place, but with so much of the flavor in milk and cheese residing in the flowers of the plants, you don't want to move them through too fast. We let the grass get a little older so there are flowers. We want the flavors, we want to encourage more biodiversity, not just because it's the right thing to do, but because it makes the cheese taste better.

"We had taken all the seminars, but then we took a pencil to all of what they told us. We got a battery-powered fencing setup and realized that there are so many situations where we don't even need fencing. The sheep perceive the tall grass like a fence—it's poverty-based fencing. Dave started to observe all of this. Around the ponds, he let the sheep move through and moved them out quickly. The USDA folks said they'd never seen a property with so much diversity."

The Falks' land sits in the bottom of the valley on marginal soils. Almost half of the 200 acres is devoted to wildlife and habitat restoration. One evening, Aaron and I follow the sound of the frogs down to the pond and come upon a blue heron feeding on duckweed.

Just above the pond, built into the hillside, is a heavy wooden door. Inside is 1,800 square feet of cavern filled with three thousand rounds of cheese. On the walls are petroglyphs painted by Mary that depict members of the family. The air is dank and moist and heavy with spores and molds that are encouraged and even worshipped. Orange and green and gold and brown, the molds cover the exteriors of the cheeses and send their threaded strands into and throughout the interiors, infusing them with life and flavor.

"I wanted the caves in the wildlife refuge because I wanted to capture every piece of mold and pollen and all of the representations of the flora that are down there," Mary explains later. "I wanted the tule fog coming off of the pond and the wetlands to enter the caves. Things attach to moisture. When you go out there, you can smell them. Everything has to be real for the ingredients to have real flavor."

Mary sent some of their product to cheese guru Steven Jenkins in New York City. A couple days went by. Then they got a phone message saying, "You have made a world-class cheese."

"It was the milk," Mary says, "the flavor of the north coming into the cheeses. It was a combination of the phenomenal grass, great milking, great animal health, and an understanding of the science. The science allowed me to customize the cheese. How could I make a cheese that best reflected the grass and the environment and get those flavors into the mouth in one bite? I knew the alchemy, but I also knew how important the molds and the pollens and the native bacterias are. So the caves were critical because they held the moisture level. We wanted to place a concentrated piece of Wisconsin into every bite."

She tells me how Wisconsin has the tightest regulations on cheese producers, that the state wanted them to wax the wood the cheese was aging on. But Mary says cheese can't breathe on waxed boards. So, when the inspectors returned, the Falks had put the cheese on cedar boughs. Mary says, "They were pissed. They wanted to know what we are going to do about pieces of cedar that are stuck in the rind." "I'll charge more for those!" she told them.

As we stand in the caves, Mary excitedly shows me a beautiful gold strain of mold that has just populated one of the rounds. "When I started doing this, I never dreamed I would get so turned on by mold," she tells me. Molds are tiny plants with microscopic roots; she's using cheese like fine soil to farm her molds. She tells me that the molds deliver complex, tiny fragments of earth, mushroom, bitter, sweet, and tangy, which come together to create complex flavor.

She describes a young man who purchased a round of their cheese and later wrote them a letter raving about it, adding that he took it with him backpacking in the Rockies. "You can imagine my horror. The smell of those cheeses is so strong, I was terrified that the bears would have eaten him."

The Falks are the only people in the whole state of Wisconsin who are making a living on sheep. Just a living. This isn't any high-tech, heavily capitalized dairy operation. From the Orv's Pizza truck-turned-cooler to the homemade milking platform, everything has been patched and pieced and thrown together. Once again, I am amazed at what can be produced with virtually no resources other than energy, will, and creativity.

Like so many other farmers we visit, the Falks say that the best way to save the family farm is through the kids. David tells his two boys that if they want to farm, he'll be happy, but if they don't, that's fine, too. They tell me that after having employees, they've decided it's better to invest in the kids and create a successful enough operation that they will want to get involved.

Their eleven-year-old son, Andy, takes Aaron and me on a tour of his favorite places on the land. We visit the remains of a decaying old log farmhouse that has trees and bush growing in and around it, and then sneak up on some of the sheep resting inside an old farm wagon. When we cross the road that bisects the farm, I comment on the custom sheep-crossing signs on the road. Between giggles, Andy tells me about an old woman who regularly pulls up just past the sheep-crossing sign, comes to a full stop, looks both ways, and, if all is clear, zooms off with her tires screeching.

The signs don't stop the bears, cougars, wolves, and dogs that move through the bustling wildlife corridor that includes the Falks' land. The Falks have a simple solution: they raise their own beautiful white dogs, a cross of Polish mountain dog and Maremma sheepdog, from puppies. Growing up alongside the sheep, the dogs are fiercely protective of them and treat the animals like family, watching over them and even acting as lead animals as they move through the farm.

As we are saying our good-byes, David tells Aaron, "If there's ever a nuclear attack and you're in Wisconsin, come join us in our cave." I can think of worse places to escape to. I imagine crowding into the cool bunker, already full to capacity with busy mold spores, all of us surviving to build the next civilization on wheels of living cheese.

Cheese was humanity's first processed food, our first attempt to trap and preserve life and sustenance for a future meal. In a way, cheese making, like fire building, is an act of human will and rebellion against the relentless demands and capricious fortune of foraging, hunting, and eating to live.

For a moment, I flash back to the Campos kitchen, where the glowing *horno* seems like the hot yang to the cool yin of the cheese cave. I realize that the alchemy of both suggests a powerful optimism; at some point our ancestors had to imagine that they would still be around when the fire and the mold had finished their work.

♣

Comida de Campos Flour Tortillas

MAKES 12 TORTILLAS

While we were at the Campos's farm, Margaret was on a rant about tortillas. "Nobody makes their own anymore!" she exclaimed. For such a staple food, it's amazing how the quality of store-bought tortillas has plummeted, replaced with thin disks that feel and taste more like cardboard than like corn or flour. This recipe was adapted from the one Margaret sent us. Made with fresh lard, these tortillas are delicious and very simple to make. Everyone will appreciate a warm, homemade flour tortilla—especially with a bowl of spicy chile verde.

3 cups all-purpose flour, plus extra for dusting
1 tablespoon baking powder
1 teaspoon salt
⅓ cup good-quality fresh lard, chilled
1 cup plus 1 tablespoon water
1 tablespoon vegetable oil

Combine the 3 cups flour, baking powder, and salt in a large bowl. Add the lard in small spoonfuls. Using your fingertips, gently toss the lard around to coat each piece with the flour mixture—this helps the lard to cut in evenly. Using a pastry cutter or 2 knives, cut the lard into the flour mixture until there are no large lumps in the mixture. Add the water and mix to form a firm but sticky dough. gather the dough into a ball and knead briefly in the bowl, about 6 turns—be careful not to overknead. Coat the dough ball with ¹/₂ tablespoon of the oil, cover the bowl with a kitchen towel, and let rise in a warm place for 20 to 30 minutes.

Preheat a cast-iron griddle over medium-high heat and coat it with the remaining ¹/₂ tablespoon oil. Divide the dough into 12 equal portions and form each portion into a ball. Working with 1 dough ball at a time, on a lightly floured work surface, use a rolling pin to roll the dough into a flat tortilla about 10 inches in diameter. Place the tortilla, rolled side down, on the griddle. When the tortilla begins to bubble and brown, about 1 minute, flop and cook on the second side for another 15 to 30 seconds. Repeat the process with the remaining dough, stacking the tortillas in a kitchen towel and covering to keep warm and soft as they come off the griddle. Serve warm.

Grilled Corn on the Cob with Chile Salt and Lime

This recipe is an embellished version of the corn we ate right out of the wood-fired horno *(clay oven) at Margaret and Eremita Campos's place. The whole unshucked ears were dipped into saltwater and thrown into the coals of the* horno. *When the corn was removed from the sealed clay chamber almost twenty-four hours later, it was golden and slightly charred, with an amazing smoky flavor. We don't expect that too many of you will have a* horno *sitting in the corner of your kitchen, but a wood or charcoal (or even gas) grill will work for this simple recipe.*

SERVES 6

¼ cup kosher salt

Dried red chile powder, such as ancho or cayenne, to taste

2 limes

6 ears fresh corn in their husks

Prepare a fire in a charcoal grill or preheat a gas grill.

Combine the salt and chile powder in a small bowl, adding as much chile as you like. Cut one of the limes in half and cut the other lime into 6 wedges. Set the chile salt and limes aside while you grill the corn.

Peel back the corn husks but do not tear them off. Remove the silk and then pull the husks back over the cobs. Grill the corn over medium heat for 8 to 10 minutes, rotating every few minutes. The husks should be nicely charred and the corn should be tender and juicy. Peel back the husks but leave them attached to the cob—they make a convenient handle to hold on to while eating the corn. Rub the halved lime down the length of the cobs and sprinkle them with the chile salt. Serve immediately with the lime wedges.

Chile Verde

I'm not normally a big fan of pork, but the meat that Margaret Campos pulled slow-cooked out of the wood-fired horno *was a real treat. Despite having virtually no seasoning except salt, it was moist and tender and delicious. This chile verde recipe is inspired by Margaret's cooking, with the addition of some onion, tomatillos, cumin, and cilantro to the sauce, and potatoes added to the dish. It makes a tasty little stew.*

3 pounds pork shoulder, cut into 1- to 2-inch chunks

Kosher salt to taste

Freshly cracked black pepper to taste

1½ tablespoons good-quality fresh lard, or olive oil

1½ pounds poblano chiles (about 5 peppers)

2 to 3 serrano chiles

1½ pounds tomatillos (about 10 tomatillos), husked and rinsed

½ cup chopped fresh cilantro, plus extra sprigs for garnish

½ teaspoon ground cumin

1 medium white onion, thinly sliced

6 cloves garlic, thinly sliced

2½ cups water

1½ pounds small red-skinned potatoes, scrubbed and quartered

Warm flour tortillas for serving (optional)

Preheat the broiler.

Generously season the pork with salt and pepper. Heat a large Dutch oven over medium-high heat and add the lard. When the lard has melted, add just enough of the pork pieces to cover the bottom of the pot—don't crowd the pot, or the meat will stew rather than brown. Brown the pork evenly on all sides, 8 to 10 minutes total. Using a slotted spoon, transfer to a plate. Put the remaining pork in the pot and repeat the process. Set the pot with the pan drippings aside.

Put the chiles and the tomatillos on a baking sheet and broil until the skins begin to bubble and char, about 5 minutes. Flip them over and broil until charred on the second side, about 5 more minutes. Set aside to cool.

When the chiles are cool enough to handle, peel back the blackened skin with your fingers. Discard the skin, core, and seeds. Put the chiles, tomatillos, chopped cilantro, cumin, and any juice that has collected on the baking sheet into a food processor or blender. Process the mixture to a smooth puree, scraping down the sides of the bowl as needed. Set aside.

Preheat the oven to 325 degrees F.

Return the pot with the pan drippings to the stove top and heat over medium heat. Add the onion and a generous pinch of salt and cook until the onion is tender, about 7 minutes. Add the garlic and cook for 1 minute. Raise the heat to medium-high and add the chile puree. Cook the puree, stirring constantly, until it thickens and turns a darker shade of green, about 3 minutes. Add the water and stir well. Season the sauce with salt to taste (about $1^{1}/_{2}$ teaspoons).

Return the browned pork and any accumulated juices to the pot. Cover and bake in the oven until the pork is very tender when pierced with a fork, $2^{1}/_{2}$ to 3 hours.

Meanwhile, put the potatoes in a medium saucepan with water to cover by $1^{1}/_{2}$ inches. Season the water generously with salt and bring to a boil. Reduce the heat and gently simmer the potatoes until tender, 10 to 12 minutes. Drain and set aside.

When the pork is cooked, remove the pot from the oven, add the potatoes, and return the pot to the oven for about 10 more minutes—just long enough for the potatoes to mingle with the sauce. Spoon off the fat on top of the sauce (leaving a little, if you'd like). Taste and adjust the seasoning, if necessary. Transfer to a warm serving bowl or platter and garnish with the cilantro sprigs. Serve with warm flour tortillas, if desired.

Biscotti with Apricot, Green Pistachio, and Hyssop

MAKES ABOUT
4 DOZEN BISCOTTI

This recipe was inspired by Odessa Piper, whose L'Etoile restaurant is a celebration of the foods of Wisconsin even in the depths of winter. Odessa describes Mary Falk's Trade Lake Cedar sheep-milk cheese with flair, telling us that it possesses "sun-ripe sweetness, herbal notes, and a piquancy." The cheese inspired her to create this biscotti in which she adds glacéed apricots, green pistachios, and fresh anise hyssop. In this adaptation, we suggest lightly poaching dried apricots in simple syrup.

POACHED APRICOTS

½ cup sugar

½ cup water

⅔ cup roughly chopped dried apricots

⅔ cup green pistachios

1 teaspoon aniseed

1⅔ cups all-purpose flour

½ teaspoon baking soda

½ teaspoon kosher salt

2 eggs

¾ cup sugar

1 teaspoon pure vanilla extract

¼ cup finely chopped fresh anise hyssop or fresh mint

1 tablespoon chopped orange zest

Preheat the oven to 350 degrees F.

TO MAKE THE POACHED APRICOTS: Combine the sugar and water in a small saucepan and bring to a boil. When the sugar has dissolved, add the apricots and reduce the heat to medium-low. Gently poach the apricots, stirring occasionally, until tender but not mushy (an apricot should offer a bit of resistance when pierced with a small sharp knife), 2 to 3 minutes. Remove from the heat and let the apricots cool slowly in the syrup. (If the dried apricots are especially soft to begin with, remove the pan from the heat immediately after you add the fruit to the hot sugar syrup.) Drain the cooled apricots and let sit for about 10 minutes to dry a little.

Meanwhile, toast the pistachios and aniseed. Spread the pistachios on a baking sheet and bake until lightly toasted, about 5 minutes—the nuts should still be bright green. Set aside to cool. Leave the oven on. Heat a small sauté pan over medium-low heat, add the aniseed, and toast lightly, stirring frequently, about 1 minute.

Combine the flour, baking soda, salt, and aniseed in a small bowl. In a large bowl, whisk together the eggs, sugar, vanilla, hyssop, and orange zest. Add the dry ingredients and toasted pistachios to the egg mixture and stir with a wooden spoon until well combined. (The dough is stiff and sticky—it may be easier to mix it with your hands.)

Divide the dough in half and place one half on one side of a baking sheet lined with parchment paper. Use your hands to form the dough into a chubby log about 12 inches long. (It's not necessary to smooth the surface of the dough; it will even out in the oven.) Repeat the process with the other dough half, leaving about 3 inches between the logs.

Bake for 35 minutes. Transfer to a wire rack and let cool for at least 10 minutes. Reduce the oven temperature to 300 degrees F.

Using a serrated knife, cut the logs on the diagonal into $1/2$-inch-thick slices. Arrange the biscotti on a wire rack (or 2 racks if necessary) and place the racks directly on the oven rack. Bake the biscotti for a second time until golden brown, dry, and crisp; 10 to 15 minutes. Remove the racks from the oven and let cool.

❨

CHAPTER 5

CLASSICAL AND JAZZ

IN A TRANQUIL SLIVER OF SOUTHWESTERN WISCONSIN, NOT TOO FAR from where Minnesota, Iowa, and the Badger State come together, bottomland fields of silt loam weave gently among the woods and pastures along Spring Creek. This is farm country in the most traditional sense: the roads are lined with rolling hills and tidy homesteads, the precise image most folks would conjure if they closed their eyes and thought "farm."

In this land of archetypes, Harmony Valley is a classic organic farm by the most established and refined definition. That's clear from our first glimpse as we round a bend and a field of strawberries appears, perfect rows winding and arcing through a narrow valley, each row a mirror of the other and the creek that meanders alongside. The alleys between the rows shimmer with pale green blades of Japanese millet. Windrows of rich compost border the field for more than 100 yards, and a 50-foot wall of wooden bins waits to be filled with the overflowing harvest of roots, fruits, and tubers still ripening in the fields.

There is order on this land; every plant, every row, every field seems to be obsessively well tended. No gaps or spaces testify to failed transplants or uneven irrigation, no nibbled or mottled leaves hint at pests or deficiencies, no undersize fruit suggests weak soil. I reflect on my own perfectionist tendencies, how I've struggled on my own farms to find the balance between wild and cultivated, and I wonder what kind of person has achieved such control over 200 acres.

Richard de Wilde is standing next to his 1998 4WD Chevy pickup, looking out over a field of kale. There's a case of 30-08 Springfield silver-tip rifle cartridges alongside the gearshift; a bag of tobacco, some rolling papers, and a lone red cipollini onion sitting on the seat. I don't normally get all gaga about kale, but the field is as deep a green as anything I've ever seen—not the crazy, pumped-up, rank green that comes from too much ammonium nitrate or urea, but deep and blue and forestlike. These plants are vibrant and well formed, with huge, turgid leaves, each standing up straight as if they've been told to pose for my camera.

"I get snapshots in the mail of someone's kid eating a piece of our squash or corn or a carrot," Richard is saying as I finish the last photograph. "There is an enclosed note that says that this is Johnny's first meal. Eighteen years later, we're providing the food for Johnny's wedding. At the market, they'll introduce their kids to 'our' farmer. There are these beaming kids standing there that have been raised on our food. It makes me feel 10 feet tall. How many people have that kind of job satisfaction?"

Richard farmed for ten years in a suburb of Minneapolis until the land was condemned by the state to become on- and off-ramps for a new industrial park. He moved to Wisconsin in 1984 to farm on 11 leased acres of what is now Harmony Valley Farm. "He cleaned the place up," his wife, Linda Halley, tells me, "built this house, invested an enormous amount in the soils. But it soon became clear that the owners really didn't plan to sell." Linda and Richard imposed a moratorium on building any more infrastructure, until years later when the owners decided to sell. "People told me that it's so insecure to be farming on someone else's land," Richard adds, "but, in the early years, I'm not so sure that I could have covered the mortgage if I had one."

Linda had returned home to Wisconsin in 1994 with the hope of working on her family's farm three hours southeast of Harmony Valley. "I had this idea in the back of my head that I could grow veggies and make a living," she says. "I asked my uncle about some of the little fields on the place, and he said, 'Sure, go ahead.' The first year, I grew light things because I didn't want to carry around all that weight. The next year, I got some help and we diversified into melons and berries. I tried to figure out what was going to make more money. I looked into CSA and I thought, 'Oh, my God, I don't know how to grow food like that.' So I went looking for someone to teach me, and I met Richard."

When she saw Richard's flawless crops, she assumed they couldn't be organic, that he had to be slipping some nitrate fertilizer or malathion into the mix. "My

father was still there, making me think that I couldn't do without the chemicals. I talked to Richard at his end-of-the-season potluck and told him I'd come back in April and work for a year." She became the crew supervisor that first year and has been the self-described "go-to girl" ever since. "Richard is the production manager," she says. "I'm the everything-else person. I field 50,000 questions a day."

"I was still planning to go back to doing my own CSA," Linda remembers. "My uncle was expecting me to come back, and I had planted asparagus and strawberries. But I realized that farming is hard and lonely, and Richard agreed to start a CSA, so I stayed."

Both Richard and Linda had sons from previous relationships. During his first visit to Harmony Valley, Linda's son, Adrian, who was five at the time, announced that he ate only meat and potatoes. "Not at my house," Richard told him. "We have a rule—we never say bad things about the vegetables."

Nearly two years later, the stepbrothers began warming to the new family dynamic. "Things started to improve when they got to be the 'melon boys,'" Linda says. "It's hard to employ a seven-year-old and an eleven-year-old, so we decided that if they had their own crop to sell at the market, they could feel independent.

"Richard is a bit of a control freak," she continues, "so he wasn't going to just let them select a variety that wouldn't work out. They said they wanted to grow yellow watermelons. They started them in flats and planted them in the fields we prepared. When the boys got behind on the weeding, even after they weeded their little butts off, we'd have to go and rescue them. They spent a lot of time arguing and throwing clods of dirt at each other. Every ten minutes Adrian would ask, 'What time is it?'"

As she talks, I look over at Aaron and remember the hours spent arguing over farm chores. It often took longer to negotiate terms with him than it took to actually do the milking, weeding, or harvesting. My inner debate always raged about how much I could push him on the farm without pushing him the other way, especially when his peers were biking to the Taco Bell down the street and drinking cow's milk from the supermarket, not goat's milk from their own backyard. I always shied away from offering money as an incentive; I wanted him to choose for other reasons. But as I listen to Linda's story, I wonder whether I made things harder than they had to be.

"The deal was that they had to give us all of the melons to fulfill CSA, but they got to keep the rest for the market," Linda explains. "They would make up to $600 a market. That's when Adrian started to feel like part of the farm. People still come to the market looking for the melon boys."

Harmony Valley Farm is not the traditional contiguous holding: the average field size is 2 to 8 acres and there are fifty of them, tucked away and bordered by creeks and dirt roads, ringed by hills of maple and oak, wild apples, black rasp-berries, and sumac.

Walking the land in my sense of the concept isn't easy to do here—everything is too far apart. Some folks would call Richard and Linda's operation small, but size is relative. In new-millennium America, their farm would be small at 200 acres, a large one would be 10,000 or more. U.S. Secretary of Agriculture Earl Butz's proclamation to farmers during the late sixties to "get big or get out" has been echoing ever since.

People's perception of scale is influenced by the relatively recent idea that farms should be big and far away from the communities they serve. Most folks would say that the scale I farmed at Fairview Gardens is too small to be economically viable, yet it continues to prove otherwise to this day. As a society, we no longer have a concept of what an appropriate community-based scale would be for our farms. They have become factories cranking out product, reducing valuable living soil to an inert medium for holding plants up in the air and turning independent farmers into cogs in a corporate machine.

To me, Harmony Valley Farm seems huge, an impression that is reinforced by the semitrucks lined up, ready to receive bins of roots and tubers and squashes and melons. Richard refers to Harmony Valley as a small farm that tries to use big-farm technology. "Why would you tie one hand behind your back," he asks, "when there are tools that make it possible to thrive?"

There is no shortage of tools here: thirteen tractors, two subsoilers, a chisel plow, harvest wagons, a one-row root digger, a skid loader, a Wildcat compost turner, miles of irrigation pipe, and hundreds of bins. Like everything else, the fleet of Farmall Super A's and C cultivating tractors, built in the 1950s, are restored and well maintained, without a trace of rust to be found.

At the morning work meeting, instructions are given in Spanish and English and eventually translated into Laotian for the Hmong crew members. "My liberal self wants everyone to be one big, happy family," Linda tells us, "but it doesn't always work out that way." In the fields, the Hmong keep to themselves while they clean garlic and shallots or pick edamame soybeans. The Mexicans work together, doing most of the harvesting and cultivating, and the white men and women— mostly young—drive tractors or do management chores. The separation is at least temporarily suspended every day at mealtime, when the entire crew gathers for a spirited homegrown meal prepared by a cook hired for the farming season.

When the work meeting ends, I hop onto a harvest wagon pulled by one of the Allis-Chalmers tractors. Twenty Mexican men and women head down the main road about half a mile, eventually turning into a field full of immaculately culti-vated salad greens. Richard speaks about keeping the fields free from weeds almost as fanatically as Bob Cannard talked about encouraging weeds to flourish. When I mention leaving weeds in the fields as an alternative strategy, Richard scoffs. I realize both he and Bob are right, both successful within the terms that they have established for themselves.

The cabbages here are the size of basketballs, the leaves on the kale and chard enormous, with a kind of vigor that can be supported only with scrupulously maintained soils. This isn't some soil-mining operation where fertility is sucked away with each harvest and not renewed. Compost from dairy manure and bedding, along with foliar applications of fish meal and kelp, mined micronutrients, and cover crops of oats, peas, and vetch are the time-honored ingredients for maintaining and building soils here. Richard tests the soils religiously every year, and a soil biologist visits and advises the farm.

Buried in the silt and sandy loam soils, Harmony Valley's heart seems to be in its root crops. We drive with Richard from field to field, harvesting samples of every imaginable edible root. They all seem to pull effortlessly. Even a 2-foot-long daikon radish lifts from the ground as if someone is pushing from below. The exception is the burdock root; the roots must be 2 or 3 feet long. I suggest that a backhoe might be an appropriate harvesting tool.

The Chioggia beets, an Italian heirloom with pink outer flesh and concentric pink and white circles inside, would normally be delicately proportioned at about 3 inches across. Here, they are the size of my fist, and nearly perfectly round. The rows of golden beets are full, with none of the gaps typical of this poor germinator.

I rub a beet against the leg of my jeans, take a bite, and pass it on to Aaron. I am only slightly distracted from its dense, rich texture by the soil that is still attached. Richard seems mildly surprised to see us munching roots raw, but Aaron has been eating like this since he was three years old, often passing up on dinner after a day of grazing in the fields. I tackle a burdock tail; it is chewy and infused with a flavor and musk of everything deep and dark and earthy. I finish with a small piece of daikon radish. Crisp and bright and refreshing, it clears my palate and cleans my mouth.

Although it's true that anyone can grow a beet, not everyone grows them like I see them here. To consistently produce volumes of perfectly formed roots, week after week, is not easy. I am humbled by these beets. When I look at them in the fields, and bunched and boxed in the shed, my mind's eye sees years of experimentation and refinement of skill. But maybe it's also about staying put long enough, getting to know a place just like another person, becoming intimate and close, being there. I have done those things, but I've also been restless, distracted by my desire to spread the word, needing to get out and away from the farm to tell my story and those of other farmers.

"Who's eating all of these turnips?" I ask, partly to take my mind off my beet inferiority complex, but also curious to see fields and fields of a food that is under-appreciated in California. "There's a tradition here that when it gets cold, we make stew and put in turnips," Linda replies, and I picture classic Midwestern winter meals drawn from the root cellar. "In the winter, we're the only ones locally with storage, so Odessa Piper depends on us," she adds.

Odessa's name comes up often in conversations around these parts. Her L'Etoile restaurant, in Madison, is known for serving regional food year-round. Not so difficult in California, but quite an accomplishment in Wisconsin, where production grinds to a halt in late fall. In the winter, farmers such as Richard and Linda provide Odessa with a steady supply of roots, the critical foundation for her winter menu. Richard says Odessa has "given parsnips and rutabagas credibility." Her root mash is renowned and would make a rutabaga lover out of anyone.

"I didn't like root crops when I came here," Linda admits. "I still don't like turnips, although, roasted and glazed and eaten with lamb, they're okay. Richard always says, 'Eat your roots. It's the season. You must eat your roots.' It's easy to turn people on to a Charentais melon, but just try to turn them on to burdock."

"We grow different crops for different reasons," Richard says. "We grow sweet corn to make friends; it's hard to make money growing sweet corn. The roots we grow to make money, and then we have friends and money. We also grow roots for our employees so that they have work year-round."

They also grow for their chefs, an important—and fashionable—relationship that can get a little out of hand. "These chefs really think that farmers are going to fall down and die for them so they can sell them something," Linda says. "People look to us to grow any root. Some chef saw this tuber-rooted chervil on a Web site, and he called and asked us to grow it immediately. I'm thinking, 'Excuse me—it's August. Get real!' Then I go to the Web site, and I find out that it's impossible to grow here—it grows in a Mediterranean climate."

On Fridays, all of Harmony Valley is focused on preparing for the Saturday market and the weekly CSA distribution. The crew fills bags with tomatoes: one large striped German, four Odoriko pink, one Goliath, and a couple of Carolina Golds. Onions, garlic, and carrots, a cantaloupe and a watermelon, and four ears of sweet corn are carefully sorted and weighed before going into a share box.

At 9:45 A.M., Gregory, who manages much of the packing, brings a sample box up to Richard for his scheduled box inspection. The box is meticulously packed, each item precisely positioned so that everything fits together like a puzzle. The box inspection is emblematic of the whole operation; there's an expectation that everything be in place, each piece gliding and meshing with each other. I can imagine Richard and Linda waking up at night with some inspiration about an obscure item they could include in the share or a new way of organizing the box. That kind of thing has happened to me the night before a big farmers' market. I wake up designing the market display in my head, tomatoes piled high next to basil next to garlic, peaches and plums flanking the sides, flowers backdropping the whole display.

Richard studies the box quietly. He has a slightly puzzled look on his face and then says he has a feeling something is missing. "There are onions and garlic. Do we have time to put some peppers in the box so they can make a complete meal?" When the quality-control session is over, Richard checks his watch, smiles proudly, and says, "Ten o'clock and the box check is done—not bad!"

He hands me a "Harmony Valley Farm CSA Member Manual and Calendar." The manual lists all the Madison-area delivery sites and times, and details the mechanics of the program—the pickup, the newsletter, the choice box, fruit shares, and how to bow out gracefully if things don't work out. There is a two-page spread titled "Don't Rip That Box," with photographs and detailed step-by-step instructions on how to properly flatten one of the boxes for return to the farm.

Each day of the calendar has little notes: "Look for strawberry blossoms/ Mother's Day," "Linda and Richard's anniversary, hope this helps you remember,"

and "Dig roots and put in storage during every spare moment." I'm amazed at the energy and effort that have been put into the calendar/manual. Richard tells me that by having 440 members in the CSA program, they can rationalize the investment in these kinds of important details. "If you've only got 30 members, how can you even consider doing this kind of thing?" he asks.

On the last night, I ask them whether they think there's any compromise in becoming heavily mechanized and shipping some of their foods long distances. As soon as I ask, I realize how absurd my question is. Of course they've made compromises. Each time we get out of bed, turn on the light, use a piece of paper, or get in the car, we compromise.

As hard as we may try to make our farms into manifestations of our highest social and ecological awareness, there are a million compromises a day inherent in growing food for people outside our family. If it's positive examples we're after— and I believe there is nothing more important—Richard and Linda's work provides one based on present-day reality, one that working farmers can relate to. It's not controversial or eccentric; there are no cosmological planting charts on the walls guiding each activity, no complex theories espoused on insects or soil fertility. Nobody here is eschewing technology. But the food is abundant, the soils rich and in good tilth, and the community investment clear and established.

As a role model, Harmony Valley's scale gives it respectability, the equipment and facilities provide an air of agricultural normality, the large staff is impressive. It's a well-founded, classical, mixed-production farm, but one where individual, social, and environmental health do not have to become a casualty of eating.

"All of the machines on this farm are simple tractors from the 1950s," Richard tells me. "To say I don't like machines or I don't like grease is to say I'm just going to break my back. Duh! The more food that you can sell, the more chance you have of making a living. I see so many farmers who are only forty-two years old, and they are tired. 'I don't have enough money, and I'm tired and my back is shot,' they say. But it requires a certain volume to get any kind of efficiency. If you're not working efficiently, you're going to burn out.

"We have this old FMC root digger," Richard continues. "In the fall, my job is to ride on it and keep things adjusted as it travels through the field. I ride that root digger counting bins, counting tons in my head, knowing that if all goes well, there will be money in the bank and bonuses for the crew. Then there's this moment when the temperature is perfect, the insects are gone, and I look up and around at the hills and at the trees changing color, and there's an eagle flying up the river. Then I remember that this is why I'm doing this work."

☙

AMID AN ANIMATED DISCUSSION ABOUT FOOD AND CONSUMPTION and entitlement and obesity and the role of the Midwest in bringing understated but powerful change to the world, we drink wine and champagne and eat wild-mushroom salad, local sweet corn chowder, free-range chicken cooked with grilled Harmony Valley cipollini onions, Wisconsin farmstead cheeses, and black-plum tarte tatin. This is how the talk and food flows at L'Etoile, Odessa Piper's celebration of Wisconsin ingredients. I had always heard about L'Etoile and its focus on regional ingredients, even in the peak of winter. I often used the restaurant as rebuttal when someone jumped on my case for waxing poetic about regional food when I was lucky enough to live and farm in Southern California. It's one thing to keep a menu alive with local foods in the peak of winter in Berkeley or L.A. It takes courage and real creativity to come up with an enticing January menu in Madison, Wisconsin, when it's fifteen below zero, and there's 3 feet of snow on the ground. Now I was finally seeing L'Etoile for myself, though admittedly in summer, when the choice of Wisconsin ingredients rivals that of any in the world.

The next day, with Odessa as our guide, I spend the morning photographing the well-loved Dane County farmers' market, where 250 farmers and 20,000 eaters from all over the state come together on the grounds of the state capitol building for the great exchange. There is symbolism here—the Jeffersonian idea of the inextricable connection between a healthy democracy and a sustainable agriculture played out at the feet of the state's seat of government.

Odessa introduces us to her favorite farmers, telling us a bit of their story, describing in passionate detail the particularities of the foods they produce, how she uses them, and how each one is unique. I take a number of photographs, only to discover—too late—that the film is not loading properly in the camera. Aaron consoles me by comparing our morning experience to a Tibetan sandpainting, impermanent, a momentary flash.

In the afternoon, we search the market for Bob and Ellen Lane's Future Fruit Farm stand. Future Fruit Farm is the largest pear orchard in Wisconsin, producing heirloom pears and apples in an unreliable climate. Along with a reputation for flavorful fruit, the Lanes are known for operating on the edge of fitting in. "Bob's going to scare the shit out of you," Odessa warns Aaron after giving him a hug goodbye. "But he has deep-rooted wisdom. Bob's like agricultural jazz."

We walk the whole market, trying to locate the Lane stand. On the second round, we find mother and daughter standing behind two small card tables with a few boxes of plums and apples. It's a small and understated display. Had I not been searching, I would have passed it by, assuming it was the harvest of someone's back-yard fruit trees. First impressions are hard to let go of, and I'm struggling to picture a serious farm behind this meager display.

Ellen introduces me to her twenty-five-year-old daughter, Selena, and tells me that in their fourteen years of doing this market, Bob has never attended, that he always stays on the farm. A friend gave them T-shirts labeled "Bob's Wife" and "Bob's Daughter." Ellen and Selena wore the shirts and made a sign that read "Bob's Fruit" and another one labeled "So, Where's Bob?"

Bob Lane does, in fact, exist. We find him on their farm, an hour due west from Madison, near Ridgeway, Wisconsin, lying down with his ragtag, tattooed, pierced, and dreadlocked crew after a day of spreading compost. The Lanes planted their 32-acre orchard twenty-four years ago. The seventy-five hundred trees are primarily old heirloom varieties: fourteen varieties of pears, twenty-four types of apples, and a small number of plums and Asian pears. The Lanes were rightfully expecting to be unique. Here, the farms are all dairies; no one else in the area has this kind of operation, and with good reason. Few farmers anywhere can afford to try something that requires this much work with this much risk of extreme weather, small harvests, even crop failure.

I know a little bit about risk myself; at every farm I've started, I've had locals telling me what works and what doesn't. During the first year on our farm in British Columbia, the mailman, the electrician, the bank teller, even the person doing the drywall in the house, all provided me with a list of when to plant, how to do it, and, most important, what products would never work. I proceeded, as I always have, to try the very things people told me not to try. Now, asparagus stands 6 feet tall in the bottomland field everyone said was too wet, figs thrive and produce as if they were on the coast of Sicily, not on the coast of Canada, and Charentais melons litter our summer fields in a climate everyone said could never support them. But the Lanes' experiment seems grander still, with risk and improvisation on a scale that would give me pause.

The farm is visually beautiful. Fruit trees roll across the top of an extended rise. One of Bob's paintings hangs on the chain-link fence that keeps out the deer; piles of straw and manure settle into the ground beneath small sections of native oaks and ash and maples that dot the orchard.

The fruit trees are in rows, like those in any other orchard, and ladders and boxes are stacked near a shed, all providing some sense of agricultural normalcy. But when I walk closer, I notice that there is not much fruit. It's August, yet only the occasional tree is appropriately laden for this time of year. The few fruits that still ripen seem like forgotten stragglers, as if I'm viewing the trees after a not-so-careful harvest. When I look even closer, I notice the subtle, striking palette of the fruit—rich golds and reds, mottled burgundy blushed on a golden green background, dusky brown, and shades of ripe green. The shapes are small, delicate, and uneven, some like large teardrops, some almost round, like well-placed ornaments. The feeling is old, almost wild, and I realize that these trees are direct descendants of immigrant dreams; they are the progeny of a small packet of fruitwood transported in a shirt pocket from favorite trees in the Old Country to propagate all across the New World. Commercial orchards of these varieties are all but gone in favor of uniform, predictable varieties that ship well. But here, in this orchard, they gather like old friends.

After the dependable, totally practical, and well-planned approach we just saw at Harmony Valley, this place feels like improv. I look at this orchard, and I can almost hear Bob Lane riffing, with Moonglow and Comice and Aurora pears forming the notes in a spontaneous performance. I'm wondering whether this is what Odessa Piper meant by "agricultural jazz." If so, then Richard DeWilde is like Benny Goodman working off a well-written score. Here, it's all Miles Davis, taking chances, never really knowing what note will come next. If I put the practical out of my mind for a moment, if I ignore the signs of risk, I can see what Bob must have found irresistible: the beautiful, vulnerable juxtaposition of these treasured varieties brought together into a strange composition that will be played out only here.

As it turns out, I will have to form most of my impressions of Bob by observing his work. Bob himself seems taciturn, inclined to drop out of the conversation and speak up unexpectedly, usually to volunteer a strong opinion and then return to his own thoughts.

When he hears that we've just come from the market in Madison, he tells us that at the age of twenty, he was one of the first growers to sell in that market along with a group of other radicals, and it's clear that he still values his radical roots. Ellen reminds us that Madison, with its progressive attitudes, used to be referred to as "the third coast." My mother went to school in Madison for a short time with a planned major in veterinary science (she's never liked animals), and a close childhood friend of my brother's blew up the mathematics building at the University of Wisconsin during the Vietnam War, not knowing there was someone working late inside.

The Lanes are steeped in the history of this area, and, although their appearances don't give it away, they fit squarely within the time-honored tradition of old hippies. Ellen tells me that when they got married, they wanted to live in a large, urban cultural center and become "starving but famous" artists. Bob decided early on that the arts were in trouble, so they chose a different kind of trouble: fruit farming. Ellen continues to teach dance, delivering fruit after dance class in pink-lavender tights. Bob still paints, but, as Ellen points out, "The farm is his primary expression."

Bob's paintings cover the walls of their barn-style home. Over a dinner of pasta and homegrown tomato sauce, I try to engage him in a discussion on the relationship between art and agriculture. The most I get is a mumbled comment from which I pick out only the phrase "the patterns of nature."

I, too, came to farming as an artist, not as an agriculturist. My only formal education after high school was in the arts, and I had no agricultural training. I often find that people are surprised or even bewildered when they discover that a farmer can also write or take photographs or play music. It's the stereotype image in their brains of a farmer as slightly stupid, dressed in overalls, with a pitchfork in his or her hands. When you consider that farming is one of the few professions in which the practitioner is out on the land every day observing nature, it's hardly a surprise that many farmers are inspired writers, musicians, and visual artists.

I sometimes feel that good farming is the greatest form of artistic expression. Farmers create the bridge between nature and human nourishment. Food as the product of the agricultural arts goes beyond any image on the wall of a gallery or museum. Good eating, in that sense, could be considered one of the most integrated forms of art appreciation.

"When Bob first met me, I was doing a solo dance concert," Ellen tells me. "I came on stage as a green bean, with a choir singing a green-bean opera. The performance was written to connect kids with food and good eating. My bean character was really proud to be a nourishing food. All of a sudden, this sugar cube comes floating down and the bean exclaims, 'No, don't put sugar on me!'

"This was about the same time I dug up my parents' suburban backyard to plant food. My father flipped out."

On Bob's side of the family, his mother wouldn't tell anyone that her son farmed. "Now, they brag about it," Ellen says.

I remember when I was still living at home, my brother, who was eleven years older than me, came home from college, hair down to his waist, with some "new" ideas that didn't sit so well with my father. I'll never forget my dad standing up at the dinner table and, with a great deal of indignation, proclaiming that 'your brother needs a special farmer to grow his food for him,' referring to the fact that he was now into organic food. We laugh when I tell that story now, both because I have become that "special farmer" and because my dad has become a champion of my work.

The Lanes have the only commercial pear orchard in Wisconsin, 6,000 fruit trees dropped in the middle of a bunch of dairy farms. Extreme weather events and risk of disease have pushed most commercial fruit growing into the more arid, predictable climates of the western states. The marketplace demands a level of cosmetic perfection that requires growers to go through the most amazing contortions to produce for a society that has been trained to equate no blemishes and large fruit with goodness. But how many times has someone bit into that perfect-looking pear or apple, only to find it has no flavor or that its texture has been compromised?

The Lanes take a different approach, growing older, highly flavorful varieties and using creative strategies to educate their customers that large fruit with a

perfect complexion does not always equate with rich taste and texture. Ellen tells me about the buyer from a major natural-foods company who requested that she FedEx a sample of their pears. After receiving them, the buyer called and told her that "these things are golf balls—they won't fit into our slots." Ellen apologized and explained to him in a deadpan tone that "we've talked to our trees, and they just don't listen."

Newcomers at the farmers' market in Madison, where the Lanes have maintained a presence for seventeen years, commonly walk right past their Aurora, Luscious, Seckel, or Moonglow pears. The fruits are small, oddly shaped, and blemished, and, after a lifetime of seeing big, yellow, well-groomed supermarket Bartletts, the Lanes' pears look a bit homely. Most folks would never come up to you and tell you how ugly your child is, but they don't hesitate to make comments to the farmer if the food they're looking at is outside their normal frame of reference.

Ellen is proud of the homely look of their fruit and often responds by agreeing with customers who disparage the look of certain varieties. She refers to the Luscious as "the ugliest pear around" and then waxes poetic about its buttery texture and flavor of "butterscotch and honey." By the time she finishes her spirited description, even the most hardcore skeptic can be seen filling a bag. Ellen describes how she and Selena sit behind their stand at the market, eating fruit instead of hawking, and hand out samples to people who walk past. They watch and count the ten steps it takes for a passerby to process the taste, whirl around, and come back.

Placing a guarantee on a car or a radio is one thing, but on a pear? The Lanes provide a guarantee that every piece of fruit will be the "best you've ever tasted." They tell me that no one has ever come back unhappy.

Few people, even those who love the Lanes' fruit, realize that it is something of a small miracle that it grows anywhere near the Madison farmers' market. Aside from climatic challenges that are difficult to overcome, heirloom varieties are not always known for prolific or consistent output. The trees themselves are durable, but here they must be almost individually coaxed to give their best harvest over the course of a very long and arduous harvest season. It takes judgment and skill to pick this fruit; each is ready in its own time, unlike in a commercial orchard, where fruit is harvested en masse, ready or not.

Bob describes the trefoil, clover, brome, and wildflowers that grow under the trees, providing support to the mason bees and blue orchard bees that pollinate the trees more completely than the honeybees so typically used in commercial plantings. He mixes calcium-rich bat guano, volcanic rock dust, seaweed, rock phosphate, and composted manures and places them along and beneath each row of trees. And, starting in late winter, almost every week throughout the spring and summer, he's out protecting his fruit with oils and clays and elemental minerals.

But, ultimately, it's a strong dose of blind financial faith that really keeps this place going. Bob tells me that the varieties that wait the longest to come into production are often the best, that planting an orchard is like starting a family—it's a lifetime commitment: "It's something you're bound to."

"Each tree is like an only child," Ellen says. "Selena has 7,000 brothers and sisters."

On the road, we've been hearing a lot about slow food, but it doesn't get any slower than this. Plant a pear or an apple tree and you can wait as much as five years for serious production. A good orchardist is patient and knows that careful actions taken today can yield good fruit that will serve generations to come. Planting an orchard is an act of hope: it requires vision and imagination, especially at Future Fruit Farm.

This particular spring, the Lanes' pear and apple trees were loaded with fruit, bringing great hope and promise for the year. Special attention was paid to the orchard, to pest and disease control, to summer pruning, and to the very time-consuming and expensive job of fruit thinning. By late July, the Lanes were preparing for a bumper harvest, the largest crop they had ever had, and quietly planning on what they would do with the much-needed extra income.

Saturday, July 26, was clear, sunny, and hot. Work wrapped up early, and the small crew was hanging out talking near the house. There was a distant rumbling, and a mellow thunderstorm began. Then the sky turned black, the temperature plummeted thirty degrees, and lightning and rain came down in sheets. At 3:15 P.M., the hail came, large hail, up to a half an inch in diameter. Exactly thirteen minutes later, the hail stopped, the sky cleared, the sun came out, and the Lanes' fruit crop was devastated. More than half the crop had dropped.

For several days, no one could bear to go near the orchard. Eventually, they would sneak in and then out again, just to get a glimpse.

Bob was ready to quit. "We had to take out loans from the farm crisis bureau," Ellen says. "I told them that I felt endangered. He told me that, compared to some others, we're not in bad shape, and that we should take out our loans and get what's left of our crop in."

Bob tells us that he was going to stand on a street corner in Madison with a running chain saw, yelling, "I will cut down my orchard if you don't support us!"

"My father was seething about the hail," Ellen says. "'I don't know why you chose this occupation,' he told me. 'Dad, you are just about to go grocery shopping. Did it occur to you that there is a farmer behind every one of the foods that you buy and eat?'"

The Lanes are not new to fruit loss and damage from weather. In 2001, Ellen distributed a "Pear Saga" she had written to her customers, explaining the reduction in their crop: "1) Below-zero temperatures for long periods over the last winter caused dormant fruit buds to become unviable. 2) During fruit bloom this spring, the temperature zoomed abnormally into the high 80s and caused the pear trees to bloom all at once (they normally bloom two times, giving the tree two chances for pollination). During this onetime bloom, a windstorm kept the bees from getting to the blooms, so pollination was greatly reduced. 3) THE PEARS WE DID GET ARE PERFECT AND EXCEPTIONALLY SWEET!"

There is a P.S. on the bottom of "Pear Saga 2001": "Please note that although there are both good and bad years for every crop, we farmers are too regularly experiencing extremes in weather conditions that put our crops and ourselves more at risk. Please help take care of our planet's health so that we can continue to grow good food."

The 2003 "Pear Saga" read, "Due to weather conditions and severe storms over the past weeks, which caused broken branches and fruit falling off the trees, our crop has been greatly reduced. Our prices reflect what we need to remain sustainable. We hope you enjoy our difficult-to-grow and out-of-this-world-fantastic organic Future Fruit Farm pears."

There is a sense here that one farmer's crisis is everyone's crisis. At a time when less than 2 percent of the population is growing the nourishment for the rest, shouldn't everyone who eats share the farmer's ups and downs? Ellen's communications to her customers are gentle reminders of that critical relationship between farmer and consumer. "This is bigger than us," she says. "We can't quit."

I get the feeling that the Lanes' survival is based to some degree on their sense of humor. It's a "pearadox," considering the hard times that weather has brought on them, that they continue to be light, Ellen says. "Greetings from pearadise," she jokes, or, "No, don't go to Pearis; you simply must go to the pearamids."

At the market, the fruits themselves speak to customers through signs placed above each variety: "Hi, I'm from around here, I taste better, I didn't have to travel from far away." But for all the humor, I also know that this latest loss, scarcely a month old, is nearly as harsh as any farmer can sustain.

The night before our departure, Aaron and I are sleeping in the van in the Lanes' orchard. In the background, we hear the same reggae song playing over and over and over. It's close to 3 A.M. when Aaron drags himself out of bed to find the source of the loud music. There, crashed out in the front seat of his pickup, is Bob, with Steel Pulse blaring.

In farming, risk and disappointment come with the territory. We prepare ourselves and the land as well as we can, but we have no control over what nature gives out. Most farmers I know do it for the love of it. Some succeed financially; most of us at some point have to deal with loss. The power and influence of our work is not so much based on all our successes, but, rather, on what we can learn from our losses and our failures and what we can pass on to those who come behind us. Some, like the Lanes, risk more than others in an effort to test the many subtle possibilities that can be captured in a lifelong dance with an heirloom orchard.

Days after we left the Lanes, I found myself reflecting on their situation, struggling to make sense of it. I puzzled over their choice of where to farm, what to grow, and even questioned how they fit into this story. Then I reached into the cupboard of the van and pulled out the last pear they had sent along with us. I could see why neither Aaron nor I had eaten it. It was small and misshapen, with patches of scab and a not-particularly-attractive brownish yellow skin. I hesitated at first and even considered tossing it out. Then I took a bite. The texture was like butter, and the flavor burst into a thousand different experiences bouncing around in the interior of my mouth. I could feel Bob and Ellen and Selena within that little piece of misshapen fruit, a little difficult to understand from the outside, but complex, unexpected, and more than a little daring inside.

♣

Winter Root Mash

SERVES 4

This recipe was adapted from the root mash Odessa Piper prepares with Richard de Wilde and Linda Halley's celery root and Jerusalem artichokes. It's rich and earthy, and delicious served with a pat of butter and sprinkled with crunchy sea salt.

1 medium celery root, peeled

1 large parsnip, peeled

½ pound Jerusalem artichokes (about 7 small to medium artichokes), peeled

2 medium parsley roots, peeled

Kosher salt to taste

2 pounds potatoes (about 3 large potatoes) such as Yukon Gold or Yellow Finn,
    peeled and each cut into 8 pieces

¼ cup unsalted butter, at room temperature, plus extra for serving

About ½ cup heavy cream, half-and-half, or milk, warmed

Freshly cracked black pepper to taste

Sea salt to taste

Cut the celery root, parsnip, Jerusalem artichokes, and parsley root into pieces of similar size and shape—about ¼ inch thick. Put the roots in a medium saucepan with water to cover by 1 inch. Season the water with a generous amount of salt—it should taste almost like seawater. Bring to a low boil, reduce the heat, and gently cook until all of the roots are completely tender when pierced with a knife, 25 to 30 minutes—be sure to check each variety of root vegetable. Drain and spread the roots out on a baking sheet to dry in a warm place, about 5 minutes.

Meanwhile, put the potatoes in a separate medium saucepan with water to cover by 1 inch. Season the water in the same manner as the root vegetables and bring to a low boil. Reduce the heat and gently cook the potatoes until they are completely tender when pierced with a knife, about 25 minutes. Drain and spread the potatoes out on a baking sheet to dry in a warm place, about 5 minutes.

While the roots and potatoes are still warm, pass them through a food mill and into a large bowl along with the ¼ cup butter. Stir in about ½ cup warm heavy cream, or enough so that the puree reaches the desired consistency. Season the mash with pepper and more salt if necessary. Serve with a pat of sweet butter sprinkled with crunchy sea salt.

Winter Root Vegetable Soup

This is just good, old-fashioned root soup that tastes like Thanksgiving in a bowl. It's the
perfect winter soup, reliant on the amazing diversity of roots that Richard de Wilde and Linda
Halley grow and that can be stored so well.

SERVES 6

1 tablespoon olive oil

2 tablespoons unsalted butter

2 medium yellow onions, cut into ½-inch dice

1 teaspoon chopped fresh thyme

Kosher salt to taste

2 large carrrots, peeled and cut into ½-inch dice

1 medium celery root, peeled and cut into ½-inch dice

1 medium potato such as Yukon Gold or Yellow Finn, peeled and cut into ½-inch dice

1 medium turnip, peeled and cut into ½-inch dice

1 medium parsnip, peeled and cut into ½-inch dice

2 medium parsley roots, peeled and cut into ½-inch dice

1 bay leaf

7 to 8 cups water

¾ cup chopped fresh flat-leaf parsley

Freshly cracked black pepper to taste

Heat a large Dutch oven or heavy-bottomed stockpot over medium heat and add the olive oil and butter. When the butter has melted, add the onions, thyme, and a pinch of salt. Gently sauté until the onions are tenter, about 7 minutes. Add the diced root vegetables, bay leaf, and about 7 cups of water—the water should cover the vegetables by about 1¹/₂ inches. Season the soup with salt (about 2 teaspoons) and bring to a boil. Reduce the heat to medium-low and gently simmer the soup, stirring occasionally, until the vegetables are tender, about 1 hour. Transfer about 2 cups of the soup to a blender or food processor and puree until smooth. Return the puree to the pot and stir to combine. Add the parsley and simmer for 5 more minutes. season with a generous amount of pepper and serve.

NOTE: If parsley root is unavailable, substitute with 1 medium turnip or parsnip

Asian Pear Watercress Salad with Toasted Walnuts

SERVES 4

Bob and Ellen Lane produce fourteen varieties of European and Asian pears, many of them older heirloom varieties with homely looks but delicious flavor. Pears, walnuts, and watercress are a classic combination. European pears are more common, but sweet, crisp Asian pears are perfect for salads.

¾ cup walnuts

¼ cup extra-virgin olive oil, plus 2 teaspoons

Kosher salt to taste

1 small shallot, finely diced

3 tablespoons Champagne or white wine vinegar

½ pound watercress

1 Asian pear, cored and thinly sliced

Freshly cracked black pepper to taste

2 ounces Roquefort or other blue cheese (optional)

Preheat the oven to 350 degrees F.

Spread the walnuts on a baking sheet and toast in the oven, stirring occasionally, until light golden, about 5 minutes—be careful not to overtoast the nuts. Transfer to a clean kitchen towel. Wrap the nuts in the towel and gently rub to remove the skins. Discard the skins and transfer the nuts to a small bowl. While the nuts are still warm, drizzle with the 2 teaspoons olive oil and season with a generous pinch of salt. Toss well and set aside to cool.

Combine the shallot and vinegar in a small bowl with a pinch of salt and let stand for 10 to 15 minutes.

Meanwhile, trim the tough and fibrous stems off of the watercress—you should end up with small, tender sprigs of watercress. Wash the watercress in a large basin of water and spin dry. Set aside.

Whisk the ¼ cup olive oil into the vinegar and shallot mixture, and taste the vinaigrette with a watercress sprig; you may want to add a little more olive oil or an extra drop or two of vinegar. Combine the watercress and pear slices in a large bowl and season with salt and pepper. Gently toss with just enough vinaigrette to lightly coat the greens. Arrange the salad on a serving platter or individual plates. Crumble the Roquefort over (if desired) and sprinkle the toasted walnuts on top. If you have any vinaigrette left over, drizzle a little on the pears and around the plate. Serve immediately.

Cele's Old-Fashioned Pear Cake

Ellen Lane's mom, Cele, originally made this cake with Italian prune plums, but Ellen prepares it with their own Seckel pears. Both versions work well—they're homey and delicious.

½ cup unsalted butter, at room temperature, plus 2 tablespoons melted

All-purpose flour for dusting

1 cup whole-wheat pastry flour

1 teaspoon ground cinnamon

1 teaspoon baking powder

¼ teaspoon sea salt

1 cup sugar

2 eggs

6 firm but ripe small pears such as Seckel, cored and cut lengthwise into quarters

Preheat the oven to 350 degrees F.

Brush a 9-inch round springform pan with the 2 tablespoons melted butter, and dust the pan with a thin, even layer of flour, tapping out the excess. Set aside.

Whisk together the whole-wheat pasty flour, cinnamon, baking powder, and salt in a bowl. Set aside.

Using an electric mixer, beat together the ½ cup butter and the sugar on high speed until pale, light, and fluffy. Scrape down the sides of the bowl, add the eggs, and beat again until well combined. Using a rubber spatula, fold in the dry ingredients just until combined. Transfer the batter to the prepared pan and neatly arrange the pear quarters on top, skin side up. Bake for about 1 hour, or until the top is nicely browned and a toothpick inserted into the middle comes out clean. Let the cake cool for 10 to 15 minutes before removing it from the pan.

NOTE: To prepare the original version with Italian prune plums, use 12 plums, pitted and halved, in place of the pears.

CHAPTER 6

☾

MARGINS

In a Chicago Starbucks at 9:00 a.m., women wearing pink and lavender spandex line up with men in white shirts and ties and a crew of fire-fighters from the 30 East division to order their macchiatos and lattes and Americanos. Everyone has a cell phone attached to the side of their heads, chattering away as if their whole lives existed somewhere else.

Outside the large glass windows that keep us cool and clean and safe, the Cabrini-Green housing project looms like a sixteen-story prison complex, its buildings entirely enmeshed in wire, walls blackened by smoke and windows broken and boarded up. Built in the fifties to warehouse poor, unemployed, and primarily black residents, it has worked no better than similar experiments across the country and gained a national reputation for poverty, violence, and desperation.

In the shadow of Cabrini-Green, two 1-acre plots of land are protected with 10-foot-high chain-link-and-concertina fences. A closer look reveals that one of the plots boasts forty varieties of heirloom tomatoes. Striped German, Green Zebra, Black Russian, and the rest of Ken Dunn's tomato plants grow in the composted remains of apple- and cherry-pie filling, and the uneaten arugula salads and filet mignon from local high-end restaurants. Dunn has laid 1,000 tons of compost on this site over a sealer layer of clay and wood chips, just a fraction of the 15,000 tons of urban waste disposed of in this city each day. As I walk between the sweet, pungent rows, the ground springs back like a sponge, and if I closed my eyes and plugged my ears, it would feel like I was walking on the floor of a virgin forest.

The tomatoes don't seem to mind the constant noise or bad air or the poverty that surrounds their little island. The plants are tall and robust and absolutely loaded. Their world is rich in nutrients and reflected warmth and light from the pavement and surrounding buildings. They thrive on the attention of local chefs who are thrilled to tell their clientele that the tomatoes on the menu were harvested down the street, that they picked them up on the way to work.

There are no red barns or silos here, no fields crowded with corn or pastures dotted with cows or sheep. Amid tall skyscrapers, crowded sidewalks, and expansive parking lots, green life finds the margins where soil has survived. Urban farmers seize available light and space under a veil of uncertainty, never knowing when the plans for a new high-rise or retail complex will get approved and the land they farm will be buried under the next necessary or frivolous building.

Dunn's little tomato forest may exist on the edge, but it is not alone. All across this country there are little sanctuaries like this, most of them community gardens where urban residents—often immigrants from agricultural parts of the country and the world—can grow the seeds and the foods of their rural roots. On abandoned lots, between buildings, on narrow slivers of land along streets and sidewalks, every city now has elements of guerrilla gardening, where trash and rubble are traded for food and flowers.

Beyond the community-gardening movement, a handful of professional farmers like Ken Dunn have tapped into an even more compelling possibility: the idea that unused urban lands can generate jobs and serious quantities of food. These farmers are challenging the common misconception that food must be grown far from where most people live. Instead, every neighborhood in every city could have its own  farm with orchards and greenhouses and a public market. These could become the new town squares, balancing the hardscape of buildings and pavement with fertile soil, lush plantings, and fresh foods. Local residents could take part during their breaks from work or at the end of the day. There could be classes and workshops on cooking and growing, as well as celebratory meals making use of the farm's yield. In this scenario, urban citizens might expand their definition of honorable work to include farmers, who, instead of laboring on the distant margins, are welcomed into the fabric of the urban tapestry.

In the meantime, Ken, like all pioneers, has to make his own welcome. He wrenched his current site from the City of Chicago, as he has two hundred other sites over the last thirty-five years. There are some 6,000 acres of vacant plots within the 200 square miles of this sprawling city. Most of them are controlled by the city's fifty aldermen, who oversee their wards like urban land barons.

Farming or gardening acts as a placeholder, something city officials or developers can point to as a benevolent gesture while they await permits for the next Nordstrom or Whole Foods Market. "If you can't buy the land to feed the city, you have to adapt," Ken says with the offhand confidence that comes from more than three decades as an urban land gypsy.

Ken was born and raised in Partridge, Kansas, in a Mennonite farming family. Growing up, he watched as his community gradually lost its respect for natural systems and got sucked into heavy machinery, big bank loans, and insecticides and fertilizers. The soil became depleted and compacted, and required more and more powerful equipment to break it up. The insecticides and fertilizers became more necessary and expensive.

Ken left the family farm to study philosophy at the University of Chicago and came to the conclusion that "there are only a few great ideas, and only a few ways to implement them." The great idea that inspired him to thirty-odd years of work started with recycling and led logically to farming. All good farmers are recyclers, but for Ken, the image of a city renewing itself on its own garbage became irresistible.

His wife, Christine, joined him in 1999 after a stint as an art student at the Chicago Art Institute. After she graduated, she was looking for something to do that was socially relevant. "What does an artist do to be in the world and answer some of the wrongs of society?" she asks. "It seemed odd that someone would come to Chicago to do agriculture, but here I am."

Urban farming is inevitably homeless farming, and so Ken has developed a system of movable farms that allows him to build soil and then move it when the tenure of a site ends. The entire contents of the Dunns' current farm were hauled eighty-eight blocks, almost 10 miles from his previous farm, at 66th and Harvard. Next year, it will take sixty truckloads to move this farm and all its priceless soil to Oak and Larabee. Ken has accepted that he will have to keep moving; he knows that urban planning and development is about buildings, not about food and farms. His unwritten agreement with the city is that officials will advise him on the approximate tenure for each site and will continue to provide new sites to move to.

The key to the Dunns' movable feast is the 10,000 cubic yards of compost they produce each year from city waste at Ken's longtime recycling facility a mile and a half from the University of Chicago. By closing the nutrient loop and returning

precious waste to the soil, Ken and Christine are reclaiming at least some of the soil fertility hauled away from the nation's farmland to feed its cities and never returned. They are also building a portable annuity for themselves in the rich, recycled soil they make out of the everyday life of Chicago.

I watch as a large skip loader mixes loads of cookies and pie filling, muffin batter, truckloads of geraniums, Krispy Kreme doughnuts, melted frozen strawberries, 2 barrels of honey, and 6 frozen ducks, along with manure from the local police stables and wood chips from the city's Bureau of Forestry. Fertility once destined for the landfill is now processed by the staff at the recycling center, many of whom once lived on the margins themselves, homeless or unemployed.

The compost piles stand 15 feet high and are 200 feet long. Dunn explains that some food-processing company might lose a cotter pin from one of its machines and have to dump 3 tons of cookies on the assumption that it landed in the dough. He'll receive a discarded 55-gallon drum of honey with a label that reads, "Lacks clarity." I have to wonder how the bees—who spend a lifetime generating a single teaspoonful—would feel knowing that the product of their labor lacked clarity.

Feral dogs have adopted the compost piles, Ken says. "When I arrive with raw material, they will grab an uneaten steak and head off to their dens." At Ken's gardens around the city, colonies of parakeets that multiply and build their nests in electrical transformers always attack his early pea crops. I can imagine there must always be some species ready to move in, that gardens or compost piles become havens for any urban wildness that remains.

"The root of our problem is assuming that we can make nature irrelevant," Ken says. "We just keep storming through." As he speaks, I realize it's not just Mother Nature he means, but human nature at its most elemental. How long can we ignore our need for sustainable food sources and build cities where the closest real food source is hundreds, if not thousands, of miles away?

That afternoon, Ken takes me on a tour through Chicago in a 1980 Mercedes-Benz station wagon loaded with farm tools and boxes. He wants me to see the sites where he has done his own brand of urban renewal in the marginal places most tourists never notice. He points out the tenements where he did recycling, the tiny patch of trees he culls for dried branches and leaves; he knows where every speck or remnant of nature is in this city.

Like two real estate developers scouting for their next big deal, we take turns spotting future opportunities. On busy Lafayette Avenue, he stops in front of his dream site, a 6-acre parcel surrounding a derelict three-story brick landmark, the former country estate of nineteenth-century developer and politician John Raber. Here, surrounded by towering skyscrapers, he believes he could make a more permanent mark on the life of Chicago.

"It gives you a feeling of awe and wonder when you look at the skyline of this city," he remarks. "The engineering, the skill, the money. This whole city is built out of the topsoil of the Midwest. The traders and middlemen exploited the farmers, and, in turn, the farmers exploited the land. This huge capitalist machine scraped up the soil of the Great Plains to build this city." From this point of view, it seems only fitting that Ken would spend a lifetime recycling the spoils of that economy back into soil.

We return that evening to a gathering in the Dunns' garden beneath Cabrini-Green. We watch as chefs arrive for a personal tour, gingerly parking their SUVs on the dirt track that runs along one side of the garden. Card tables are laden with wines and cheeses and olives and the best carrot cake I have ever eaten. And, of course, tomatoes: every color, shape, and size spills across the surface of a large, makeshift table that is the gathering's centerpiece.

Outside the towering barbed-wire-topped fence, residents from the housing project walk by, pausing long enough to look in at the strange sight of men and women in starched white jackets and checkered pants with wineglasses in hand, looking a little lost in this world of plants and soil. I overhear a woman who has been involved with the garden describe being here at night, looking out at the illuminated skyline and listening to the pop, pop, pop of guns being fired in the neighborhood.

Ken says it used to be common for a few kids to scale the fence and destroy the garden just for sport. I remember that one of Ken's detractors pulled me aside at the farmers' market and said he "should be growing for the community, not fencing them out." But Ken's perspective is simple: no fence means no product, no product means no income, no income means no garden, no garden means no jobs. "We need to get beyond this sentimental notion that we can make ourselves feel good by not putting up a fence," he tells me. "Generosity is shown either by employing people and paying good wages or by providing quality food for them."

I drift away from the crowd and wander to the fence. Up about six stories in one of the Cabrini-Green buildings, a young black man—maybe Aaron's age— stands on his wire-encased balcony, fingers pushed through the mesh as he stares into space. I turn around and am facing another world, the Gold Coast skyline, the heart and center of high finance, illuminated and glittering. My attention turns back to the tomatoes that surround me. Could this small farm and those like it become the bridges between those two worlds?

At the moment, Ken's farm, the housing project, and the city itself are simply neighbors, separate worlds that are just beginning to have a new kind of exchange. "One of the things that keep people clinging on to the old models is that they think there is no alternative," Ken says. "But this is a living alternative."

The next day, we meet Christine at the rear service entrance of the Frontera Grill, where she is delivering produce. Their toddler, Soren, sleeps in his car seat, completely enveloped by boxes of produce. Christine opens the back hatch and Frontera chef Tracey Vowel selects from boxes of Amish Paste, Black from Tula, and Oxheart tomatoes. While all this is going on, Ken is rummaging through a fleet of garbage cans behind the restaurant, sorting and separating salad scraps, meat trimmings, and corncobs, the majority of which will go into his compost. He is one of those people who look at garbage and see soil and food.

Tracey tells me that Ken "is relentless—he's here every day, taking the waste away. You go over to the garden at Cabrini and see what they've done, and you feel like you have some hand in what they're producing. It feels good." Initially, Ken was hesitant to sell to restaurants. "Before we met some of the great chefs we work with now, it seemed like a lot of restaurants were being run on anger. I was afraid that our lettuce would wilt as soon as it entered some of those kitchens."

The economics of farming in the city are such that selling to high-end restaurants is a necessity. Even at $3 a pound for tomatoes, it's tough to make, or to pay, a living wage. There is no wage parity between farmers and other professions anywhere in this country, but in a city like Chicago, the discrepancy is extreme. "We have to make it work within the existing economy before we can develop a just economy," Ken says. At the Dunns' garden gate, there are a few boxes of tomatoes, both green and red. Most locals walk by and say, "Give me a tomato," but the older folks come to buy, saying that it reminds them of Alabama or Georgia, where they came from. They can buy the same tomatoes being sold for $3 a pound to Frontera or the Ritz-Carlton for $1 a pound here. "We couldn't sell less expensively at the gate," Christine says, "if we weren't selling to the restaurants."

At 6:00 A.M. the next day, I've arranged to get onto the rooftop of the spotlight factory next to the garden to take photographs. The city is just beginning to wake up; the first light gilds the sleek spire of the Hancock Building. The early shift at the Starbucks across the street is just arriving to turn on the lights and warm up the cappuccino machines. Commuters swish by on elevated tracks, beating the rush to work.

In this light, the greens and rich browns of the garden beneath us are accented by dots of red and yellow, fruit hanging heavy from mother plants. Just outside the fence that separates the garden from the street, a family makes its way back home to the housing project, eating potato chips and drinking Cokes and tossing an empty can up and over the fence.

❧

WE NAVIGATE THE MAZE OF FREEWAYS THAT THREAD THROUGH AND OUT of the city. We're headed south about an hour and a half to the rural black community of Pembroke Township, near the town of Hopkins Park. The rows of buildings and houses give way to rows of corn, mile after mile of it, acre after acre, as if the whole damn country is one big cornfield.

Along Highway 17, a high-speed two-laner, we see dozens of pickups parked on the edge of a 10-acre corn trial. A sign marks each row of hybrid and genetically modified plants with a number and the name of the company that created it.

We slow down, park the van, and join the latecomers as they make their way into a giant, steel tractor shed. Inside, a representative from the Chicago Board of Trade is in midspeech, tossing out condition-rating indexes, outlooks, prospects, and volume projections to the blue-jeaned crowd. It's the annual meeting of the local Corn Growers Association, but, instead of corn, the discussion is about futures trading, the Brazilians, and how shrewd the Chinese are. We linger inside near a collection of building-size tractors, hoping to hear something—anything—familiar. I would have expected local growers to be griping about local issues, such as the year's weather or pest problems. But these growers are serving a global market where their corn is destined to become the corn syrup in kids' breakfast cereals. It's close to harvesttime, and the main issue facing these farmers is international trade and how it will affect their bushel price.

We leave before the meeting is over and follow John Thurman's directions to his family's L&R Farms, about half an hour south. We take the turnoff toward Hopkins Park, cross the railroad tracks, and bear left at the Bible Witness Center. The road turns to dirt, and the pampered, unvarying corn and soybeans are replaced with ramshackle clapboard houses, trailers, and rusting vehicles scattered across a dusty landscape of undisturbed and self-sufficient weeds. Every face at the corn growers' meeting was white, but out here they're all black. Everyone we pass looks at us as if we've made a wrong turn and gotten lost.

There are no numbers on the houses; our directions say only to go left at the third curve at the top of the hill. As we make the turn, the road becomes so sandy that we must keep moving or sink in. At the crest of the hill, we turn into a sparse compound of about half a dozen dilapidated buildings. Plastic hangs over some of the windows, turkeys graze in and around old cars, and piles of pipe, boxes, and equipment are strewn around the common area. Six or seven teenage kids look up as we knock on the door of a small, unpainted wooden house. A woman points out three rusting 20-foot trailers, lined up like railcars, home to John and Ida Thurman and their seven youngest children.

As the woman is speaking, a young man offers to find John. When John and Ida appear from a small building behind the trailers, it is getting dark. We shake

hands, and I deliver a gift of tomatoes from Ken Dunn and smoked salmon from home. Once formal greetings are exchanged, there is an awkward moment as we search for common ground. On a whim, I take out one of my harmonicas and begin to blow a slow blues in the key of G. The kids look over and move in a little closer, and everyone seems to loosen up. When I play the final note, Ida rolls her eyes with pleasure and tells me it reminds her of home in Mississippi, and the old-timers who used to sit around playing blues while she was growing up.

L&R Farms is lovingly named after John and Ida's fathers, L. D. Patterson, of rural Mississippi, and Roy L. Thurman, who farmed the land we're standing on now. During the 1940s, Roy Thurman raised many of the same crops John and Ida still produce: watermelons, beans and peas, squash and okra and sweet potatoes, along with chickens, turkeys, and hogs.

The Thurmans own the 27 acres surrounding their home. The remainder of L&R Farms includes 20 leased acres near Hopkins Park and another 15 acres they lease or barter in exchange for produce and work. Although many of Pembroke Township's citizens own land, this remains one of the most economically depressed rural regions in the entire country. Farmers here haven't had the support of farm extension and development agencies until recently, and now it may be too little, too late. Many locals are selling to outside developers and land trusts—Ida says 10 acres recently sold for $22,000. "This community really wants to help them-selves, keep their heritage, and pass on their land," she says of those who remain, "but there is no funding for start-up costs and little infrastructure to do anything." Even the roads are not paved.

The old savanna landscape is dotted with legacy oaks and clumps of spear grass and sassafras. The soils are so sandy that in some places it's like walking on the beach. Where fields have been cultivated and later abandoned, saplings sprout up along the edges, filling the void, moving in to clothe and protect exposed ground. The chickens—built to prosper on the margins—scratch and scrape for tiny, forgotten morsels. The summer heat and humidity are thick; if I got dropped here without knowing better, I'd think I was in Georgia or the Carolinas.

Although insects, plants, and chickens thrive in this heat and humidity, humans slow down to survive. I find it hard to imagine how I would rise above the oppressive weather to farm day after day. The moments when one can truly enjoy this environment seem brief and fleeting: early in the day, in the balmy darkness before the sun rises, immediately after a rain, or just after sunset, before the mosquitoes come out to hunt.

Nodding toward their makeshift home, John says, "It's not hard to see that we're sure not keeping up with the Joneses." He and Ida chuckle. Then he adds, "but we're only poor in dollars."

Along with the normal vagaries of changing weather and markets most farmers have to deal with, the Thurmans have one primary, overarching concern: the intense pull of the urban world on local youth.

They watched their two eldest kids leave the land and go off to the city. Veronica, now twenty-seven, joined the navy. Jessica lives in Gary, Indiana, with her three children. Ida says that when the grandkids visit, they are afraid of the livestock. "It's weird seeing my own grandchildren so scared of everything natural."

Seven kids are still at home. Twenty-one-year-old John works alongside his father. Monica, nineteen, does the farmers' market. Joseph, eighteen, Joshua, sixteen, Jacob, thirteen, Ida, eleven, and Maya, ten, all help out before and after school, just as farm kids have always done. The Thurmans are obsessed with inspiring them to continue, providing some sense of honor and respect to a way of life young folk are not exactly flocking to.

Knowing that their neighbors shared the same urgency, they started a youth-training program that teaches kids farming and marketing, leadership and organizational skills, and "the value of giving back to the community." The hand-folded, photocopied brochure for their Youth Training Program includes a list of requirements for taking part:

1. Participate four days or more per week.

2. Follow work/safety rules.

3. Join a credit union.

4. Practice regular savings.

5. Attend meetings.

6. Respect other enrollees.

7. Provide community service.

8. Take vegetables home.

9. Share what you learn with others.

The back cover closes with the words: "We have looked into the past and accepted the future. Agriculture is art, our heritage, and our future. It is our duty to preserve this small piece of Mother Earth. Our future depends on it."

At the Thurmans', the phrase "family farm" keeps turning over in my mind. Most folks use the family to keep the farm together; the Thurmans seem to be using the farm to keep the family together. And for John and Ida, family extends beyond bloodlines to what they call "the rural village." As an example of the village mind-set, John explains that he and Ida joined forces with local farmers and activists to start the Pembroke Farmers Cooperative in 1999 to help black farmers in the region sell their products more effectively. John and Ida and several others in the local community were beginning to expand their food production and develop outlets in Chicago. Every weekend, a parade of rundown pickups and vans would leave Pembroke for the same markets in Chicago. They realized it would be better to join forces to buy seeds and equipment and to transport and market their products

together. With several grants, they hired staff, set up an office, and bought a refriger-ated truck to haul produce and chickens to processors and stores and restaurants.

The common thread among the participating growers is their commitment to organic methods. This did not originate out of some deep philosophical commit-ment but because it was what they and their parents and their grandparents had always done and because their financial circumstances wouldn't allow anything else. John describes the cooperative's work as "nothing special—just a group of hard-working people trying to make something beautiful."

The collards, sweet potatoes, beans, and pasture-raised chickens the Thurmans grow provide food for the locals and for a neighborhood in Chicago that would otherwise never see any fresh food. Once a week, John, Ida, and the kids make the trek into Chicago to sell at the Austin farmers' market, in an all-black neighbor-hood that does not have a single grocery store.

"I just want to run a farm," John says tersely when I ask about all the energy he puts into organizing his family and neighbors. "I'll do anything I can to make that happen. We've had to get into all sorts of stuff to do that. It's been a big, nasty mess of a thing to create profit from this area and keep the money out of the hands of the overseers."

Choice here is a different concept than it is for most people. For John and Ida, farming is their greatest challenge, and their greatest opportunity. As small farmers, the Thurmans are on the very edge of an increasingly marginalized group; as black farmers, they are statistically on the margins of the margins.

"It was our vision to have this for the children if they choose it," Ida says. "The elder children have chosen a different path. It's tough, but I understand. We are committed to leaving something here for whoever wants it. Our eldest son, John, is really dedicated to the work on the land. He tells me that this is his future. He's doing this for himself. We are low income, we are limited, we have to pinch pennies all the time, not much movie time, but we're building relationships inside our home.

"I feel we're truly blessed. Every time we have problems, we keep our faith, and something always comes through. We're close, we work together, we play together, we communicate. The kids are learning to take care of the plants and the livestock, they're learning business skills when they go to the market, learning to talk with people, and customers give back a lot of gratitude. We care about other people, and, because we are farming, we have a unique ability to show that care through our products. As a family, we're out there working together, carrying on conversa-tions in the fields; we're closer than we would be otherwise. When families are separated and away from each other, different influences come in. Here, we can stay in touch and support each other."

At midmorning, Ida announces that we are off to see the elders. We all pile into our van and drive across the maze of dirt roads that intersect derelict fields and second- and third-growth forests. In the middle of an overgrown crabgrass lawn, we pull up in front of the home of 80-year-old Herbert Wallace. The Thurmans lease the 5-acre field of bottomland that sits behind and down the hill from the house in exchange for produce and some work around the house.

Inside the dimly lit house, I can just make out a figure in the corner. From the darkness, Herbert welcomes us in and is happy to talk food and farming. He tells us that when he used to farm the field himself, he would carry a salt-and-pepper shaker in his shirt pocket and just graze, and we chat about the unique pleasures of fresh-picked snacks. When John and Ida hug him goodbye, they remind him that they'll be back later to mow the lawn and harvest some Mississippi beans that are growing near the house.

"They are the ones who was here before us—they kept this place together," Ida says passionately as we leave Herbert's place and head up the dirt track to visit Ms. Ellen, who is still farming at ninety. "They are our teachers," Ida insists. "Though we may not be related by blood, they are still a part of us because they have made this community. Being away from my home in Mississippi, away from my people, they help me feel connected."

From her seat on the porch, Ms. Ellen waves her arm in the direction of the sea of soybeans planted right up to her back door. "Everything used to be woods round here . . . all them corns and soybeans, all woods," she says as she launches into the kind of personal history John and Ida treasure. "Since 1946, when I got here, I've been farming. The backbone of society. All hard work. Rough and tough. I'm ninety years old and still planting my seeds. Fell in the dirt the other day and got right back up." She throws her head back and roars with laughter.

I reflect on how much adversity this woman has seen in her ninety years, how she can still fall down and get back up again, and that she's still planting seeds. I remember watching one of my Hopi friends in his late eighties sitting in the hot desert sun, holding an ear of blue corn that had been saved for seed, the feel of its kernels providing comfort and connection. My friend Hiraam used to crawl on all fours to work in his garden because his legs would no longer support him. Plant-and-soil people must all be alike, drawing sustenance from seeds and soil, never ready to give them up.

There is an incessant high-pitched beeping emanating from inside Ms. Ellen's house as she talks. I stop the conversation to ask whether she hears it. "Hear what?" she says and continues the conversation. The beeping continues, and I smell something burning. I ask her again. "Oh, I'm burning my food!" she screams and dashes off.

As we get up to leave, she gives us each a warm hug, grabs our heads, and looks directly into our eyes. "You be good to your kids," she admonishes us. "They're paying attention. Watch what you do! Be good to people!" We drive off, and I notice that the van is very nearly out of gas. The nearest gas station is 15 miles away in the town of St. Anne, now that the three gas stations in nearby Hopkins Park have closed along with the grocery stores and pretty much everything else.

When we get to St. Anne, John asks us to drop him off at the dentist to have a tooth pulled while we fill up with gas. While we wait for John, we cruise the predominantly white town past an active and thriving supermarket, car dealerships, a bank, a bakery, and a number of stores and restaurants.

When John rejoins us, we drive back to Hopkins Park for a meeting with the mayor. We arrive at the city office building without an appointment, but Mayor John Dyson is happy to take some time to talk. With his large frame, shaved head, and warm smile, Mayor John has an imposing presence. He divides his time between the responsibilities of mayor and his role as local preacher.

"We've got to inspire our youth to be proud, not ashamed," he tells us as we settle in comfortably for the sermon. "We can't separate the land and the people. We've got to get these kids to appreciate the art of agriculture, not just the science. You only get that out in the dirt. Dirt can reform you. We need to give our kids somewhere to go. We have to invest in rural activities for rural youth so they don't need to become city wannabes. It's about giving them self-worth and removing the shame of their environment. Why do young country boys wear street clothing? Why the exodus to the bright lights of the city, only to miss the country life that Mama and Daddy told them to hold on to in the first place? How do we change the tide? How to make available funds, programs, honest actions, and hope for the art of agriculture?"

I can almost hear the silent amens coming from everyone in the room. Amen, Mayor John, amen.

There is so much good intention and insight here, but I am struggling to understand how conviction will prevail in this battle to preserve alternatives for the next generation. I want some simple answers, some explanation as to the huge gap between insight and reality, between the inspiration I am hearing and the poverty and discouragement I see.

Instead, talk turns to lunch. We stop to visit with 77-year-old Vestine and her husband, Leslie. From a kitchen that is not much bigger than the one in our van, Vestine cooks us up a late-afternoon feast of corn bread, collard greens, and rib tips, which she serves with hot peppers on Styrofoam plates accompanied by a can of Diet Pepsi. We sit on a picnic table with a small fire burning in the yard outside her old wooden house.

The food is rich with flavor, the corn bread smoky, with kernels of meaty corn that taste real, not like the sugary hybrids you get in the supermarket. The greens are slow cooked, imbued with the flavor of the bones she cooked them with. The pork, pulled off the open fire, tastes like it has been basted in some secret sauce passed down over generations. We've been on the road eating with some of the best chefs and farmers, but this meal is satisfying like no other. I compliment Vestine and her barbecue-tending husband. She seems thrilled to have company, and her toothless smile lights up her face when we rave about her cooking.

We arrive back at the Thurmans' place just as the big yellow school bus pulls up in a cloud of dust. Jacob, Ida, and Maya get off, drop their books in the house, and immediately head out to the fields. I pull Aaron away from a drawing he is doing, seated in the open door of our van. The Austin market is tomorrow, and there's still plenty of picking to do. When the fields nearest to the house are picked clean of squashes and pink-eye/purple-hull and Silver Crowder beans, we load the rusty blue cargo van with boxes and travel in convoy several miles along dirt roads to one of the Thurmans' leased fields to finish harvesting.

The field, situated on fertile bottomland at the base of a small hill, is rich, black, and friable. I feel a twinge of envy at the sight of that gorgeous soil. The field has been freshly worked and seeded, except for a peculiar 20-foot-wide swath of weeds that extends the full length of the 15 acres. Beneath the weeds are a small number of straggly watermelons and squash, the sole survivors of the rains that flooded this field during July and drowned the spring planting.

"We took the kids out to see this field after it flooded," Ida says. "They were really discouraged, but it's a good thing for them to learn that what you put in doesn't always turn out."

The harvest goes until there isn't enough light to see your hands in front of your face. While we wait for the van to arrive to pick up newly filled boxes, Aaron plays food football in the dark with John Jr. and Joseph using peppers and eggplants. The mosquitoes are so bad that the kids have to keep running to keep them from landing and biting. Each time the pepper or eggplant ball breaks, everyone gathers around to eat the pieces.

At 4:30 the next morning, we all gather round the Thurmans' van, now loaded for market with beans and greens and melons. The vehicle won't start, so we fumble in the dark to locate and hook up jumper cables. Eventually, the engine catches and starts, and the boys jump in for the two-hour drive to the Austin market in Chicago. John, Aaron, and I follow behind the Thurmans' rickety van, occasionally getting flagged down to troubleshoot a new noise or smell coming from the engine. It's incredible that this is the only transportation these folks have to rely on.

John prepares me for the realities of the Westside Chicago community we are about to arrive in. His father delivered food into this community in the 1940s. "It's a family tradition," he says with a twinge of sadness. He tells me there are twelve-year-old kids in that neighborhood who, because of the violence, don't expect to live to be twenty.

At the market, John lets his kids do all of the setup and sales. He stands in the background, chatting with old friends and watching with obvious pride. "We love the way the kids get such positive reinforcement for what they do," he says. "We do recipe swaps. That's a beautiful thing. We watch people put down their money and say, 'I'm going to spend this right here. You pick it out, but tell me how to cook it.'"

The crowds descend on the Thurmans' stand, and piles of food rapidly diminish. It's here that I see John's real satisfaction, a sense that all the struggle is well worth it. He tells me it's like "putting real life into somebody."

I am always fascinated how food, like nothing else, keeps people connected to their roots. People migrate from anywhere in the world and always find a way to grow or get the foods from their homeland. It's the ultimate connection, the one thing that every culture holds on to. Here we are in Westside Chicago, in an environment as far removed from the rural South as you can get, yet piles of black-eyed peas and okra and collards are transporting people across miles and years. It's a passionate scene played out by people who left the South many years ago, and by some who have never been there but feel connected to the crops and drawn to the farmers who grow them. It's a phenomenon of the farmers' market that I've felt myself: as you touch hands and exchange food with eager people, an electric current seems to run between you and them, connecting both back to a world that for a moment seems to make perfect sense.

I overhear John responding to a woman who has just heard the story of his flooded fields. She wants to know all about him, where he's been, why he works so hard, what keeps him going against such odds. I expect to hear him express some discouragement, maybe even seek out sympathy. Instead, he expresses pride and, loud enough for me and his young sons to hear, says, "If you've farmed for five or ten years, you can run the world. It ought to be a law that you have to farm before you can do anything else."

☘

Salsa Fresca

Aaron and I joined Ken and Christine Dunn for a memorable evening at Frontera Grill. For three hours, we sampled just about everything on and off the menu. As always, the food tasted so much better knowing the history of its ingredients and eaten with those who had produced some of them.

This is a standard salsa fresca, made with ripe heirloom tomatoes, finely diced onion, jalapeño peppers, and lots of lime. Tasha DeSerio, who tested the recipes for the book, told me she added a few glugs of olive oil and spooned it over grilled flank steak and sliced avocado. She said it was delicious alongside fresh corn tamales. The olive oil is not traditional, but neither is growing tomatoes on the streets of Chicago.

1 pound ripe, fragrant heirloom tomatoes
1 small red or white onion, finely diced
2 to 3 jalapeño peppers, seeded and finely diced
½ cup roughly chopped fresh cilantro
Kosher salt to taste
Fresh lime juice to taste

Core the tomatoes, cut them in half crosswise, and squeeze out the seeds. Using a sharp knife, cut the tomatoes into 1/4-inch dice. In a medium bowl, combine the tomatoes, onion, jalapeño pepper to taste, and cilantro. Season the salsa with salt (about 1 teaspoon) and a generous amount of fresh lime juice (1 1/2 to 2 tablespoons). Stir the salsa to combine and let stand for 5 to 10 minutes before serving, to allow the flavors to mingle.

NOTE: For the best texture and flavor, serve the salsa within an hour or so after it is made.

Garden Tomato Sauce

Every fall, we convert hundreds of pounds of perfectly ripe tomato cosmetic rejects into our annual supply of sauce. It's a ritual that marks the end of the summer season, and, put into jars, it provides us with our own version of the endless summer. Each year's batch is slightly different, informed by the weather, the changing soils, and the success of our dry-farming techniques.

This is a simple, fresh tomato sauce, but it's totally and completely dependent on perfectly ripe, sweet, heirloom tomatoes, good olive oil, and fresh herbs!

MAKES ABOUT 4 CUPS

6 tablespoons extra-virgin olive oil, or to taste

1 medium yellow onion, cut into ¼-inch-thick slices

1 medium carrot, peeled, halved lengthwise, and cut crosswise into
    ¼-inch-thick slices

Kosher salt to taste

Hot red pepper flakes to taste (optional)

5 cloves garlic, chopped

4 pounds ripe, fragrant heirloom tomatoes, cored and cut into
    ½-inch-thick wedges

¼ cup chopped fresh basil

Heat a large Dutch oven or heavy-bottomed saucepan over medium heat. Add 3 tablespoons of the olive oil, the onion, and carrot and season with a pinch of salt and red pepper flakes, if desired. Cover and gently cook, stirring occasionally, until the vegetables are tender, about 10 minutes. Add the garlic and cook for 1 minute, then add the tomatoes and stir to combine. Season with salt (about 1½ teaspoons). Cover again and cook, stirring occasionally, until the tomatoes are very juicy, 10 to 15 minutes. Uncover and continue to cook, over medium heat, stirring occasionally, for 30 minutes. Add the basil, and cook for 5 more minutes.

Pass the sauce through a food mill fitted with the coarse blade into a medium bowl. Discard the skins and seeds. Stir in the remaining 3 tablespoons olive oil, or to taste. Taste and adjust the seasoning with salt, if necessary. If it's too acidic, also add a pinch of sugar, or, if it's too sweet, a drop of red wine vinegar. If the sauce is too thin, return it to the pot and cook it down until it reaches the desired consistency.

Corn Bread

SERVES 10

The meal Aaron and I shared with John and Ida Thurman's 77-year-old friend, Vestine, and her husband, Leslie, was memorable. The corn bread was served with rib tips and slow-cooked greens on a Styrofoam plate with a Diet Pepsi. There were no cookbooks in sight, the kitchen was the size of a large closet, and the equipment consisted of a small stove, an open fire, and a pot and a pan. I don't know whether it was the heat of the day or the warmth and generosity of these people, but I can still summon the taste of that meal and the feeling of that afternoon.

Vestine bakes her corn bread in a small pan, but this one is cooked in a cast-iron skillet—it's a little more romantic, and you can't beat the crispy crust. And, although many Southern recipes call for white cornmeal, this one can be prepared with either yellow or white.

5½ tablespoons unsalted butter
1½ cups cornmeal
½ cup all-purpose flour
2 tablespoons sugar
1 tablespoon baking powder
1 teaspoon kosher salt
1 egg
1¼ cups milk

Preheat the oven to 400 degrees F.

Melt 4 tablespoons of the butter and let cool slightly. Combine the cornmeal, flour, sugar, baking powder, and salt in a medium bowl. Whisk the egg and milk together in a small bowl. Add the melted butter and milk mixture to the dry ingredients and stir to make a smooth batter. Heat a 10-inch cast-iron skillet over medium-high heat. Add the remaining 1½ tablespoons of butter to the pan. When the butter is melted and foaming, pour the batter into the skillet. Bake until the corn bread is golden brown and a toothpick inserted in the middle comes out clean, about 25 minutes. Serve hot out of the oven.

Vestine's Collard Greens

Vestine makes traditional Southern-style collard greens with smoked pork broth. She adds a small chuck of salt pork to her broth as well, then chops the salt pork and adds it to the greens. The salt in the salt pork is enough to season the greens—which are traditionally served highly seasoned. They go perfectly with corn bread, of course.

SERVES 6 TO 8

SMOKED PORK STOCK
1 smoked ham hock, rinsed
2 ounces salt pork
1 gallon water

4 pounds collard greens, stemmed and cut into ribbons
    about 1½ inches thick
Freshly cracked black pepper to taste

TO MAKE THE STOCK: Put the ham hock, salt pork, and water into a large Dutch oven or stockpot. Bring to a boil, reduce the heat, and simmer until the stock has a rich, smoked-pork flavor, about 3 hours. Discard the ham hock. Remove the salt pork with a slotted spoon, cut into small pieces, and set aside. Refrigerate the stock until chilled, or preferably overnight.

Skim the layer of fat from the surface of the stock. Pour 8 cups of the stock into a large Dutch oven or heavy-bottomed saucepan (reserve the remaining stock for another use). Bring to a boil over high heat and add the collard greens a handful at a time, waiting until each batch wilts into the stock before adding the next. When you have added all of the greens, add the reserved salt pork. Reduce the heat to medium-high and cook, uncovered, until the greens are silky and tender, about 25 minutes. Season the greens with pepper (the salt pork should provide plenty of salt). Drain any excess liquid from the greens and serve.

CHAPTER 7

SCIENCE AND CIVICS

As we passed through upstate New York, Aaron caught a Greyhound bus and headed to Montreal for a few days with friends. I'm on my way to Strafford, Vermont, with my new traveling companions: a slab of bacon, some veal chops, and a piece of honey-cured ham, all parting gifts from Amy Kenyon and Craig Haney at Skate Creek Farm, near East Meredith, New York. It's strange cargo for someone who was a vegetarian for fourteen years.

I had deliberately sought out Amy and Craig's farm because of my own ambivalence about meat, veal in particular. I had seen the pictures of boy calves standing in tiny wooden crates, collared and chained, spending their whole lives in the dark. And though Amy told me that she had never seen farmers raise veal that way, she knows that, as with most things in farming, the veal issue is not so black-and-white, and not all calves get to live on peaceful pastures.

Amy grew up on a 300-cow dairy farm witnessing a basic reality: in order for cows to keep lactating, they must be bred. The female offspring become the future milkers, but most of the male calves are sent off to veal producers. When Amy moved a few miles away to her own place, she was determined to deal directly with the issue facing farmers such as her parents. "It is important to me to close the loop for dairy farms by finding a place for every animal that's born there. There is no infrastructure for the bull calves.

"Maybe we're trying to prop up something that's being done badly to begin with," she reflected. "The veal is harder to sell, we haven't yet been able to come up with a consistent product, and it's more work, but it's my mission, and I want to see anything that's born at a dairy treated well."

Amy and Craig now produce pasture-raised chicken, beef, pork, lamb, turkeys, and veal on a former dairy farm along bucolic Kortright Creek. Their meat is highly regarded, and their choice of what and how to farm is clearly conscious and deeply individual, based on their experience, on what they know most directly. It occurs to me that one of the privileges of a farming life is the ability to choose a path based on that kind of firsthand experience, an opportunity that often isn't available in our secondhand society.

Of course, choices don't come without contradictions, even uncomfortable ones, and that's true in a food system that must support our survival, often imperfectly. The fact is, in large-scale food production, few options are entirely pure. Ironically, even an innocent-looking organic carrot is often fertilized with

the manure from big beef-producing feedlots, where millions of cows are ware-housed in squalor. In my own mind, I'm not sure whether reciprocity between the organic farm and the feedlot is an unholy alliance or the beginning of something better for both.

I've made my own choices and compromises, and, inevitably, my farm, my relationships with my customers, even the taste of my crops reflect my personal moments of inspiration and delusion. As I head into New England, fragments of words, images, and food collide in my mind, and I consider the individuals I've met on this trip, farmers who might be lumped together under the banners and slogans that attach to "organic" as it becomes more mainstream. The farmers I've seen have no such consensus or homogeneity of thought, method, or food. I smile at the image of them as a group portrait. If I put them all together at one table, I can imagine the almighty arguments they could have even as we built a banquet from their unique foods.

I munch on the last of the Goliath tomatoes from Harmony Valley, sheep cheese from the Falks, and pear butter from the Lanes. As I have done with each of the farms' bounty, I carry Amy and Craig's meat on to my next stop. Tomorrow's breakfast at Earl and Amy Ransom's sprawling Strafford Organic Creamery will be Skate Creek bacon, eggs from Earl's brother Barry, a puffball mushroom from one of the upper pastures, homemade cinnamon buns, and coffee ice cream.

☙

WHEN I ARRIVE AT THE RANSOM FARM, IT'S LATE AFTERNOON, AND THE fall sky is already darkening. Earl takes me into one of the walk-in coolers for what seems like a kind of initiation. He hands me three old-fashioned glass bottles of milk and asks me to compare the color and consistency of cream-line, homogenized, and skim milks. It's a test to see whether I will notice the differences. Even in the bad light, I pass. The skim looks more like milk than the typical watery whitewash, the homogenized has color and body, and the cream-line is downright thick and yellow.

Stacks of milk crates filled with empty bottles returned from the day's deliveries are piled nearby. Earl bends over to pull out a note from one of the bottles: "We love your milk, thanks for producing something that tastes like Vermont."

Although the milk certainly has its fans, it's really ice cream that has brought attention to Strafford Organic Creamery, and not just because of the almost mystical lure of "homemade" or the cultural passion for all things ice cream. Here, it's down to a sweet science—not in the laboratory sense of the word, but in the most elemental and alchemical sense. The chemistry here begins literally in the pasture and figuratively in the relationship between the Ransoms and a food they truly love, so much so that, during my two-day visit, they serve it with breakfast, lunch, and dinner.

We grab some ice cream from the freezer room—strawberry, experimental ginger, and coffee—and head back to the house. The harvest moon is up now, the

cornfield just below the house is shimmering, backdropped by the silhouette of the mountains in New Hampshire beyond. When we get to the house, four or five homemade pizzas are waiting on the counter while several apple pies bake in the oven. Amy has prepared this culinary fete while carrying her baby boy, reading stories to her three-year-old, and handling orders for milk and ice cream. For a moment I flash home to Jeanne Marie, telephone under her chin, Benjamin on her hip, shucking sweet corn and shelling fava beans for dinner. I remember the relief I heard in her voice when I called earlier in the day and she reported that we finally had rain.

The Ransoms' house, originally built in the '50s, partially burned down in 1973 and was rebuilt before winter the same year. Earl's father, Woody, graduated from Harvard with an architecture degree and went on to work with Buckminster Fuller, designing and building geodesic domes. His mother grew up in Redding, Pennsylvania, came to Vermont on a whim, met Woody, and never left. Earl and his two brothers grew up in this house, which started as a prefab from Sears, Roebuck and Co., and, with Woody's architectural influence, morphed into an eclectic, masculine, rough-sawn mix. Earl's brother Barry is legally blind and runs an egg operation with six hundred laying hens. Younger brother William, who used to do some maple sugaring, is off at school, studying sculpture at Bennington.

Earl delights in telling me the colorful history of the land, illustrated by two well-worn photo albums. Woody bought the original 100-acre farm in 1963 for $4,500 when it was occupied by a back-to-the-land commune. He let the commune continue to operate while he did the work to create a farm. He cut 1,200 trees and milled them to build the barn and cleared the land using two teams of Belgian horses. Eventually, he graduated to using a small bulldozer and a backhoe. He left individual trees strategically spaced in the center of each of the pastures so that as the shade moved, so would the cows, and, as the cows moved, so would the manure, preventing it from accumulating in any one place.

The property now totals 600 acres, half of which is farmed, and yields 10,000 pounds of milk and 800 pints of ice cream every week from a herd of thirty Guernsey cows. Aside from the vacuum pumps used to run the milking machines, everything at the dairy is run on gravity: The milking barn sits at the top of a small hill, and the cooling tanks and the bottling and ice-cream rooms are built in succession going down the hill. The milk moves from the milking parlor to the cooling tanks and then to the bottling and ice-cream plant without the use of a single pump.

At first, I marvel at these simple innovations. Then I realize that it didn't exactly require a Harvard degree in architecture to figure out that using gravity is a good idea, or that trees provide shade and that cows will follow it. It's just that so much of agriculture has lost any relationship to common sense. We've got this idea that things need to be complicated to be any good, that simple solutions can't possibly be as good as technological ones.

It's late by the time we've finished sampling ice cream and hearing Earl's colorful tales of the farm's history. I leave the house and climb into the van to sleep. At about 4:00 A.M., a familiar sound penetrates the deep reaches of my dreams, and an eerie chorus of yapping coyotes comes into focus. As I come around, I realize I'm not actually in the West and I don't have to get up to protect the chickens or check the geese. It's Earl who will trudge through the damp pasture to carry a 70-pound newborn calf back to the safety of the barn.

A few hours later, I head straight to the milking barn to watch the daily ritual. From the doorway of the milking parlor, I talk with Earl as I watch him move through the thirty-cow Guernsey herd. Like pruning or cultivating, milking is one of those repetitive jobs that allows the mind to wander. If you're alone and it's early in the day, great ideas and schemes take shape, poetry is written on the pages of the mind, full political debate bounces around inside your head. Earl seems happy to have company, pleased to have someone who will listen to some of the ideas he's been experimenting with in the privacy of his brain.

He describes how milk fat suffers from being pumped and churned and sloshed around, that it acquires a metallic taste—not so much from the pipes, but from being exposed to air. "The more gently it's handled, the better," he says. "Butterfat and air don't go together very well." I think about all the years I milked goats by hand, how I could create more foam from the intensity of the milk hitting the side of the bucket than the best Italian cappuccino machine. I didn't know any better.

Earl says an old-timer in the area told him his ice cream is the best he's ever had, then asked, "What cows are you milking, Guernseys?" Earl loves hearing from older local folks like that, from people who can pick out variations in flavor other than sweetness. "It's more gratifying to satisfy people who remember real food than the new gourmet crowd," Earl says. I echo the sentiment, remembering how often people at the farmers' market ask only if our corn is sweet, and are surprised or occasionally disappointed to discover the subtle range of corn flavor in an heirloom variety. "These hybrid supersweet corn varieties are terrible," I grouse. "You bite into them, and it's like you've just received some sort of mainline injection of sugar. But do they taste like corn?"

"Sabrina, get out!" Earl yells as a cow with the largest udder I've ever seen tries to get back into the milking parlor. "You can't come back—you're all done!" he says, shooing her away. As she walks past me, she swishes her tail, sending a large plop of fresh Guernsey shit all over me.

I ask Earl if he thinks you can actually taste the farm and the region in the product, and he launches headlong into a favorite topic.

"If I go and buy Guernsey milk from a farm in Ohio—and there's some great Guernsey farms in Ohio—their milk is going to taste different from mine. If they're growing the same plants on their soil, it will be closer, and if their climate is close to mine, it will be even closer, but it's still never going to be exactly the same. The French have taken this to the extreme. But I think they're on to something. Taste is terribly complex, as I'm sure you know, but the thing that goes into taste is mostly smell. Your tongue can only taste four things, or maybe five is arguable. But you can smell hundreds of thousands of things. And the thing about food, and especially food with fat, is that it absorbs what's around it. You can test this. If you put a sponge out somewhere, it will absorb volatile compounds that are in the air. If you put it next to a pile of manure, eventually it will absorb the smell of the manure. Milk is an excellent example of this transference.

"So, if you have a cow that is on an IV, and all she is getting is plain sugar and amino acids, but not actually eating anything, she would still produce milk. And the milk would taste like nothing. But if the cow is out in the field and she is breathing dust and a little bit of manure and she's breathing dandelion flowers and red clover and maple leaves, or whatever—all those smells, when they go into her lung, the compounds that make up the smells, they're attached to gas and the gas dissolves in her blood. That blood goes cruising around inside of the cow, and the whole cow becomes suffused with this smell.

"It's fairly subtle. If you were to cut a cow open, you wouldn't smell it, because there's just not that much of it there. But milk is a great absorber of smell. If you took a glass of milk and put it next to a fish in your refrigerator, the milk would taste like fish."

"It reminds me how most people think that goat milk tastes 'goaty,'" I add. "But it doesn't. It tastes goaty only if it's been left outside near a male goat or it hasn't been cooled or handled right."

"Yeah, this is exactly the same thing," Earl says, "but on a much more refined scale. If you've got lactating animals that are out breathing fresh air, their milk is going to have that particular characteristic. If my cows are out in a field tomorrow that's got blackberry bushes and Queen Anne's lace and orchard grass, red clover, and around the edge of the fence there's some comfrey growing that particular day, if you were really good, you could smell that stuff and you could say, 'These cows were grazed on an east-facing slope, in September, in Vermont.'

"For the most part, those volatile aromatic compounds are fat soluble," Earl continues. "They're going to stick with the fat. And you can accentuate those characteristics, or you can hide them. With our ice cream, we start with the fact that we love the way cream tastes. I mean, I like just straight, heavy cream. I think it's delicious. I like butter, too, without salting it or any of the other stuff. Even without culturing it. Fresh butter is a beautiful thing."

Before they started making ice cream, Amy and Earl attended a two-week ice-cream course at Penn State. They lasted fifteen minutes in the Better Ice Cream through Chemistry class. "They show you a movie about stabilizers and tell you that you can't make ice cream without them," Amy says. "They show you ice cream holding its form even after it's half melted. People were frantically taking notes. When we revealed that we were planning to do things differently, they said, 'No way.'"

One year later, the Ransoms' ice cream was already overshadowing other established products in blind tastings.

"Our idea is that ice cream should start with a base that tastes like cream with some sugar in it," Amy continues, "because the sugar accentuates the flavor of the cream. Some, not too much. We knew we wanted it less sweet. And I'm still convinced you can taste that weird stuff—carrageenan, guar gum, locust bean."

"The stuff that leaves a film on your mouth," I say. "So, out of that experience, you decided less sweet. Anything else?"

"More fat," Amy says.

"It seems to me," I suggest, "that the challenge is in maintaining a scale that's livable. It seems like there is a tendency for an operation like this, especially when you start getting successful with value-added product, to want to expand, to get too big."

"I'm very dedicated to producing the ingredients ourselves," Earl responds. "We have a certain carrying capacity on this land. We can only grow enough feed for so many cows here. Once we pass that, then we can't physically do it. I could start buying food for the cows, but then the quality of our product goes down."

On our second evening together, Amy and Earl organize a babysitter, execute a remarkable transformation into nice-looking street clothes, and usher me to the car for an evening out. Amy drives Earl and me at high speed along back roads to a small restaurant that serves their ice cream. Along the way she tells me she was raised on Jell-O and Dream Whip. I make an ignorant comment that implies the ice cream is Earl's creation. "It's my ice cream," she says in an irritated tone. "I did the recipe."

I tell her that she can let me out on the side of the road.

"Yeah, you can walk home," she confirms. "Actually, what you said isn't entirely untrue. It's a weird dynamic in a marriage. At the core of my being, I am grateful not just to be here with Earl, but to be here and doing this. I thank my lucky stars I can do this work. I didn't think this is where I'd end up, and it's better than anything I can think of."

I mention Jennifer Greene and how she didn't want marriage because she felt she'd end up in the home or the office, like so many women on farms do.

"When I first met Earl," Amy says, "I was in the barn almost every day if I didn't have class. I milked the day before Cliff was born, and I have only milked sporadically since then. Girls are definitely better at milking, but Earl's not a poor substitute. He's very good at taking care of the kids, but he can't do anything else at the same time, and our world would fall apart if I weren't here in the house. There's not really any way around that."

The conversation drifts to the local-food movement. Amy questions the way it's being presented. "This whole idea that's being put forth, that if you don't buy locally, farmers will go out of business, makes people think they're saving our farm by buying our milk. We want people to buy our milk because it's good milk. I hate the 'buy locally' thing. Try local foods, and if they're not better, then buy from California. I'd like to challenge the farmers of Vermont to make things that are world class, and for the people to support that. I don't want to ask people to buy my stuff out of charity or out of some belief system. It's the pleasure equation instead of the guilt equation."

They tell me about debuting their ice cream at a local Slow Food event in a now-defunct café in Strafford. "We hit it lucky," Amy says. "I finished freezing it and ran down to the event. People stopped in their tracks, and we were like rock stars!"

"And the cows?" I say. "Don't they get a lot of credit for your success?"

"Well, we probably don't give them enough," Amy replies.

The next day, on Earl and Amy's suggestion, I drive into the town of Barre to check out the Farmer's Diner, which serves Ransom milk and ice cream. The place is so unassuming that I drive by it a couple of times. When I go in, the waitress greets me, gives me a menu, and then slaps the order book down on the table. "What do you want, honey?"

The place looks like an ordinary diner. There's the long Formica counter lined with Naugahyde-covered swivel seats like the ones I used to spin around on while waiting for my milk shake when I was a kid. There's a jukebox in the corner, and cakes with thick icing sit on shiny metal pedestals with plastic covers.

The thick, plastic-covered menu lists a hamburger for $5.50; meatloaf with gravy, potato, and vegetable for $7.95; a grilled cheese sandwich for $3.50. But on the cover is a photograph of a local farmer. Wendell Berry's rallying cry "Eating Is an Agricultural Act" is printed on all of the staff T-shirts and on the plastic-covered place mats. On the back of the place mat, I discover that the majority of the ingredients are from the immediate region: eggs from Stowe, bacon from Barre, tomatoes from Thetford and Plainfield, steaks from Starksboro, and milk from Strafford. It's good local food without the attitude (or the price) that is normally part of the program at most restaurants that use local ingredients.

I order a vanilla milk shake, and the waitress returns with the stainless-steel container cold and full with a spoon and a straw stuck in the center. "Sorry it's so thick," she says. "We just put in too much ice cream." I accept her apology and eat the whole thing with a spoon.

My hamburger and fries arrive, and I ask the waitress for the origins of the pickles. She yells across the diner to the cook, "Hey, Chad, are our pickles Vermont grown?"

"The potatoes are from here," Chad answers. "The lettuce is from Cedar Circle Farm, but the pickles aren't from here—they're from Massachusetts."

It's refreshing to see a place like this acknowledging farmers. As I drive back to the Ransoms', I consider how anonymity, as much as poor prices, development pressures, and lack of help, is forcing farmers off the land. Farmers' markets, CSAs, and now even local diners are helping put a face back onto our food.

Although the Ransoms don't exactly seem like the grandstanding type, they aren't into being anonymous, either. The cows have names, not numbers, each regarded not as a milk machine but as a separate personality. I reflect on Amy's comment that "it's nice not to have to deal with the whiny bulk-milk truck driver." I can imagine that transferring milk from cows you know by name and lovingly care for into a bulk tank truck where its unique flavor is mixed with milk from everywhere to be processed and moved to anywhere would be as thankless and anonymous as you can get.

"In terms of satisfaction, overall quality of life, you can't really beat this," Earl tells me later that day. "But there's a huge amount of responsibility that goes along with owning land, too. We benefit from owning the land, but the land—if it's not benefiting from us being here, then we're all losing something.

"Of all the things I'd like to give my boys, I want them to be able to die as old men on this land," Amy adds. "I actually have three more goals: I want my children to be respectful, I want to make pickles, and I want to personally eliminate all of the flies from this farm with my swatter."

That night, I decide to hang out with the cows. They have just been put onto a new field of oats with an understory of alfalfa and timothy grass. When their eyes catch the moon, it looks like all thirty of them are looking right at me. I move slowly amid their munching and chewing and loud breathing, the ecstatic sounds of cow contentment. I imagine I am swimming in the ocean and a pod of whales has moved in around me. I sit down, and a few of them put their heads down and sniff and check me out, their udders hanging full and low. In spite of their massive size, I feel safe and protected sitting on the cool, moist grass in the moonlight, imagining the scents of the night air and the tender oats swirling around in their bloodstreams, infusing their cream with the chemistry of this moment.

❧

AFTER AN AFTERNOON AND EVENING AT THE TUNBRIDGE COUNTRY FAIR, and a night camping on the streets of Barre, I make my way east, toward coastal Maine and Eliot Coleman and Barbara Damrosch's Four Season Farm. I'm carrying 4 quarts of Strafford Creamery ice cream—two vanillas, one coconut almond (do they grow coconuts and almonds in Vermont?), and my all-time favorite, black raspberry. It will be two days before I reach Eliot and Barbara's place, so this particular sharing of foods proves to be a little challenging. An hour into the trip, I check my stash and discover that the ice has all melted and the cream is following suit. I buy some ice at a country store and repack the load.

I stop to take a rest an hour west of Bangor, Maine. I know I'm supposed to be saving the ice cream for Eliot and Barbara, but I've been living with this stuff ever since I left the Ransoms', and the black raspberry has been calling to me all day. I tell myself that someone should enjoy it if there's a chance that it might not survive the trip. I give in, eat some, and then lie down and fall into an ice-cream slumber.

In Maine's interior, fairy-tale villages give way to pulp mills, Wal-Marts, and run-down trailer homes. Along the coast, lobster traps and fishing boats and restored villages appear, and the wealth that has moved in from the south manifests itself in picture-perfect seaside homes.

The road into Four Season Farm passes in and out of rocky beaches and inlets. The soil looks like beach sand, and I wonder how anyone could be growing anything out here, much less the four-season harvest Eliot and Barbara are so renowned for. As I walk around the fields and greenhouses, I am struck by the exactness, the precision, and the consistency of each of the plantings. The beds are 30 inches wide, immaculately cultivated with laser-perfect straight lines of intense greens and reds, full rows from end to end. It is a level of technical skill and detail that reminds me of my visits during the eighties to see many of Europe's master farmers.

This land belonged to Scott and Helen Nearing, the extraordinary couple whose life and writings became the inspiration for thousands of young people across the country to take up the simple life, living lightly on the land. Scott and Helen moved to this 140-acre plot in 1953 from Vermont, having left the farm they had started there when a new ski resort was approved in view of their land. Scott was seventy years old and Helen fifty when they moved to this land and started over again, developing water systems and putting in gardens that would feed the hundreds of visitors that came flocking for their wisdom.

Eliot talks about helping Scott start construction on a new house in the 1970s. "We threw saws and axes into wheelbarrows and trundled down the driveway to where the new place was going to go in. Scott took this little bow saw out of his wheelbarrow and went over to the first sapling and cut it off and looked at it, and there was just a 1-foot piece of firewood in there. He cut that off into his wheelbarrow and dragged the rest over and threw it over the bank. I was standing there thinking, 'Man, you're in your nineties. You're going to cut the driveway by hand? Come on, let's get chain saws and bulldozers, you know?' And the lesson from it was that the process is what you enjoy; the goal is meaningless. Scott enjoyed the process."

Eliot initially came here with his first wife in the fall of 1968 to visit the Nearings. Helen suggested that he buy the back half of their place. Scott wanted the same $500 for the 60 acres he had paid twenty years before. After all, he "hadn't done anything to it," and he didn't believe in unearned income. Helen suggested $2,000 for the 60 acres. Eliot and his wife "bargained" upward and offered them $2,500 but she stuck to her $2,000. Years later, Eliot and Barbara sold off a few sections to friends for the same $33 per acre they originally paid. The Nearings' work and inspiration are carried forth by Eliot and Barbara, along with friends and neighbors who live along this stretch of Maine coastline. We walk along a system of footpaths that connect families and homes. As the woods open up into one homestead, Eliot yells out to announce his arrival. It feels like the Nearings are still alive and present here in the way folks are living, in the gardens, in the handmade buildings, and most of all through the strong sense of sharing and community.

"It's interesting how we are and we aren't children of the Nearings," Barbara is careful to point out. "The Nearings were militant vegetarians, especially Helen, but almost nobody in our gang is. We're all omnivores. The thing that is common, and this isn't any intentional community, mind you—because that would completely ruin the whole thing—is the fact that with incredible ease, without even thinking about it, we share equipment and services."

We visit the home where Scott and Helen Nearing lived, now established as the nonprofit Good Life Center. Young couples live here for a period of one to two years on a rotating basis, maintaining the gardens and keeping the Nearing lifestyle alive. Eliot tells me the Nearings were unusual because they actually walked their talk, and it is clear that they had a profound influence on his life and work. I can't help but reflect on those who have been mentors and influenced my life—David Brower, John Collier, Wendell Berry—and I remember that none of the genius, the ingenuity, the perseverance, the love of land that I have witnessed over and over on this trip stands alone. There is always some individual who came before whose life provided the model and the inspiration.

Eliot and Barbara describe the weekly ritual. Every Wednesday, there's a potluck dinner, and all the neighbors have a sauna together. Each neighbor has a hand-built sauna, so the gathering moves from farm to farm.

"We have a good friend who's an alternative rabbi," Eliot says. "I was telling him, 'Everett, nobody up here is religious.' And he said, 'Wait a minute, Eliot. Isn't it true that you and your friends, on one certain day a week, go into a certain building that is reserved for a special use, go through a certain ceremony, and partake of food afterward?' And I said, 'Yeah, sauna.' 'It's your religion,' he says."

"Ours is built next to our pond," Barbara says. "All winter we maintain a 3-foot-diameter hole in the ice at the end of our dock so we can plunge in."

"The rest of the pond is for hockey," Eliot adds. "We have games every afternoon. A bunch of total loonies."

During the seventies, Eliot says, this was the perfect hippie farm. "We all worked naked," he reminisces. "I had a timekeeper to make sure that when the stand opened, we all had clothes on. At ten o'clock every morning, someone would scream, 'Pants dance!' and everyone would run around trying to figure out where they'd left their goddamn pants. One day Frank didn't hear the cry; he was down at the well, bunching carrots. They'd brought in a load, and he was tying and bunching and washing them. He cut all but 4 inches of the tops off so they wouldn't wilt, and I wanted that for the compost. So Frank was sitting there naked with a whole pile of carrots, and he suddenly heard people coming in, so he picked up some more carrot tops, threw them over himself, and just sat there."

I observe as Eliot prepares one of his signature greenhouses for its transition out of summer crops and into winter greens. Barbara gleans the last of the basil just in time, just as plants are being pulled and loaded up for compost. I admire the speed with which Eliot works, and reflect on my own style of moving quickly through farmwork. This past summer, I watched in disbelief as an intern working with us sat with legs crossed next to a row of vegetables, pulling one weed at a time. When there are a million things to be harvested or cultivated, speed and efficiency can make the difference between economic success and failure. It's one of the more difficult things to explain to someone who has never worked in agriculture: the need to be thorough and detail-oriented but to move fast.

I watch and photograph as Eliot methodically pulls out each of the plants from the finished summer crop, lays a string line along the edges of the bed, broadforks the whole bed, applies compost, alfalfa meal, crab meal, and a little sul-po-mag, and rakes it all in. He then marks the newly prepared bed using a modified landscape rake with alternating teeth extended. I love the meticulousness with which he finishes by transplanting a crop of Rouge d'Hiver lettuce. Standing by and silently watching someone else work is a little awkward, but it is such a refined and graceful performance, perfected by years of repetition, that I don't dare interrupt.

Everything in Eliot and Barbara's house seems to revolve around growing and cooking and eating. There are books everywhere, and Eliot's office contains one of the most extensive libraries on natural agriculture I've seen. I ask about his favorite books, and he hands me a sheet titled "The Fertile Dozen" that lists titles such as *Make Friends with Your Land,* published in 1948, *The Stuff Man's Made Of,* from 1959, and *The Soil and the Microbe,* from 1931. His deep respect for those individuals who have paved the way is evident, as is his dedication to constant improvement of his craft. Our conversations are peppered with this endless quest to push our work as farmers to another level, to find just the right variety, hand tool, or way of planting or cultivating.

Eliot's own books have provided a generation of market gardeners with the tools and techniques to proceed on their own. His seminal *New Organic Grower* reveals in great detail the techniques for growing for market on a small scale. His *Four-Season Harvest* provides the template for growing food year-round, even in the harshest northern climates.

Eliot's techniques are rooted in his endless questioning, so, inevitably, discussion ranges over the many things that go into our chosen science—economics, politics, even public relations. He expresses admiration that Fairview Gardens was able to achieve a measure of financial success on such a small piece of land. He tells me that on an acre and a half he is producing $100,000 per year. (Fairview grosses more than $700,000 per year on 12.25 acres.) When people are critical of my emphasis on economics, I remind them that the best land-preservation, food-security, and farm-ecology strategies lie in getting young people involved with farming. And the best way to do that is to show them that there is an economic incentive to do so. They've got to see that they can make a decent living. How else is anyone going to take us seriously, and how can we do what we do if we can't make it financially?

"You can say what you want about capitalism," Eliot says, "but economics is just a great way of keeping score. If you're a competitor in anything, you want to know whether you're playing up to your potential."

We continue our discussion over a lunch Eliot prepares—open-faced cheese sandwiches on a bed of turnip greens and spinach with tomato sauce on top. Barbara looks at our farmer's lunch, laughs, and refers to it as "boy food."

"If you're an organic farmer, the hardest thing is the economics," Eliot says while we eat. "Across the road is a very high-priced development on 400 acres. These people'll say, 'Wow, we just love your produce, but it's so expensive.'

"I was curious about this, so I've been researching it, and it turns out that as recently as 1940, the average American spent one-third of their income on food."

"And we now spend less per capita on food than any other industrialized country in the world," Barbara puts in.

"It's 14 cents on the dollar," I add.

"What people are missing is that they now have the money to eat really good food," Eliot says. "If you want medical insurance instead of sickness-amelioration insurance, the best medical insurance you can buy is good food."

"This is the one thing that makes my blood pressure go up more than any other," I say. "It's one of the reasons at Fairview that I couldn't be at the produce stand or the markets anymore. Most people are pretty loyal and supportive, but you always get a handful who give you that 'too expensive' line—usually with the BMW keys in one hand—and what can you say?"

"Oh, I had the best line at our stand, years ago," Eliot replies. "I'd look out to the parking lot, and I'd say, 'What's that you drove in on? Oh, the BMW. How come you bought that instead of the Ford Fairlane?' And they'd say, 'Oh, God, Fords are made of tin. They're just shitty.' And I'd say, 'Well, you just answered your own question. We're selling BMW s. You know the difference in cars. There's just as much difference in vegetables.' And that was my most effective answer."

It always shocks me to realize how crucial communication and advocacy are becoming in the new agriculture. It's as if what we are doing is so foreign to twenty-first-century society that we have to become a voice for the land, be able to articulate what it's like to grow soil that is alive and food that carries that life. We've got to add writing and speaking to an already long list of required agricultural skills: welding and carpentry and plumbing and electrical, marketing and refrigeration and biology and botany.

"We had a produce manager at our local food co-op," Barbara says. "This guy was really dispirited. Somebody explained that his problem is that he really wanted to work for a more political cause. That amazed me. He just didn't get how political and powerful working with good food can be."

Today's politics have become even more complicated, as longtime members of the so-called organic movement find themselves at odds with some of their organic-industry colleagues. A movement that was based on the simple goals of regenerating soil and growing food for local communities has become an industry requiring a vast bureaucracy of organicrats to inspect, police, advise, and manage a comparatively small handful of folks who are actually doing the work of organic farming. Once again, the marketers have taken over a grassroots movement and turned it into an industry. The impulses of social change and forward thinking must now share space with the economic priorities of industry, and, often, the balance seems unequal.

Ten years ago, organic farmers hardly qualified as a demographic, and we went unnoticed by anyone with something to sell. Now, my mailbox bulges with slick catalogs containing every imaginable product for the organic grower. For a long time, I just ignored it, but then I started to think, "Maybe I'm not doing a good job because I'm not buying some of these things. Maybe I'm missing something here; maybe this stuff will make me a better farmer."

"We have set up a world where we are only interested in treating the symptom," Eliot says, "preferably with a product that you have to buy. Because someone makes money when you're treating the symptom. And that's why organic agriculture is never going to become the form of agriculture, because, when it's done right, it only makes money for the farmer. If I'm doing this correctly, I'm not buying anything.

"The bad guys are trying to re-create chemical farming in organic farming and make it an input system," Elliot continues with what he describes as his most current rant. "But this kind of farming is based on information input, not product input."

"I've always said it's management intensive," I add, "rather than resource intensive."

The beauty of Eliot's system is that it is incredibly simple and self-determined. It requires none of the high-tech, fuel-intensive methods you would expect when you're talking about growing fresh vegetables in the winter in Maine. Simple greenhouses run without dependency on nuclear power, coal, or foreign wars to ensure a steady supply of energy. In fact, he seldom requires any electricity to keep these winter crops warm and alive. Instead, cold frames and greenhouses act as the primary protective shells. A layer of diaphanous floating row cover rests gently over the vegetables, providing additional protection and maintaining even temperatures while letting in light and moisture. The result is that, outside the cold frame, it may be coastal Maine in December, but, inside, it's Massachusetts in October, and, under the row cover, it's Pennsylvania. Propane heaters are in place to keep the houses just above freezing. It's all part of a system that requires the farmer to pay attention and think rather than buy.

Later, over a dinner of lamb stew, mashed potatoes, and yellow watermelon, we talk about chefs and how, despite the evolution in food awareness, farmers are not always given the credit they deserve. Sure, many amazing relationships have been forged between farmers and chefs, and many great chefs are providing critical support for their local farming community. However, the end product almost always gets presented as the chef's creation, instead of a collaboration among the chef, the farmer, the soil, the sunlight, and the earthworms.

Eliot tells me that New York City chef Dan Barber makes fresh food taste even fresher. I can attest to that. Aaron and I spent a memorable evening at Dan's Blue Hill restaurant, partaking of a two-and-a-half-hour multicourse meal while sitting outdoors at tables lit by candles and Manhattan moonlight. I could taste the farmer's work in each of Dan's dishes. Rather than hiding the ingredients beneath an array of "here I am" disguises, Dan stood quietly behind each dish, placing the farmer and their food into the forward position. By the end of the meal, I felt as if I had taken a tour across the agricultural landscape of the Northeast.

I spend part of the last afternoon wandering alone, taking pictures out in the greenhouses and around the edges of Four Season Farm. At every farm, I like to have time on my own in the fields or with the animals. I'm amazed at how every place has been such a strong reflection of individual personalities. Here, it's as if every project has a question associated with it: "If I do this, will it create this result?" There is a personality type associated with what I see here; the work is pursued with precision, control, formal science, and discovery. This well-honed discipline is reflected in the continuous harvest and the way Eliot and Barbara address the evolving and overlapping needs of each season in a climate where the margin of error is nonexistent.

It's mid-September, and most folks in these parts are putting in their firewood, gleaning and canning and freezing the last of the summer's bounty, winterizing their homes, and turning in crop residues. Eliot, meanwhile, is out preparing ground and planting.

It's weird, like I'm in some sort of time warp: it feels like fall—I even get the occasional whiff of winter—but this farm is abuzz with springlike activity. I have known that one of the centerpieces of Eliot's work is to show what is possible on a small piece of land in a northern climate throughout the year, but, for some reason, it still tweaks me. It's a little like jet lag, where, after an international flight, you feel like pieces of your psyche are scattered across continents and trying to catch up.

Here, all the seasonal stereotypes are turned upside down, especially for a guy like me, who escaped the never-ending farming season of Southern California for parts north so that I could actually take a break in the winter.

I've always said that I look forward to the day when individuals and families put farmers out of business by growing their own. The usual objection people raise to this possibility is that not all climates are equal. Eliot's system provides a model, a way for individuals to envision a year-round harvest no matter what their climate, and a way to spread a sense of self-determination and everything that goes with it.

Ultimately, "organic" has got to be more than some *Good Housekeeping* seal of approval, and even though people will always need farmers, the more people can participate in and question their food system, the more they will benefit. For those of us who have grown up in this movement, it seems natural to advance from technique to science to teaching to politics. I guess that's the evolution of anyone who achieves some mastery and independence: they want to see people engage, think, and join in, and not passively wait to be told what is safe, or valuable, or even possible.

♣

Warm Apple Pie with Vanilla Ice Cream

SERVES 8 *I've never thought of myself as particularly patriotic, especially within the current definition of the word, but place a piece of well-made apple pie in front of me and I'll be pledging allegiance to the land. This one, made with butter and sour cream, is basically a classic American apple pie with a splash of brandy. Of course, it must be served with a good ice cream. Unfortunately, Earl and Amy Ransom's handcrafted ice cream is available only in Vermont.*

PIE DOUGH

2 cups all-purpose flour, plus extra for dusting

1 teaspoon sugar

1 teaspoon kosher salt

7 tablespoons cold unsalted butter, cut into ½-inch square pieces

7 tablespoons cold salted butter, cut into ½-inch square pieces

3 tablespoons sour cream

3 to 4 tablespoons ice water

FILLING

½ cup sugar

1 tablespoon all-purpose flour

½ teaspoon ground cinnamon

½ teaspoon kosher salt

3 pounds apples such as Gravenstein or McIntosh, peeled, cored,
   and cut into ½-inch chunks

1 tablespoon brandy

1½ tablespoons unsalted butter, at room temperature, cut into small pieces

1 egg yolk

2 teaspoons heavy cream

Vanilla ice cream for serving

TO MAKE THE PIE DOUGH: Combine the 2 cups flour, sugar, and salt in a large bowl. Add the cold unsalted butter. Using your hands, gently toss the butter around to coat each piece with the flour mixture—this helps the butter to cut in evenly. Using a pastry cutter or 2 knives, cut the butter into the flour until the mixture has the texture of coarse oatmeal. Add the cold salted butter, gently toss again to coat each piece with the flour mixture, and quickly cut again until the larger pieces are about the size of lima beans. Spoon the sour cream into the bowl and sprinkle in 3 tablespoons of ice water. Using your hands, lightly toss the mixture between your fingers to moisten it evenly. The dough should look raggedy and rough but hold together when you gently squeeze a small amount in the palm of your hand. If not, add 1 more tablespoon water. Form the dough into a brick shape—be careful not to knead it, just squeeze it gently into one solid mass. Cut the brick in half crosswise. Wrap each half tightly in plastic and press each package into a flat disk. Refrigerate for several hours to relax the gluten and chill before using.

Position a rack in the lower third of the oven and preheat the oven to 400 degrees F.

On a lightly floured work surface, roll out one dough disk into a 14-inch circle. Brush off any excess flour on both sides with a dry pastry brush. Transfer the dough to a pie dish and trim the edge of the dough even with the edge of the dish. Refrigerate the pie shell while you prepare the filling.

TO MAKE THE FILLING: Whisk together the sugar, flour, cinnamon, and salt in a small bowl. In a large bowl, sprinkle the apples with the brandy. Add the dry ingredients and toss well to combine. Set aside.

On a lightly floured work surface, roll out the remaining dough disk into a 14-inch circle and brush off the excess flour. Heap the filling into the chilled pie shell and dot the top with the room temperature butter. Carefully fit the top crust over the apples. Trim the top crust about $1/2$ inch beyond the edge of the pan and fold it under the bottom crust. Crimp the edge in a decorative fashion. Whisk the egg yolk and heavy cream together in a small bowl and brush the top crust with the mixture. Make a few small decorative cuts through the top crust for the steam to vent. Bake until the apples are tender and the crust is beautifully golden, about 50 minutes. If the crust browns too much before the pie is done, tent the pie with aluminum foil, or if just the edges are browning too much, cover the edges with strips of foil. Serve warm, with vanilla ice cream.

Panna Cotta

SERVES 8

This is the perfect dessert to showcase the high-quality products Earl and Amy Ransom (and their Guernsey cows) produce: it doesn't hide the natural flavors of the cream and the milk and the pastures. Panna cotta—"cooked cream"—is lightly sweetened custard that consists primarily of milk and cream. It's made with gelatin as opposed to eggs, so it's especially light, and it's very easy to make. You can serve it with fresh berries or your favorite compote.

Vegetable oil for greasing
3 tablespoons cold water
One ¼-ounce envelope unflavored powdered gelatin
One 2-inch piece vanilla bean
3 cups heavy cream, preferably not ultrapasturized
1 cup whole milk
¼ cup plus 1 tablespoon sugar
Pinch of kosher salt

Lightly grease eight 4-ounce ramekins with oil. Place the ramekins on a baking sheet and put them in the refrigerator to chill.

Put the cold water in small bowl, and sprinkle the gelatin evenly over the water. Set aside to soften.

Meanwhile, slice the vanilla bean lengthwise and scrape out the seeds. In a medium saucepan, combine the vanilla seeds and bean, cream, milk, sugar, and salt. Heat the cream mixture gently over medium heat, stirring frequently, until it just begins to simmer. Remove from the heat and let cool for about 10 minutes.

Stir some of the warm cream into the softened gelatin to dissolve it. Then, stir the gelatin-cream mixture back into the remaining cream. Strain the cream through a fine-mesh sieve, and pour into the ramekins. Cover lightly with plastic wrap or a piece of parchment paper, and refrigerate until the panna cotta has set, about 4 hours (or overnight.) To serve, run a small, sharp knife around the rim of the ramekins, and invert the ramekins onto dessert plates, gently tapping to release the cream.

Mâche and Beet Salad

Mâche, also known as corn salad or lamb's lettuce, is one of the earliest spring greens to grace our northern table. We plant it in the fall and watch in amazement as it rides out the snow and cold and wet, magically appearing bright and green and ready to eat in early spring. Of course, Eliot Coleman and Barbara Damrosch have turned the seasonal stereotype on its head, making mâche just one more note in a diverse composition of fresh foods produced in the north.

At home, we harvest several beet varieties for our salads. Our favorites are the Italian Chioggia, with its pink flesh and concentric white circles; golden beets, for their sweet flavor and outstanding color; and the elongated, deep-red Cylindra. Each of these varieties has distinctive textures and flavors, and the colors are outstanding when served together. Remember to isolate the red beets until assembling this salad to keep the color from bleeding onto everything else.

4 medium red or golden beets

2 tablespoons plus 1 teaspoon red wine vinegar

1 tablespoon plus 1 teaspoon balsamic vinegar

1½ teaspoons Dijon mustard

Kosher salt to taste

¼ cup extra-virgin olive oil

4 ounces mâche (about 2 cups)

Freshly cracked black pepper to taste

2 ounces fresh goat cheese, chilled (optional)

Preheat the oven to 400 degrees F.

Trim and wash the beets and place them in a baking dish large enough to hold them in a single layer. Add enough water to cover the bottom of the baking dish and cover the dish tightly with aluminum foil. Roast until the beets are tender when pierced with a small, sharp knife, about 45 minutes. Set aside and let cool.

Meanwhile, in a small bowl, whisk together 1 tablespoon plus 1 teaspoon of the red wine vinegar, the balsamic vinegar, mustard, and a pinch of salt. Whisk in the olive oil and taste with a leaf of mâche; you may want to add a little more olive oil or an extra drop or two of vinegar. Set aside.

When the beets are cool enough to handle, peel them and cut them into small wedges. In a small bowl, combine the beets with a pinch of salt and the remaining 1 tablespoon red wine vinegar. Toss well to combine.

Put the mâche in a large bowl and season with salt and pepper. Gently toss with just enough vinaigrette to lightly coat the greens. Place the greens on a serving platter or individual plates. Toss the beets with the remaining vinaigrette. Nestle the beets around the greens. Crumble the goat cheese on top, if desired. Serve immediately.

Sautéed Greens with Garlic and Hot Pepper

SERVES 4 TO 6

"Boy food" is the term given to describe the simple, quick, and nutritious meals Eliot Coleman prepares for himself and his farmworkers when Barbara Damrosch is away. Eliot prepared this dish for me in minutes while carrying on an in-depth farmer's rant on soil fertility.

The mesclun mix Eliot grows can be used for a salad or a stir-fry, so he often sautés the mix and tosses the greens with noodles or eats them with fried eggs and sliced tomato. Or, as he did when he served me, he piles the greens on toasted bread with homemade tomato sauce spooned on top.

This simple recipe for sautéed greens with olive oil, garlic, and hot pepper can be made in minutes and used for several boy-food meals. The greens are especially delicious with hot peppers preserved in vinegar, rather than with dried pepper flakes.

3 tablespoons extra-virgin olive oil

3 cloves garlic, finely chopped

Hot Peppers Preserved in Vinegar (page 249) or hot red pepper flakes to taste

2 pounds tender, young Asian salad green mix (about 10 cups)

Kosher salt to taste

Heat a large sauté pan over medium-high heat. Add the olive oil, garlic, and preserved hot peppers and sauté for about 1 minute—just until the garlic is fragrant. Add the greens in large handfuls, adding more when a batch has wilted, and cook until all of the greens have collapsed and wilted. Season with salt and serve warm or at room temperature.

Aioli

MAKES ABOUT 1 CUP

Sadly, most store-bought vegetables don't lend themselves to being eaten au naturel—they've been on the road for too long, traveled too far, and often didn't have much flavor when they left the fields. As a result, most vegetable dips have to be pretty loud, as the vegetables have been reduced to tasteless instruments, mere conveyances to carry dip to the mouth.

A well-made aioli can actually enhance the textures and flavors of raw vegetables rather than burying them. Before dinner, Barbara Damrosch served a beautiful selection of Eliot Coleman's home-grown best that we munched with a deep-yellow aioli made with a neighbor's fresh eggs.

Barbara occasionally adds a pinch of saffron or the homemade paprika she makes by drying their own peppers and pureeing them in a blender.

3 cloves garlic
Kosher salt to taste
1 egg yolk
1 cup pure olive oil
Fresh lemon juice or red wine vinegar to taste (optional)

Using a mortar and pestle, pound the garlic with a pinch of salt into a smooth paste.

In a medium bowl, whisk together the egg yolk and half of the mashed garlic, then slowly whisk in some of the olive oil, a few drops at a time. As the mixture begins to thicken and emulsify, add the olive oil in a slow, steady stream. (If the aioli becomes too thick, add a splash of water and continue adding the olive oil.) Once all of the olive oil has been added, taste and adjust the seasoning with as much of the remaining mashed garlic and salt as you like—keeping in mind that the garlic is lightly seasoned with salt already. If the aioli tastes a little flat, add a drop or two of fresh lemon juice or red wine vinegar.

Serve the aioli for dipping with vegetables such as heirloom tomatoes or baby carrots, or blanched green beans, beets, or cauliflower, or steamed artichokes or new potatoes.

NOTE: If the aioli separates, or "breaks," pour the broken egg and olive oil mixture into a measuring cup and repeat the process with another egg yolk, first whisking the broken mixture into the egg yolk, drop by drop, then whisking in any remaining olive oil.

CHAPTER 8

☾

HEART LAND

I LEAVE ELIOT AND BARBARA'S PLACE ENERGIZED, IMAGINING A revolution of small-scale, year-round farms, independent and self-sufficient, beholden to no one but their neighbors, buying as few inputs as possible, selling as locally as possible. I picture them serving equally independent communities that consider the term *organic*—if they use it at all—as just a starting point for dialogue between farmer and customer. I think about the different values, priorities, and influences that motivate the farmers I've met and how my own convictions and experiences have gradually come together into a highly personal blend of attitude and practice. I wonder sometimes if I'm just one more crotchety dreamer—which is, I suppose, a redundant description of a small farmer. We all think, like John Thurman, that we should run the world.

With my mind still churning, I pull into New London, Connecticut, and wait in the thick, foggy evening to board the ferry for Orient Point, Long Island. Without Aaron to talk to, I've become fully absorbed in my own grand visions of Michael's Better World. My thoughts shift to my upcoming visit with my dad in a few days. He's agreed to take Aaron and me on a tour of our agricultural roots in Sussex County, Delaware, a trip I used to make as a child with my grandfather, the last time when I was twelve. It's been a long time since I've been back to Sussex County, and Aaron has never been there. I'm beginning to wonder what this trip into the past will feel like after everything else we've seen.

When I pull into Satur Farm, it's ten o'clock. I drive blindly around the dark property, trying to find a quiet place to park away from the refrigeration compressors that are rhythmically churning on and off, as if they're having a loud conversation in a language I can't understand.

I awake to the Spanish chatter of the farm crew arriving for work. When I emerge from the van, Paulette Satur's husband, Eberhard Mueller, is waiting to greet

me. He has the flu and looks pale and tired. We exchange introductions, and he rushes off to attend to some chore.

The sky is gray and foreboding, and there is a frantic energy about the place. When I see Paulette, she tells me that Hurricane Isabel is sitting out in the Atlantic, waiting to pounce. They are worried about the storm, anxious to get as much harvested as possible before it arrives. She jokes wanly that they won't have to harvest after the hurricane comes through.

I catch up with Eberhard and jump into his pickup truck, and we head out to the fields in high gear. Satur Farm is 200 entirely flat, sandy acres on the North Fork of Long Island. Seemingly endless rows of 5-foot-wide, laser-perfect beds score the land into a geometric patchwork of green romaine, Lolla Rossa, and oak-leaf lettuces, arugula, radicchio, and mustards that stretch as far as the eye can see. Satur Farm produces a ton and a half of organic lettuce a week, which is shipped to restaurants in New York City, including Eberhard's own hot spot, Bayard's, on Hanover Square.

Eberhard mounts a tractor with a high-tech European salad harvester on the back and takes off in a frenzy, barely allowing the two Mexican workers time enough to get on. He speeds up and down a bed of arugula as the machine cuts the tender leaves and conveys them up to the two workers, who desperately try to keep up as they fill bin after bin.

Eberhard is surely one of the few chefs in America who also drives a tractor, and in fact he seems to be something of a heavy-metal aficionado. There is a flotilla of tractors, tillers, precision seeders, cultivators, fertilizer injectors, and harvest machines, most of which appear new and imported from Europe. The latest acquisition is a hydraulic cultivating and fertilizer-injection machine. It looks like a giant insect moving down the rows; its operator taut with concentration like a video-game player. The large bin in the front of the machine carries a mixture of bagged fertilizers: blood meal, bone meal, sul-po-mag, and an organic 4-2-4. As the machine runs down the field, it drops the mixture alongside each row of plants. Cultivators at the back of the machine dig it all in.

I could not find any compost piles here, and, when I ask about them, I'm told there isn't enough space for composting. Eberhard explains that this is "precision farming," as if to suggest that composting is a little old-fashioned.

I wonder to myself whether Eberhard and Paulette would be surprised to see the comparatively tiny scale that I farm on and how compost dependent I am. Seeing all this equipment, all these trucks full of food coming and going, and this businesslike operation, makes me feel for a moment like what I grow is inconsequential. I remind myself that I've tried working on a larger scale, that I made a conscious choice to work small. There's nothing wrong with technology; I just like to be able to combine it with hand labor.

It's hard to imagine giving up, for example, the discipline of hand-cultivating fields. It's possible to do the same job from the seat of a tractor, but hand cultivating feels more direct and enables me to see things up close that can't be seen any other way. When I decided not to use chemicals to farm, it wasn't as much about rejecting chemicals as it was about getting away from the idea of farming based on the model of inputs in, products out. If I substituted steer manure for nitrate fertilizer or botanical oil for malathion, I would certainly be handling safer substances, but I would still be tied to inputs that had to be produced or mined somewhere else.

Perhaps most intangibly, I wanted to participate more directly in my farm's fertility. I wanted to start with the soil and make it as self-sustaining as I could. I didn't totally understand it at the time, nor do I completely now, but I saw a farm as a community, and, as such, it needed to be inclusive of all the parts: the wildness, the people who work on it, those who are nourished from it, the water that flows through it, every form of life from the tiniest soil microbe on up. Satur Farm's elegant and efficient operation reminds me that the thing I wanted most to experience was something different, an unpredictable intimacy with nature, the rewards of seeing soil improve, frogs and insects return, and ecosystems take hold. As usual, my mind has strayed far afield, and I realize these thoughts say less about Paulette and Eberhard's farm than they do about me.

Paulette calls us in for a quick pasta lunch, saying apologetically, "Here you are, in the home of the great chef Eberhard Mueller, and his wife is cooking a meal for you." Paulette is actually the driving force behind Satur Farm. A former wine-sales executive with a degree in plant physiology, she knows the culinary landscape and how to fill a need, first for Eberhard's restaurant and then for restaurants throughout Manhattan.

Paulette and Eberhard's contacts in the restaurant world have given them an uncommon access to chefs and buyers. Most of the smaller producers I know deal with a handful of chefs who must buy from a number of farmers to fill their weekly needs. Paulette and Eberhard's concept makes good business sense: grow enough volume and diversity of products over a long enough season to be consistent every week throughout the late spring, summer, and fall. If I were a busy chef, I would certainly prefer not to shop around constantly for basic items.

Satur Farm is a reliable source; it's about production, consistency, about always being able to say yes to every request from every restaurant. I'm sure such reliability has helped give chefs in the region the confidence to commit to regional and organic ingredients and to promote them to their customers. This draws valuable attention to the connection between local farmers and chefs and helps people realize that ingredients have a history, that they came from somewhere and that their quality is critical to the outcome of the final dish.

The lay of the land is too flat to photograph well from the ground, so I ask Paulette whether she knows of any pilots in the area. She contacts a man who does aerial spraying, and he agrees to meet me the next morning.

John is a former Vietnam helicopter pilot turned aerial-spray pilot. I meet him at his shop, where he's busy cleaning out spray booms and getting equipment put

away before the hurricane arrives. He removes the door from his turbine-powered copter, and, with blind faith, I hop in and buckle up. In seconds we lift off smoothly, and, within a few minutes, we're over Satur Farm. We circle around, turn sideways, and dance around in the sky above the fields. While John giggles as he demonstrates his aerial aerobatics, my stomach gurgles and floats as if it is barely attached to the rest of my body. He holds steady as I lean out the door to photo-graph, but when I finish he tells me to hold on. Like a madman, he navigates just above the railroad tracks, threading the copter through a clump of trees, turning sideways, then swooping straight up into the air and down again toward the ground. At the last microsecond, he pulls up and floats the machine gently down onto a small trailer. Wow!

I thank him for his generosity and offer to give him a copy of one of my books. He follows me to the van, and we start talking about his aerial spraying. He tells me that most of his work is mosquito abatement and control of blight and beetles on potatoes. He was a major player in the aerial spraying for West Nile disease in New York City in 1999 and talks about the neighborhood politics— how this neighborhood couldn't be sprayed on such and such a date because of the Hasidic Jews or the Hispanics. Ironically, I had been in New York in 1999, the night the spraying began, and I tell him that I had to run for cover.

John says that most of the chemicals he uses now "aren't too bad," but in the old days there was some nasty stuff. The conversation is relaxed and easy until I ask him whether he's concerned about the long-term effects of spraying pesticides. At that point he gets excited and animated, his eyebrows going up and down, his arms gesturing emphatically. "We have the best food in the history of the world!" he exclaims. "Look at the Irish Potato Famine—if they had had fungicide, all those people wouldn't have died."

He asks me questions and answers them himself: "How many people do you know who have died from pesticides? No one! These people ought to go after drunk drivers, not pesticides. Organic food is a niche, but it can't feed the world." He begins aggressively paging through my book and says, "All these farmers are dependent on sprays." I distract him from the book, thank him again, ask for his card, and leave before he has a chance to read further.

I head down the road toward New York City to meet up with Aaron to see what promises to be the most unusual farm we will see on this trip, a chef/farmer connection of a very different kind.

♣

"HERE IS WHERE WE MAKE GRANOLA AND BUTTER COOKIES AND THE Galaxy cookies for the planetarium." Eli Zabar is gesturing briskly as he shows Aaron and me around part of his kingdom on Manhattan's Upper East Side.

Eli Zabar is a successful baker and retailer with several locations in Manhattan that feature many of his own products. His seven hundred employees produce everything from cookies and breads to their own ice cream, pizzas, and jams and—most remarkably—Eli's own homegrown winter tomatoes and salad greens.

The three-story brick complex that houses Eli's wholesale bakery is like a food-production multiplex. The kitchens, workshops, offices, and massive storefront retail shop culminate in what I'm really here to see: half an acre of rooftop food gardens that thrust up into the New York City sunshine.

All of Eli's facilities throughout the Upper East Side look as if they grew out

of the neighborhood in bits and pieces. This particular location started out as one little part of a building, and then it took over another part, and then the whole building, and then another building, until it became a little city within the city.

It's like a large rabbit warren full of every kind of food product and food-related activity and jam-packed with people, including a noisy group of kids who have taken over the birthday-party room.

Eli guides us through the maze of floors and buildings. "Here, we're cutting up the croissants for tomorrow; here are the pastries." As he passes by, he peels off a cinnamon bun and hands it to us, then sticks his finger into a mound of bagel dough like a farmer checking soil for moisture.

Eventually, we reach the final stairway that takes us up through a dark passage and out a rooftop door. When we surface, my eyes need a moment to adjust to the sunlight and to the extraordinary sight that surrounds us. Huge, commercial-size production greenhouses cap the rooftops, each glass or plastic structure filled with raised beds planted in greens and herbs and tomatoes. Fig trees in planters are lined up sporadically along the edge of one rooftop. Brick apartment buildings tower overhead, and, across the canyon that is 91st Street, I can see people working in another set of Zabar greenhouses. An industrial compost grinder stands at the ready, waiting for the loads of bakery and deli waste to be converted back to fertility and spread on the beds.

Inside the greenhouses, trellises and irrigation systems crisscross raised beds of rich soil. Lighting and ventilation systems filter the New York atmosphere into garden oases that smell distinctively like baking bread. As I look out through the glass and plastic walls, the city is blurred and unreal, and reality becomes the bright, tender green of new tomato transplants.

"This crop—these are all heirloom varieties—was seeded maybe in the middle of July," Eli is explaining, "and will go right into the spring." I immediately picture the greenhouse dusted with January snow, the tomatoes riding out the winter without the cashmere overcoats, pashmina scarves, and leather boots that normally protect the residents of this neighborhood. "And they'll climb up over these wires," Eli continues, pointing out the support infrastructure for the vines. "By the time we take them down, the vines will have stretched maybe 60 feet and look like spaghetti all over the damn place."

The next greenhouse over is full of salad greens, herbs, and radishes. Eli bends down to pluck a radish from the soil and offers it to me to sample, just as if he were grabbing a croissant off one of the cooling racks downstairs.

Aaron and I are in awe of the scale of this rooftop greenhouse operation. My mind races at the prospect of farms on the tops of every building in New York. I consider how much food could be produced, how many people could be employed, how it could improve the diets of local residents, what impact it would have on the urban environment.

I'm brought back to the present by the sound of a familiar refrain. "It's been a terrible, terrible summer around here," Eli is saying. "The sun just came out. We've had no sun for four days—nothing but rain." So, I think to myself, the baker has learned to complain about the weather, just like a farmer.

I ask Eli about the engineering of these rooftop greenhouses, how he dealt with issues of weight and water and drainage. "When I built the original greenhouse, my goal was to get tomatoes in the winter," he replies, and tells us how he decided to try to harness the heat of his pastry ovens. "I ran the exhaust pipes of these ovens that are going all the time throughout the buildings beneath us here up into the greenhouse.

"I had all kinds of theories," he continues. "For instance, theory one was that in order to have a really good-tasting tomato, you had to grow it in soil. And so I brought in organic soil that I bought from a guy we were buying vegetables from upstate. And then of course we had weight issues, so I had to bring in steel and reinforce this thing. I had beautiful leeks, but I didn't grow a single tomato that first year out of this greenhouse. I put lights in, and I brought in experts.

"I brought in twenty different people. Everybody had a different opinion," Eli concludes with that blend of pride, frustration, and hindsight that every farmer masters.

"I don't use lights anymore," he continues. "I found that I couldn't really measure any difference between growing with these 500-watt sodium lights and spending $18,000 on electricity. And during the period that we weren't getting tomatoes—which was January and February—we didn't get them with lights, either."

On the side beds, which aren't tall enough for tomatoes, Eli planted mizuna and baby arugula. He found that the lettuces really did well, but the passive heat

was creating very irregular temperatures in the greenhouse. Now, that is a baker's complaint. "We kind of stabilized between fifty and seventy degrees," Eli continues, "but tomatoes didn't like fifty to seventy; they liked sixty-five to seventy-five. But all the greens loved it. So, after one or two unsuccessful years with tomatoes, I went to greens in this greenhouse."

I ask Eli whether the greens that come out of a greenhouse continuously infused with bakery exhaust contain any flavor of croissant or muffin or bagel, a question I can imagine Earl Ransom approving of. Eli ignores me and goes on to talk about some of the disease problems they've had, including late blight and various funguses.

As we wander the maze of rooftop paths, I try to get Eli to talk about what he was thinking when he built this rooftop farm.

"I had opened a little restaurant that was on the other side of the street," he replies. "My original idea was that we were going to do something very special and grow fresh food for it all year-round."

I ask him whether he needed some kind of special permit. "It's an ordeal," he replies, "because there's nothing in the zoning code in New York City that permits this. I don't know what we got it under, but I do know that it was something other than greenhouses. There's nothing called 'greenhouse' in Manhattan. This is the gold coast in New York. The apartments go for millions of dollars here. This was an anomaly."

By now, we are standing alongside a row of mature Adriatic fig trees. Eli launches into a vivid description of their flavor, and I might as well be standing with a peasant farmer in Sardinia on the top of a rocky hillside overlooking an ancient gnarled orchard.

We make our way back down the maze of stairs and doors, which eventually leads to one of Eli's retail stores. I head for the produce section and watch as smartly dressed men and women daintily use a set of plastic tongs to fill bags with salad greens and herbs. The sign says "Eli's Own Home Grown." But "homegrown" is written on a lot of things these days, and I doubt that this urban crowd could imagine that the greens they're collecting are so local that the roots are still growing three stories above their heads.

♣

AARON AND I GRAB SOMETHING TO EAT AND HEAD BACK TO THE CAR. We are in a hurry now; the hurricane that everyone has been talking about the last couple days is due to hit today, and we need to get to my dad's place a few hours south of here, in Delaware. The winds have already started to kick up, and swirls of dust and paper are blowing around the streets of Manhattan. We wind our way slowly out of the city and through the Lincoln Tunnel to the New Jersey Turnpike. The winds are growing stronger, and the farther south we go, the less traffic there is on the roads. It's midday on a weekday, so I start to figure that everyone else must know something we don't.

About an hour from our destination, the temperature light on the dashboard comes on, accompanied by a loud beeping. I pull off at the next exit. The radiator is losing fluid. We scrounge several plastic bottles, fill them with water, and decide to keep going. Every 10 miles, the warning light comes on, and we have to stop and fill the reservoir. At this pace, the storm has easily overtaken us, and the van is being blown from one empty lane to another as we hold on for the ride. Just as we make it to my dad's place and get out of the car, a huge, old oak tree splits in half across the street.

This is my first visit to my father's new home, six stories up in an apartment building near downtown Wilmington. Moving from a house with a big garden was difficult for an 81-year-old after spending his childhood on farms in southern Delaware and a lifetime growing food for family and friends in his own garden.

My dad moved away from Sussex County to Wilmington when he was 15, after Franklin D. Roosevelt personally asked my grandfather to join the Works Progress Administration. My grandfather retained ownership of a collection of small farms scattered throughout the county—most of them leased to working farmers—and a general store that had been in my family since the late 1800s.

When I was a child growing up in Wilmington, my grandfather would take me downstate in the summer to visit our family farms and check up on the store. Although I knew little about the family history behind these trips, I have intense, lifelong memories of the rural characters my grandfather introduced me to and the food we shared on these ambling adventures.

My father had never really elaborated on our past, or perhaps I wasn't listening when he did. But today I'm listening. As we head downstate, he begins to unfold the tale of my great-grandfather Abel Ableman—who, in the 1870s, driven by persecution and lack of opportunity in his native Russia, immigrated to America. My dad is relishing the rapt attention of his son and grandson and the security of a captive audience. He explains how Abel became a peddler, traveling with a horse and wagon from Philadelphia, by ship to Smyrna Landing, in Delaware, then through Kent and Sussex counties, selling eyeglasses. Apparently, he was treated kindly in Sussex County, so he brought his wife, Fannie, to Delaware and settled at Shaft-Ox Corner, a small rural crossroads area southwest of Millsboro.

In 1890 he bought a property in Millsboro that had been an old inn with stables. Abel opened an adjoining store that he named simply Ableman's Store that he stocked with work clothing and general farm merchandise. The property became the Ableman homestead and remained in my family until the 1980s.

Jews in Russia were not allowed to own land, my father reminds us, and Abel cherished his newfound freedom to take title as one of the greatest treasures of his adopted America. As money accumulated from his retail business, he began buying small parcels of land and immersed himself in agriculture, at the time one of the most important industries in Delaware's Kent and Sussex counties.

As his landholdings accumulated, Abel recognized the need to promote their agricultural use. Ableman's Store started selling furniture, farm implements and tools, and—of great significance—mules. In lower Delaware, the mule was the choice for farm power during the first three decades of the twentieth century, and the old livery stables adjoining the Ableman home on State Street became the local source for these sturdy animals. After the end of World War I, in 1918, Abel's son— my grandfather, Ben—went on train trips to Saint Louis to bid on railcar loads of mules no longer needed by the U.S. Army. Back in Delaware, they were sold to Sussex and Kent farmers, along with plows, disks, harrows, and the other equipment needed to prepare land for planting, cultivating, and harvest.

My father had heard about my great-grandfather's master plan from more than a few Sussex County residents who had become successful farmers by the middle of the century. The ritual they described seemed to be pretty consistent. A young couple preparing to marry would come to town to visit the Ableman Store, along with their parents. Together with profuse business, personal, and moral advice—including what and when to plant and how to market the harvest—Abel would stake out the couple with a small tract of land, their wedding and work clothing, furniture for the home to be built on their new farm, the implements and materials necessary to till the land, and a pair of mules.

Money was in short supply in the 1920s and '30s, when America experienced its worst depression. Abel knew that the typical young couple about to "go to farming" in Sussex County had no funds to pay for either the land or the personal items and equipment. The solution was a roll of brown wrapping paper at the end of the store counter. No money passed between buyer and seller. Instead, a sheet of this paper was torn off the roll, and the prices of the land and items purchased were listed on it with the total. The sheet of brown paper was skewered on the sharp spindle back in the store office. At the end of each fall harvest, the new young farmer would come to town to make a payment. The scrap of brown wrapping paper would be retrieved from the spindle and the amount paid deducted to reach a new balance due.

Apparently, on many occasions Abel Ableman would insist on a lower payment, encouraging the young farmer to retain enough funds to be "safed up" for the winter and to provide for the spring planting. No interest was ever charged, and, despite the oppressive economy and the fact that the practice violated every principle of business or banking, there's no evidence that any of these accounts ultimately went unpaid. By the time of my great-grandfather's death, the "active" spindle was empty and the "paid in full" spindle was full.

When he married, my grandfather followed in Abel's footsteps and bought a homestead and store in nearby Georgetown, Delaware. Benjamin and Bertha Ableman continued to buy Sussex farmland, and, like Abel, they became well-known personalities among their rural neighbors. One of my grandmother's Guernsey cows apparently became famous for the high butterfat content of its milk. Physicians throughout the county prescribed this cow's milk for underweight babies. The cow died on September 28, 1922—the same day my father was born.

"I'm not sure which caused them more grief—the death of the cow or my arrival," my dad concludes. He's beaming by now, pleased with his story, excited to visit his old haunts, and thrilled to have his son and his grandson interested enough to go along and take notes and photographs.

As we get closer to Sussex County, my dad points out various places and reminisces about who lived there and what they did. He talks proudly about the warm and friendly atmosphere of the people in this region, and I can see as I never have before how this region has informed who he is, how, through many life changes, he has held on to his "downstate" nature. I remember walking with my dad from his office in the city of Wilmington to our home as a boy. I was amazed to observe him greet every single person we passed, many of them by name, and stop to talk and find out how they were doing. My father left rural Sussex County when he was a young man, but the spirit of the county never left him.

In a run-down neighborhood in Georgetown, Delaware, we stop outside the house where my dad was born and raised. The neighborhood is now home mainly to Hispanic families who work in the poultry houses and grain facilities that now dominate Sussex County agriculture. A group of young men hangs out on the corner across the street from us. I start to explain in Spanish why we are taking pictures outside this old, run-down house. I want to introduce them to my father, tell them that he was born in this house, that our family has history in this town, that my great-grandparents and my grandparents had farms here, that we were part of this landscape. I imagine that if anyone could relate, it would be people from Mexico, where family and tradition and belonging to a place are still valued. But their polite indifference tells me I could have been talking about the history of the moon.

My father directs us next to the Sussex County airport, where runways cover what were once our family's fields. As we park along the stark runways and look across the low, shrubby fields beyond, my dad talks about how he used to ride his pony through the pecan grove here, harvesting and eating pecans from the saddle.

I volunteer my own memories of cantaloupes. My grandfather and his buddy, Dewey Shehan, would cut their way through an entire bushel basket, sampling each one with a running commentary as if there was nothing else in the world to do. Aaron listens intently, quietly in the background as he has done all day, while my dad and I mine the memory of a place my son has never seen before.

We search for a parking space, get out of the car, and walk up to one of the runways. There is a fleet of private turboprop planes lined up with the names of NASCAR racing teams emblazoned on the sides. A family stands scanning the sky, and I ask them whether they can imagine that this airport was once a farm. The father gives me a strange look and then tells me that they are waiting for their son to arrive. "He's on one of the NASCAR race teams." I take some photographs of the runway and the planes as an airport employee walks by. He smiles and looks at me as if I'm some sort of car-racing paparazzo waiting to catch a shot of a famous driver. He leans over, points to one of the planes, and rattles off the name of the race-car celebrity who owns it, like he's sharing an inside scoop.

I want to find someone to tell that this was my grandfather's farm, that my people lived here, raised their families here, nurtured the land where that runway is, milked cows and kept chickens and raised vegetables.

We head toward Millsboro along back roads I traveled often with my grandfather but can barely recognize. I realize I've been re-creating a familiar rhythm with Aaron on this trip, visiting with farmers, loading up on their food, swapping stories, and lingering over meals, as I watched my grandfather do. As a young man, those were important trips for me, intimate forays into a rural way of life that was beginning to unravel. At the time, I liked to entertain my family with imitations of the Sussex County characters my grandfather knew, unaware of who they really were and the knowledge they possessed. My generation was part of a very rapid progression away from rural life and from the values that were so much a part of that life. Like young people across the country, I saw the Dewey Shehans of the world as backward, their accents, clothing, and livelihoods different from our own and from where the world was going. But, at the same time, those journeys steeped into my consciousness, provided the context for the foods I loved; I got to know the people who grew the peaches and tomatoes and corn, to meet their families and walk their land. These were my family's people, and their history and culture got passed on to me on these trips, represented in my memory by the intense smells and flavors of the summer harvest. Now, forty years later, I'm desperate to find a little field somewhere, the kind of farms and orchards I remember from that time, some little break from the corn and soybean monocultures, the pavement and warehouses that blanket the land. Caught up in memories, I'm looking for something tangible to transport me to that time, a peach or a melon to taste and savor—how can it be summer here without them? But I can find nothing in this landscape to pull the past into the present.

I have always marveled that, 3,000 miles from this past, I still find myself specializing in familiar crops, growing the summer foods of my childhood for my own family table. I think I must have stubbornly willed peaches to grow in coastal Southern California in part to carry forward a familiar crop. All immigrants who farm or garden carry the seeds and plants and foods from their homeland to the places where they move. I did it again on our new place in British Columbia, when I brought my favorite varieties of asparagus and Italian artichokes, fig cuttings, and bare-root strawberries north. As a farmer, it gives me comfort to bring my old friends with me; I know these plants and feel some security in working with them. Now, I begin to wonder whether the rest of my work—in particular, the effort to get young people involved with the agricultural arts—is somehow rooted here in Delaware.

The sun has gone down when we reach Millsboro, and I get out of the car at the entrance to town to photograph the new Dairy Queen. The driveway and land-scaping leading up to it are dotted with creepy, 5-foot-tall plastic ice-cream cones illuminated from within. I walk down the sidewalk into town. The dirt streets I remember as a kid are paved now. It's nighttime, yet the stores are still open and active, and there are restaurants with people at every table.

I'm having trouble finding the site of Ableman's Store, where my grandfather used to take me every fall to get "fixed up" with jeans and shoes and shirts for school. On the street in front of an antique shop, a large plaque tells a short history of the Ableman family in Millsboro. We walk into the shop, and I ask the young attendant whether he has any items that relate to our history. Although our name and story are plastered in big letters outside, he doesn't know anything about the Ablemans.

We head on to Dover, to the Delaware Agricultural Museum. When my grandfather died in 1976, my father donated fixtures from Ableman's Store to the museum, and we assume they'll still be on display. The museum is located across from the huge stadium where the NASCAR races are taking place, and we arrive in the middle of a race day. The museum is offering paid parking space for race attendees, so we have to explain to the surprised attendant that we are not here for the car race, that we're here to visit the museum.

Inside the museum, with the roar of race cars ringing in the background, I walk around, looking at an amazing array of old combines, reconstructed and transported farm buildings, picking and packing equipment, photos, and displays.

There's even a produce-market display with old bushel baskets, price-per-pound signs, and fake strawberries and tomatoes and peaches.

I call my dad over when I finally spot the old counter from the store. I recognize the smell, and remember standing beneath this counter as my grandfather, soggy cigar hanging from his mouth, packed up the blue jeans and the boots that I selected using brown paper off of a giant spool. I feel sad here, knowing that a piece of my family and so many other families, a piece of our culture, lies dormant on display in a museum.

I ask the director why this stuff isn't being used, why the fields next to the museum aren't being farmed the old way with the old equipment and the old varieties. She tells me they start up the tractors once a year. "A tractor isn't a tractor unless it runs," she says. I add that a tractor isn't a tractor unless it's actually working for a living.

I had always assumed I was called to farming at least in part by my memories of Sussex County and by the inexplicable urge of many young people, including myself, to dismiss the skills and life choices of their parents in favor of the greater mystique of their grandparents. I was attracted to farming as a rebel, as someone who wanted to be unconventional, experimental. It was only in time that I widened the circle from my own independent dreams into a sense of community and exchange that has become a conviction, even an urgent one about the power of food and farming as a cultural force. It was only in time that it became more important for me to be a part of rather than against something. Now, coming back to my family home, I realize the encounters with my grandfather's friends, the taste of corn and tomatoes, maybe even an echo of my great-grandfather's work, had been there as quiet, tantalizing voices, an inheritance I didn't know I had received.

My great-grandfather understood firsthand that a little land and a good start could make all the difference. He must have seen agriculture, much as I do now, as a life-affirming opportunity, best done on a personal and community-oriented scale—a way to have a rich life, rather than an affluent one. It hits me that I have ended up where he started when it comes to farming, and the revelation floods me with a strange sense of comfort and homecoming even as I pick through the vanishing fragments of his life and times. I have tried to trust in the permanence of land and soil, always understanding that all farmers are just temporary tenants and caretakers of a larger natural force. But now, as I picture the chain of lives that my great-grandfather affected, I see that, unbeknownst to me, I was a link in that chain as well. Thousands of miles away, with no knowledge of my past, I have continued his work, using a little bit of knowledge and experience to offer a model and a start to the next generation.

☙

Satur Farm Mesclun Salad with Citrus Vinaigrette

Who would know better than Paulette Satur and her husband, chef Eberhard Mueller, how best to handle their own farm-grown greens? Three thousand pounds a week of their salad find their way into the kitchens of some of New York City's finest restaurants.

Needless to say, even the best vinaigrette cannot transform greens that are not fresh and alive. If you can't grow your own, head down to the farmers' market, and buy only those greens you can still see moving.

For a more elaborate salad, try serving it with pickled beets and a few fresh grapefruit segments.

2½ tablespoons fresh grapefruit juice

1½ tablespoons fresh lemon juice

½ teaspoon sugar

Sea salt to taste

1½ tablespoons extra-virgin olive oil

1½ tablespoons grapeseed or sunflower oil

1½ pounds mesclun, mâche, or butterhead lettuce

Freshly cracked white pepper to taste

Combine the grapefruit juice, lemon juice, sugar, and a pinch of salt in a small bowl and stir to dissolve. Slowly whisk in the olive and grapeseed oils to make an emulsified vinaigrette. Taste the vinaigrette with a mesclun leaf; you may want to add a little more oil or an extra drop or two of lemon juice. Put the mesclun in a large bowl and season with salt and white pepper. Gently toss with just enough vinaigrette to lightly coat the greens. Transfer the salad to a serving platter or individual plates and serve immediately.

Bruschetta with Tomato, Fresh Mozzarella, and Basil

While the term "vine-ripe heirloom tomato" now seems to be a part of everyone's vocabulary, most tomatoes don't ripen in winter in "farms" perched on the top floors of upper-east-side New York City buildings. Eli's "homegrowns" are best eaten with as little fuss as possible. In this very simple recipe, they sit on top of grilled bread with a little mozzarella and basil, left, as they should, to speak for themselves.

SERVES 10

1½ pounds ripe tomatoes, cut into ¼-inch-thick slices

Kosher salt to taste

Freshly cracked black pepper to taste

One 1-pound loaf rustic country bread or crusty baguette, cut into ½-inch-thick slices
     (cut baguettes on the diagonal)

Olive oil for brushing (about ½ cup)

1 or 2 cloves garlic

½ pound fresh mozzarella cheese, thinly sliced

Extra-virgin olive oil and balsamic vinegar for drizzling

Leaves of 2 sprigs fresh basil

Prepare a fire in a charcoal grill or preheat a gas grill.

Season the tomatoes with salt and pepper and set aside while you grill the bread (the tomatoes benefit from being seasoned in advance).

Brush both sides of the bread slices with olive oil. Place on the grill rack over medium heat and grill until the first side is darkly grill-marked, then turn and toast the second side until grill-marked.

Rub one side of the grilled bread slices generously with the garlic clove(s) and top with a layer of mozzarella and a sprinkle of salt. Top each with a layer of tomato slices. Drizzle with the extra-virgin olive oil and a few drops of the vinegar. Garnish with 1 or 2 basil leaves and serve.

Nana's Sussex County Chicken and Dumplings

SERVES 6

When I was a child, meals at my grandparents' home were always a social and cultural experience. My granddad would stand at the head of the table like the director, making sure that no one's plate stayed empty for long. Nana spent the whole meal shuttling between the kitchen and the table, bringing out an unending parade of dishes. Although some of her creations had their roots in Russia, this one is Sussex County all the way. The dumplings in Nana's dish would have traditionally been referred to as "slippery," so much so that you'd often have to chase them around the plate.

This is a classic recipe with a few changes from my grandmother's original. Nana used shortening in her dumplings—no major sin, but we've used butter. These dumplings are made with herbs, and the broth has leeks, baby turnips, and, of course, carrots added in. This is good, old-fashioned comfort food, especially for those of us who grew up having it served to us by our grandparents around a big table, with the whole family present.

One 3- to 4-pound organic chicken, cut into 8 pieces
Kosher salt to taste

DUMPLINGS
1½ cups all-purpose flour
2 teaspoons baking powder
¾ teaspoon kosher salt
1½ tablespoons finely chopped fresh flat-leaf parsley
½ teaspoon finely chopped fresh thyme
Freshly cracked black pepper to taste
1 egg, well beaten
2 tablespoons unsalted butter, melted
⅓ cup milk

4 quarts chicken stock, preferably homemade
Kosher salt to taste
1 large leek
2 large carrots, peeled, halved lengthwise, and cut into ½ -inch-thick slices
18 baby turnips, halved lengthwise
3 tablespoons chopped fresh flat-leaf parsley

Using a large knife, cut off the chicken wing tips and the nubs at the base of the drumsticks. Trim any excess fat from the chicken pieces and remove the skin, if you like. Season the chicken pieces on both sides with a generous amount of salt and let stand at room temperature for about 30 minutes.

MEANWHILE, MAKE THE DUMPLING DOUGH: Combine the flour, baking powder, salt, parsley, thyme, and several twists of pepper in a bowl. In another bowl, whisk together the egg, melted butter, and milk, then stir it into the flour mixture to make a stiff dough. (If the dough becomes too difficult to stir, use your hands to gently knead the dough just until it comes together.) Set aside.

In a large Dutch oven, bring the chicken stock to a boil and season it with salt (about 2 teaspoons). Add the chicken pieces, return the stock to a boil, then reduce the heat to medium-low and gently simmer for 10 minutes.

To prepare the leek, cut off the roots, trim the tough, dark green tops, and peel off an outer layer or two. Halve the leek lengthwise and then cut crosswise into 1-inch pieces. Wash the leek in a large basin of cold water, agitating to remove all of the dirt. When the dirt has settled, scoop the leek out of the water with a strainer. (It's not necessary for the leek to drain thoroughly.)

Add the leek, carrots, and turnips and continue to simmer for 10 more minutes. Using a table-spoon, drop spoonfuls of the dumpling dough on top of the simmering broth. Cover, reduce the heat to low, and cook for 20 minutes without removing the lid. Taste the broth and adjust the seasoning with salt, if necessary. Carefully remove the chicken breast halves from the pot, cut the meat off of the bone, and then cut each breast half crosswise into thirds. Divide the chicken, vegetables, dumplings, and broth among warm individual bowls, sprinkle with the parsley, and serve immediately, passing the peppermill at the table.

☾

FOOD WITH A FACE

"THIS ISN'T WHAT WE EXPECTED," THE WOMAN IS TELLING ME, AS IF I am responsible for fulfilling all her expectations. "When we bought our home next to your farm, the field next to us was strawberries, not a pasture with chickens." Her exasperation cuts through the crackle of the cell phone and the roar of the torrential rainstorm that is pelting our van on the road to Virginia.

My continued role as executive director for Fairview Gardens requires that I negotiate with suburban neighbors who can't seem to accept that they moved in next to a farm. I remind her that farm fields change constantly and that we keep the animals moving, that it's bad for the land and the chickens to keep them in the same location all the time, that we try to be good neighbors, but that it's difficult to run a farm based on the changing personal needs of each of the hundreds of people who live on the edges of the land.

When she says she "puts up with the tractor" and "tolerates the work in the fields" and that she's going to organize the neighborhood against us, I start to lose my patience. I suggest that she go back and research the newspaper clippings from 1991, when a few of the farm's neighbors challenged us over roosters, touching off the grassroots campaign that ultimately secured the farm under a conservation easement through our nonprofit educational organization.

It seems that no matter how much education we do, there will always be phone calls like this and people who see fields of life-giving food as a nuisance. I imagine making a movie like *It's a Wonderful Life* in which all the farms and the food they grow simply disappear, leaving a bewildered and hungry world to wonder why it is that the supermarkets are empty. It's hard for me to imagine that my unhappy caller would prefer that her home backed up to a stucco wall rather than the ever-changing, green tapestry of a small farm. In fact, she keeps interspersing her complaints with the reassurance that she "really loves the farm" as the phone drops out of cell range and I turn my focus back to the road.

The spectacular misty mountains of Virginia loom like an oversize Hollywood backdrop left behind from some Civil War documentary. We exit the main highway and enter a quiet, rural backcountry, heading for Joel and Theresa Salatin's Polyface Farm. The rivers are swollen and muddy from the rains and the recent hurricane. Bridges are washed out, and low-lying fields turned into lakes.

Polyface Farm was not spared. One of the first things we see when we pull up is a hoop house for the chickens turned on its side, twisted and bent. The creek that runs through the place is roaring, and the fields are soggy. Joel pulls up on his tractor as we arrive. He is wearing a goofy, misshapen hat and a contagious grin. He greets us with a cheerful report on the weather and its devastation.

The 500-acre farm stretches up and over Little North Mountain. Although forest dominates the majority of the land, 100 acres is devoted almost exclusively to a

continuous circular migration of pigs, cows, chickens, and turkeys moving through the most brilliant green pastures I have ever seen.

The Salatins' pastures are diverse, with a range of red and white clovers, fescue, orchard grass, timothy, bluegrass, plantain, chicory, and wild carrot. Joel tells me that, forty years ago, there was so much bare ground you could have walked the whole farm and rarely encountered any vegetation. Now, the lush, green pastures are cropped and used efficiently, the plants are in a constant state of being pruned, and old growth is removed and new growth fertilized and stimulated. The systematic movement of diverse species of grazing animals places different kinds of manure evenly over the whole pasture. Except for a few small, lower paddocks near the house that suffered from the recent flooding and a resulting inability to move the animals on time, none of the land comes close to resembling that trampled, eaten-to-the-ground look so common in animal operations. I am amazed, considering the numbers of animals, that there are almost no flies.

Observing the Salatins' farm is like attending a dance-theatre performance. Joel, his wife Theresa, son Daniel, and daughter Rachel direct and choreograph the animals, continuously repositioning them to feed themselves and regenerate their own pastures. Every day, on land pioneered and prepared by diligent hogs, the cows, chickens, and turkeys are rotated across different pastures, each performing their unique service on the land—pooping, scratching, eating insects, and mowing in symbiotic sequence. The only things that stand still around here are the buildings.

A few days earlier, my dad, Aaron, and I had talked our way into one of the huge chicken factories that dot the landscape of Delaware's Sussex County. There, sealed inside a huge metal Quonset hut with no windows, no light, no fresh air, and no green grass or pasture to roam on, were twenty thousand day-old chicks, lethargic clusters of yellow fuzz on a bed of manure and wood shavings. When the doors were opened for our visit, the birds panicked, huddling close to the security of automatic watering devices and feeders. The ninety-degree temperatures and smell of ammonia and fecal dust made it hard to breathe.

In this system of farming, the farmer works in service of a corporate machine that owns and dictates every aspect of the "value chain," from the eggs that hatch the baby chicks to the stores that sell the processed meat. I doubt that anyone eating the "young fresh chickens" advertised on the company's colorful billboards can imagine the gap between the farm-fresh pictures and reality. It seems incredible that food for a civilized society is actually produced in this way, when, just a few hours south, a humane and ingenious model is thriving.

"Daniel runs the place—I just run around," Joel is saying, and he is only partially joking. Raised on this land and involved in the day-to-day operations from a very young age, Daniel has an enthusiasm for farming unusual for someone who has come of age in the new millennium. He is beaming as he shows us his experimental rabbit house, a multitiered dwelling he helped design and implement to model intensive protein production where space is limited. In the soft, dappled light, rabbit cages hang above a deep bed of wood chips where about thirty-six laying hens scratch away as living composters for the rabbit droppings. Approximately 1,300 pounds of rabbit meat and 18,000 eggs are produced each year in a space the size of a two-car garage. As Daniel explains the system, Joel kicks the surface off the top of the litter, revealing a bed of rich, black compost underneath.

I'm impressed with the innovation, even more so by the comfortable dynamic between Daniel and Joel. It's encouraging to see a young man expressing pride and commitment in an occupation just beginning to recover from a bad rap. I also feel a pang of envy. Although I have never pushed Aaron toward farming, I secretly hoped that he, too, might have the inclination to take over, but, these days, his interests run more to writing and painting than to farming. Aaron, Joel, and I hop onto the Yamaha Big Bear motorized three-wheeler Joel calls his "Japanese pony" and race off to feed the turkeys.

The next morning, Aaron and I watch as Daniel and Joel move an enormous chevron of chicken pens 12 feet down the pasture. One by one, in a fluid rhythm, the two men shift fifty-five 10-by-12-foot pens, each containing about seventy broiler chickens. Each of the pens is staggered to allow access and to ensure that the entire 15-acre field gets evenly grazed and fertilized. More than three thousand chickens are moved in less than an hour in this simple but elegant daily routine that provides the birds with clean, fresh pasture each and every day.

This system joins the ranks of unusual agricultural innovations I've witnessed throughout the world—the *chaquitaclla* foot plow high in the Peruvian Andes, the cabling system used only in Switzerland's steep Emmental Valley, or the radiating circular farm fields surrounding the homes in the mountains of Burundi. From a distance, it reminds me of the old photographs I've seen of forty teams of horses combining a field of grain in perfect formation. When I crouch down to get a closer look at the birds, I can hear a chorus of contented chirps emanating from the cages. Chicken is one of many languages farmers can learn to understand but not speak.

"Most guys in farming like to go home and talk about how much ground they tore up each day," Joel tells us. "I come home and tell my wife I made thousands of chickens happy."

After a breakfast of scrambled eggs, Italian sausage, and whole-grain biscuits, Joel, Theresa, Rachel, and Joel's mom, Lucille, plus a couple friends, put on rubber aprons, sharpen knives, and process one hundred fifty chickens and six turkeys through their home-built butchering facility while carrying on conversations and running an impromptu butchering class for eight members of a local Mennonite family. Joel patiently demonstrates knife and finger placement, how to extract the liver and intestines, how to prevent the meat from bruising, proper scalding temperatures for easy feather removal, and on and on. With a well-rehearsed efficiency, crate after crate of chickens are transformed from live birds to ready-to-eat carcasses. The stainless-steel processing equipment is housed under a sheet metal roof in a wooden structure open on all sides. The simple, modest setup demonstrates that small farms like the Salatins' could, if allowed to, take control of their own butchering. The steps from killing to bagging are carried out so smoothly and calmly that it shakes up all of my preconceptions about slaughter and meat processing.

Later, as we're eating dinner, I ask about permit issues.

"They tried to close us down," Joel tells us. "They said a facility that is open to the air is inherently unsanitary, adulterated."

"Isn't that inherently more sanitary?" I suggest, picturing the sealed environments I've seen in most slaughterhouses.

"That's what I said," Joel says.

"So you won that, right?" I ask.

"Yeah, we won that, but we've been politically savvy—we get our legislators involved. For Democrats, we represent the small guy, doing ecological farming that's humane and decentralized. For the Republicans, we're capitalism, small business, Chamber of Commerce stuff. So we have found tremendous support from both of them."

"Do you get inspected?" I ask.

"Well, supposedly, all the law says is that the processing has to be sanitary and unadulterated. But that could change every morning, depending on who happens to occupy the cubicle. We've had the full blessing of the head inspector in the state for several years. We were doing this for eight years before anybody came out to visit. This guy came out, and, after he watched us work, he sat with us in the living room and said, 'Boy, you make me want to have stayed on my family farm and start over again.' So, we operated until he retired.

"Then a new guy came into the office and had to establish his authority. So, the first thing they did was to confiscate all our beef at the slaughterhouse. The guy showed up on the front doorstep and accused us of selling uninspected beef. 'We have to do an investigation,' he said. 'How long will the investigation take?' I ask. 'It could take months,' he says. 'Well, what will happen to the meat?' I ask next. 'We have to throw it away,' he says.

"They had federal marshals to keep anyone from touching it. It was hell. In those days, that meat was 40 or 50 percent of our entire year's income. We immediately contacted our attorney and our legislators. The inspector basically parked out

front for a week. He'd sit in his car on the phone to Richmond, and he'd come back in and say, 'Well, Richmond says . . .' And then we'd call our delegates and get some advice. 'Okay,' he'd say, and then he'd go back out to the car. This went on for five days."

"And our butcher," Theresa says, "bless his heart, he told the inspectors and the marshals, 'In two weeks, I'm cutting that beef. I'm not going to throw it out.' He said, 'I'm going to jail—that meat is not going to be thrown away.'"

"When it finally came up to Friday," Joel concludes, "the inspector came in and said, 'We've decided that we're going to assume that this never happened.'"

"I was livid," Theresa says. "I said, 'You might pretend this never happened, but we're not going to forget this, and you're not going to forget it, either.'" I'm not surprised to hear their story, since it mirrors my own experience and those of many other farmers I know. You'd think a society losing its farmers and its farmland at a staggering rate would do anything to support those who have stayed with it. But the laws and the bureaucrats who enforce them—even the ones involved with organic agriculture—are programmed solely to enable the large-scale corporate agricultural model. Smaller, decentralized, local farming is just not in the rule books. At the farm in California, each time we were challenged, we tried to respond with education, drawing the growing population that surrounded us into an experience of small farms and local food. We held countless events and workshops and transformed most of our neighbors, based on what they were able to see and taste for themselves, into allies.

Joel calls himself a Christian Libertarian capitalist environmentalist and then describes an organization he's helped start called the Virginia Independent Consumers and Farmers Association. "Our goal," he says, "is to have an exemption from government regulation for on-farm sales, for anything that we sell directly to individuals. In other words, if you want to come around, look around, smell around, and do business with me, it's none of the government's business. That even includes scales. If you're happy that it's a pound and you think I'm trustworthy, or if it's a pack or a poke or a bushel or whatever it is, we ought to be able to do business. Because what's happening now is that the infrastructure requirements make it almost impossible for an embryonic entrepreneur to access the market. An oak tree is not planted as a 20-foot sapling. It's planted as an acorn. It is a smaller, viable life-form of that tree. You have to be able to plant a business as an acorn, not a 20-foot sapling. When these regulations require $100,000 worth of cheese-making equipment in order to milk three goats and sell your first pound of artisan cheese, it stifles someone who is just starting out. When your first item has to be locked up in a $100,000 infrastructure—"

"Nobody's going to do it," I say.

"There's no cash flow," Joel continues. "That's why this on-farm exemption is so important, because it is necessary to preserve the embryonic industry."

"Not just that," I add. "It sustains the critical relationship between the farm and the community. Small farms cannot maintain those relationships if the government insists on getting in the middle. For the government to say that I can't make a decision for myself, to tell me whether or not it's okay for me to eat Joel Salatin's chicken, that's a form of control that represents a real breakdown in our rights as individuals and in our democracy."

I tell Joel and Theresa that I have the same problem with the federal government owning the language that describes the organic movement, a movement my colleagues and I helped established without any help from anyone at the USDA.

"I think that the government had no reason to be a part of this until organic growers started making money," Joel says. "One of the biggest dilemmas facing the organic movement is how to produce something from an Eastern, holistic, living standpoint and market it to a Western, market, reductionist system."

At dinner, Theresa serves us a simple, delicious meal of meatballs, halved potatoes prepared with butter and Parmesan, cucumber slices, and pound cake and ice cream for dessert. My relationship with meat is similar to the one I have with wine: I know little about either. I don't drink wine very often, but when someone gives me a glass of something really special, I recognize it immediately and my taste buds jump to attention. Most people assume that the flavor or texture of meat is all about how it was prepared—the seasonings, sauces, or method of cooking. But I suspect that the way the animals have been raised can easily be tasted in the meat. The diversity and types of green matter they are eating, how they are killed and processed, all these things become what that animal is and what it will taste like. Eating meat here, knowing the context, provides me with a level of security and satisfaction I can never get from faceless food that comes from an unknown source. If it's true that you can taste the farmer and the land in the food, it is definitely happening here.

I admit to Joel that, five or six times a year, I think about quitting. I'm not sure whether it's the intense physical nature of the work, or not having enough help, or just the demands of balancing biology with economics. But what's amazing is that just as my brain is going down the list of all the other things I could be doing, I have some experience that pulls me back from the edge. It's usually subtle, a shift in the wind that carries the smell of a new season, a flock of geese flying over, a special cloud or a dramatic sky, or just the shimmer of a leaf. What other livelihood would allow me to kneel in the middle of a field, eating the heart out of a watermelon still warm from the sun, or to safely send my children out to graze for their lunch?

"It's not just the commodity you produce that's valuable," Joel responds. "It's the whole. And, on mornings like this, I think of people stuck in their cubicles, getting road rage, facing expressways, and I think, 'Man, I might not make much money, but, boy, what an office!'"

♣

After spending the night at a rest stop on I-64 in Indiana, Aaron and I drive a few miles to Exit 105 and stop at a Cracker Barrel restaurant for breakfast. I slip a dozen Polyface Farm eggs and a package of bacon into a plastic shopping bag and take them in with us. After I order Grandma's Special—pancakes with maple syrup, eggs, bacon, and hash browns—I hand the waitress the eggs and bacon and ask if she'd have my breakfast prepared with those ingredients. She is a little surprised but cooperative. By now, the middle-aged couple sitting at the table next to us have stopped eating and are staring at us, and Aaron has slid halfway under the table from embarrassment.

Dressed in a starched white shirt and pencil-thin black tie, the manager comes out with the carton of eggs and the bacon on a tray, returning them to us and apologizing. He tells me that cooking food supplied by customers is against company rules. I gently press him and ask him to check with his superiors. He tells me he'll check again and disappears with the tray. By now, every customer sitting within hearing distance is looking on with disbelief.

Fifteen minutes go by, and the manager returns with the waitress by his side, proudly reporting that our request has been approved by headquarters. When I ask why they changed their minds, the manager says, "They figured you're the ones eating the stuff and you've taken your own precautions."

I ask him where they normally get their eggs, wondering how they were raised and whether the chickens ever see the light of day or a blade of grass. He returns with a label that reads "Loose USDA Grade AA LARGE X 30 Dozen 256 PI595 Sell by 9/22/03" with "Use by 10/12/03" printed in bold black letters. In tiny, barely legible print at the bottom of the label is the name of the Indiana farm that produced the eggs.

Our food arrives, and I ask the waitress whether she notices any difference between these eggs and the ones they normally use. She tells me, "No question, these are yellower and look bigger, not so flat." The manager follows and tells me he's sorry for giving me such a hard time. He comments on how yellow the eggs are. I thank him for cooperating and tell him that, next time, I'll show up with a cow.

In Gibson County, Indiana, on a detour down a dirt road, we stop to photograph an old, boarded-up farmhouse. A farmer in his late sixties pulls up in his pickup.

"Got problems?" he asks by way of a greeting. I tell him we we're just taking some photographs.

"People steal from this old house," he says. "They even take the copper wiring. There must be five or six meth labs around here. We can't leave our anhydrous ammonia tanks out, or they steal the fertilizer and add it to battery acid to make the drugs." I ask him how the year has been. "Terrible," he says. "Too dry. Everywhere around has had flooding, but here, nothing." I thank him and move on.

Forty miles outside Saint Louis, we stop at a combination gas station/Burger King. When the tank is full and the gas pump switches off, we hear the speaker on the pump say, "Attention! Now that your car has been refueled, why not come in and refuel your body?"

We spend a night with my former brother-in-law in a suburb of Saint Louis. He and his wife are both new MDs. They tell me that, out of hundreds of courses they were required to take in medical school, only one was on nutrition. The housing development they live in has a written contract that specifies that no one may have a compost pile or may raise vegetables.

In need of provisions, we stop the next day at a Whole Foods store just outside Saint Louis. While I'm photographing a 30-foot case of frozen organic carrots and peas and French fries, the manager comes running up to me, flailing her arms and demanding frantically that I put away the camera. She tells me that if I continue to take photographs, she'll have to remove us from the store. Somewhat surprised both by the message and the force with which it has been delivered, I ask her why and am told it's "corporate policy," and it's her job to enforce the rules.

We continue shopping under the manager's watchful supervision. As I move through the well-stocked aisles, I notice that most of the food has been shipped in from distant ports. It's hard to find anything local. When I ask the person at the customer-service desk what percentage of the produce in the store is grown locally, in the State of Illinois, or in the United States, I am told I'll have to speak with a "team leader." He calls the produce manager.

The produce manager says he really doesn't know what percentage is from where. "We don't do things that way," he says, a little irritated with the question. He tells me that this week, the local food is Carbondale apples, and last week it was zucchini. "Two to three items at any time," he says. I ask whether the company has any policy regarding ordering from local or regional sources. He tells me that they don't, that the peppers could be from the Netherlands or Canada today and California tomorrow, beans are probably from Florida, and, for heirloom tomatoes, "it just depends." He points out the sign stating that 132 items are organic, and then proudly comments that 90 percent of the organic stock is produced by one California-based megafarm. I pick up a bunch of the white asparagus, "probably from Peru," and he starts into a semiaccurate description of how white asparagus is grown. I'm fascinated by the sweet corn. Here we are in the Midwest, where corn covers nearly every field, and this tired-looking stuff was shipped in from Florida.

The store manager follows me out when I leave and wants to know why I was photographing and asking so many questions. I tell her I am working on a book. She then asks with great concern whether I was talking to any customers. I ask her what she is so worried about. "The bigwigs from our competitors come in here and try to steal our ideas," she says. "They're in here every day." She apologizes for being rude.

When I'm away from home, if a farmers' market or produce stand is not at hand, I brave the dizzying displays of stores like this, knowing I can find something free of poison that hasn't had its genetic makeup bioengineered. But the culture of any supermarket is inherently about central control and distribution dependent on large-scale production. I find myself reflecting on how often we tend to think that the best we can do is refine the status quo.

Figuring out how to feed people sustainably is a messy process of unraveling old ideas and experimenting with new ones. To conclude that, once chemicals are replaced with steer manure, the job is done misses the opportunity to explore a wider range of social, ecological, personal, and political possibilities tied to our food system and the way we eat.

A more sustainable food system is inevitably decentralized. It should take advantage of local knowledge and solve local problems, and it must be accessible, humane, ecologically responsible, and biologically and culturally diverse. That means rethinking how our society *participates* in the food system, where food is produced and by whom, and what scale it is grown on. We've got to question the idea that a tiny handful of folks can sustainably feed the vast majority. And we've got to question whether a problem that is essentially social and ecological can be solved by science and technology.

Many of us who have been pursuing sustainable farming since before there was a Whole Foods or a National Organic Standards Board are realizing that the most important aspects of a healthy food system are relationships—interpersonal, biological, and ecological. Food shouldn't be just another fuel, grown out of sight by anonymous people, prepared and consumed as quickly as possible as if it were an inconvenience. Growing and eating food are sacred acts; we need to reclaim them from the scientists and the industrialists, the bureaucrats and the organicrats.

As I continue to solve the world's problems from behind the wheel of a Volkswagen van, we cross the river from Missouri into Kansas on Highway 70 and spot the sign for the Agricultural Hall of Fame. Aaron says that he thinks the best way to get America back into agriculture is to turn it into a spectator sport.

Imagine thousands of people showing up at the Rose Bowl or Yankee Stadium to watch pruning or cultivating or a lettuce-harvesting contest. There would be cheerleaders chanting, "Cultivate! Cultivate! Our team is really great!" Hawkers would sell carrots and fava beans and watermelon slices to a transfixed crowd.

"There's a hoeing injury on the field," the announcer would report, and, when the farmer finally stood up and limped off the field, the crowd would applaud.

They'd plow up Soldier Field in Chicago and Dodger Stadium and replace instant replays with instant preplays so folks at home or sitting in the bleachers wouldn't have to wait months for crops to grow and be harvested.

Families would gather around their TVs to watch preseason interviews with the pros, who would discuss what varieties they are selecting for the big season and how they plan to improve the soil to make it outproduce their opponents. Retired farmers would work as radio and television announcers, analyzing each competitor's techniques, moves, and strategies. Successful farmer competitors would be well paid and would sign on with Nike, which would change its Swoosh into a scythe.

After school, kids wearing irrigation boots and overalls would head past basketball courts turned into greenhouses to their personal gardens, where they would practice cultivating, planting, and harvesting techniques. Landscaping at every tract home, school, and park, even the lawn at the White House, would be worked up and turned into food gardens, orchards, small dairies, and pasture for animals.

Unemployment and hunger would end. Much of the bloated health-care system would collapse into irrelevance as good food and real work emerge from the nation's obsession with its new competitive sport. Sports facilities across the country would become so fertile that when all the farmers and fans went home and the vast stadiums lay empty, earthworms would come out and dance and carrots would burst out of the ground in an act of immaculate production.

We exit at Salina, Kansas, and take a spontaneous detour to Wes Jackson's Land Institute. Wes is a MacArthur fellow and a botanist, writer, and speaker best known for his revolutionary efforts to create perennial, polyculture grain production on the native prairie. His Land Institute is a place where idealism and science come together as Wes and his colleagues pursue long-range alternatives for sustainable world agriculture.

Though Wes is a longtime friend, I was hesitant to make this stop, not wanting to drop in unannounced and tired of explaining to people who know better why I am away from my fields in the summer. As we wind our way down East Water Well Road, we encounter hundreds of people departing and discover that the annual Land Institute Prairie Festival has just ended. We've missed the speakers, the contra dancing, the workshops and art exhibitions, but I sense the familiar afterglow of a successful event. If you were going to drop names, this would be the place, I think, as I spot some of the well-known artists and thinkers of the sustainability movement: authors Angus Wright and Mas Masumoto, Native American activist Winona LaDuke, social critic David Korten, photographer Terry Evans, and farming's poet laureate, Wendell Berry.

The first person we run into is Wendell. "Does Wes know you're here?" he asks gleefully, and, in his kind, gentlemanly way, proceeds to take us around. My hesitations are instantly dissolved as a number of old friends greet us warmly, asking about my work, about Fairview, about the new farm, and about what the hell I'm doing away from my fields in the summer. I realize that I've had my head down on our new farm in British Columbia for five years, that my sense of community has shrunk to the size of the little island we now inhabit. Here, among colleagues I have admired for years, I'm reminded of the broader tribe I still belong to.

Aaron and I sit down with a small group over a lunch of fried chicken, mashed potatoes, and coleslaw. Wendell is eager to talk about the Amish wedding he had just attended, and the barrelful of perfectly hand-peeled, homegrown Yukon Gold potatoes, later mashed and served as part of a meal that hundreds of people helped grow, prepare, and consume as a natural expression of community.

Terry Evans tells me she is going to be photographing Ken Dunn's urban tomato farm when she returns to Chicago; my neighbor Mary Laucks, who sits on the Land Institute board, remarks that it's nice to see Aaron and me in Kansas, since she seldom sees us when we're all at home in British Columbia. I take the chance to shake Angus Wright's hand and tell him how much I admired his book *The Death of Ramon Gonzalez* and thank him for shining a spotlight on the toll of chemical agriculture on farmworkers.

After days of being captive to the highways of Middle America, we have stumbled in late for the main event but still in time for an embrace, a few words, and a meal. Like any true odyssey, this one is now capped by one more unexpected experience and a touch of light wisdom from the oracles. Back on the road, we look out at rows of long, white, hot-dog-shaped tanks of anhydrous ammonia, the storage units for synthetic gas fertilizers. They flank the edge of a flat and sterile field where the same crop is planted over and over, year after year. If the soil had a voice and could summon whatever energy it had left, it would whimper for help.

Kansas gives way to a very dry Colorado. We stop just over the state border and attempt to have a meal at "Mexican #2," the only place open in the "downtown" strip. We eat something that poses as a chile relleno and then head down the road to a KOA campground that makes most highway rest stops seem like dark, quiet mountain getaways. Huge home-away-from-home casas on wheels are plugged in and humming, oblivious to the brilliant anticrime lighting and the roar of the highway.

The next morning, we stop at a cluster of towering grain elevators and watch as a semitruck pulls onto the scales and stands by for the eight minutes it takes to load it with tons of corn. All this corn is for feed and corn syrup; immense fields require millions of gallons of fuel to plow and plant and water and harvest and ship and store and process, all to feed cows and sweeten junk food. The huge silver-and-white cement monuments to industrial agriculture dominate the landscape. I am fascinated by their size, by their strange sculptural beauty, and how they stand out in this vast flatness.

In the foothills of the Rockies, we follow a long gravel road to see a gypsum mine. I climb under the locked gates and past the "No Trespassing" sign and follow the packed dirt road. After climbing for close to half an hour, I get to the edge of a cliff. There, below me, is an amazing sight: an entire mountain has been removed, shaved away until all that is left is a thin facade resembling a shell bandstand. Beneath it, a perfectly flat, white tabletop the size of a football field is plied by gigantic machines extracting and pushing around piles of white, powdery gypsum.

Gypsum is an intensive-cropping farm's version of cocaine for the soil; it provides immediately available calcium and sulfate-sulfur without changing the soil's pH and keeps heavily cropped soils from "locking up." There are holes in the earth like this all over this country, entire mountains disappeared to fertilize and remineralize mined agricultural soils. Each 50-pound bag of gypsum or rock phosphate or limestone farmers consume is tied to some extraction and natural destruction.

Back on the road, Utah looms like an alien landscape as pyramids of red rock catapult into the sky. At the Big Bend campground, along the Colorado River, Aaron and I spend the day reading, playing drums, and painting ourselves with mud. The next morning, in a predawn departure, we drive through red-rock canyons as the sun rises in a glorious spectacle of light and color.

We stop in Snowville, Utah, to get gas, and wind up in Mollie's Homecooking Café. The walls of the diner are covered in rodeo calendars, Elvis mementos, and a photo of Merle Haggard.

The cowboy-style menu promises chicken-fried steak and huge cinnamon buns. There is special mention that "all Mashed Potatoes, French Fries, and Hash Browns are made daily with Real Potatoes." The cook, Jolene, has been working for Mollie for thirty years; her daughter, Charlotte, has been waiting on tables on and off for almost ten. The local ranchers and truckers file in and are greeted by name.

I order the bacon and eggs and ask that they prepare them with the products from Polyface Farm. There is no hesitancy. A few minutes go by, and, as each egg is broken, there is a gasp from behind the grill. "These sure are yellow!" Jolene yells out from behind the grill. "The way they used to be!"

A 2000 Lincoln Continental pulls up within inches of the door, and out climbs a 5-foot, 11-inch woman with a bleach-blonde beehive that sits about a foot high on her head. She marches in like she owns the place (it turns out she does) and announces, loud enough for everyone to hear, that she's come to get some of the peach cobbler she made that morning. From our booth, I pipe up and ask her whether she used real peaches. She snaps, "What do you think this is—McDonald's or something?"

I ask one of the truck drivers how he can survive on the road eating the bad food typical of most roadside dives. Without answering, he gets up off his stool and beckons me to follow. Next to the café sits his brand-new, shiny tractor-trailer. He opens up a side compartment and reveals a barbecue and a bag of mesquite charcoal. When we return to the restaurant, I give Jolene another fresh egg and ask her to cook it up for him. He requests sunny-side up, and, when it's served, he swivels around on his stool and, with a big grin, says, "It tastes just like Grandma's."

The vast, open rangelands of Colorado and Utah give way to Idaho's huge jumbo dairies and fields of potatoes, dry beans, and hay. Nothing here is small; not the sky, or the mountains, or the distances between anything. The landscape is desolate here, dotted with big, white plastic tubes filled with hay silage and metal storage huts covered with soil and sod. A film of dust covers everything and the dairies can be seen and smelled for miles around.

In the heart of this open, sage-covered valley, my friends Fred and Judy Brossy farm potatoes, dry beans, vegetables, hay, and cows on 300 verdant acres that flourish along the Little Wood River. To me, this is Idaho at its most beautiful, spacious, and thriving, surrounded in all directions by vast rangelands that lead into the nearly unlimited country of the Sawtooth wilderness. Aaron and I pause for three blissful days in the Brossys' comfortable company. While they rush to bring in the last of the pinto bean and Russet Burbank potato harvest, we do endless loads of laundry and repair the van's exhaust leak with a piece of Fred's irrigation pipe. In the evenings, I finally have the chance to share months of stories and thoughts with people I know will understand.

On the morning of our departure, as I reluctantly pull away from the Brossys' place, I call home and find out they're picking pears. Jeanne Marie asks me what to look for with the Bosc: it's tricky to know when they're ready. I tell her to look for a deep, golden undertone beneath the rusty-brown skin. She tells me that little Benjamin insists on helping harvest the fruit, that they set him up on a box to stand on so he can reach the trees. Not too many make it past his mouth.

We chat on the phone as she shells and parboils fresh lima beans with olive oil, salt and pepper, and a few cloves of garlic. She tells me that baby artichokes are waiting for the steamer and that she'll serve them with a salad of Early Girl tomatoes, butter lettuce, arugula, carrots, spinach, and a little radish, topped with a few local grilled scallops. The meal will finish with the last of the French melons and late figs.

Benjamin tells me over the phone that he misses me, and I can picture how much he will enjoy this dinner with all his two-year-old abandon. It hits me like a physical pain that I have missed the summer harvest and the family meals that go with it. This will be the first summer I have not picked fruit from my own trees, not eaten a single melon from my own fields, or gorged on cherry tomatoes or fresh figs. Now, amid the endless expanse of corn, soybeans, and wheat, I am ready to be home. It will be difficult to return and find fields that have finished, to face dying vines and plants scorched by frost. It will be hard to have to wait until spring to put into place all the ideas and schemes bouncing around in my brain, the fruit of this summer's harvest. As I drive, I dictate ideas for Aaron to write down, as if a list will empty my brain, calm my enthusiastic plans, and somehow draw together the threads of our experience.

I went on this journey in search of a movement, as if there were some unified group of people across the country following the same path. I return home realizing that each place requires a different response, and each individual is unique in his or her creative expression. I traveled to gather new ideas, innovative techniques, seeds and tools; I return inspired. I left exhausted from too much work, worried about the fate of the earth, deeply concerned about a nation that had turned its back on its land, its food, and its agrarian roots. I return with a sense of hope and possibility. In a time when we all race about in a blind quest for more, choosing speed at the expense of everything else, those individuals whose days are spent milking and planting and harvesting, those whose daily effort requires watching and waiting and paying attention, whose job it is to nurture soil, grow food, and care for animals, are still there after ten thousand years, quietly guiding and feeding us. I started out with a sense of the importance of local solutions, and now I head for home with a conviction: I know the world must eat; I know that food must be plentiful and safe. But I also know we must aim higher still. There is a richness and complexity that come with lives lived in the pursuit of abundance—not material abundance, but that which come from good relations and careful connections: with the land, with a community of soil organisms, with the plants and animals we eat, and with other people. It's more than the food, I realize, as we make our way west to our last two stops. To gather together around food, food that is of a place, carefully brought forth by a person, is the ultimate expression of love.

♣

Roasted Chicken charred with Rosemary

SERVES 4 TO 6

Theresa Salatin cooked up some amazing meals during our visit with them. The food, which featured their own eggs and meats, was simple and delicious, without any hint of high-flying gourmet pretense.

I'm sure Joel and Theresa will get a laugh at the idea of exposing one of their pastured chickens to the following machinations, but I've eaten the results of this recipe, and it's great. The first time I saw it performed was by its creator, Marc Peel, at one of Fairview Gardens' renowned outdoor Field to the Plate cooking classes. It's the perfect recipe for all you pyromaniacs, but just remember to ignite the chicken outside! When Tasha DeSerio was testing this recipe, she got the crazy idea to fire it up in her garage. Her husband flipped out when he saw a bird on fire and black smoke pouring into the house.

The brine moistens and tenderizes the bird, especially the breast, and the charring makes it taste like it was cooked in a wood oven—which is a treat, coming out of a home oven.

BRINE

⅓ cup kosher salt

¼ cup sugar

5 leafy sprigs fresh thyme

1 bay leaf

4 black peppercorns

3 whole cloves

3 juniper berries

1 small dried red chile

8 cups water

1 whole organic chicken (about 4 pounds)

2 tablespoons olive oil

2 medium yellow onions, cut into ½-inch dice

1 head garlic, cloves separated, peeled and thinly sliced

Kosher salt to taste

Freshly cracked black pepper to taste

2 dozen fresh rosemary sprigs, each about 6 inches long

2 large carrots, cut into 3-inch pieces (optional)

2 stalks celery, cut into 3-inch pieces (optional)

TO MAKE THE BRINE: Combine the salt, sugar, herbs, spices, and 2 cups of the water in a large saucepan. Bring to a simmer over medium heat and stir until the sugar and salt dissolve. Remove from the heat and add the remaining 6 cups water. Transfer the brine to a bowl with steep sides large enough to accommodate the chicken and refrigerate until thoroughly chilled, about 4 hours. Submerge the chicken in the brine and refrigerate overnight.

Preheat the oven to 500 degrees F.

Remove the chicken from the brine and let stand at room temperature while you prepare the other ingredients. Heat a large sauté pan over medium heat. Add the olive oil, onions, and garlic and season generously with salt and pepper. Sauté until the onions are tender, 8 to 10 minutes. Remove from the heat and let cool.

Remove the leaves from 1 sprig of rosemary and chop them finely to yield about 1 tablespoon. Stir the chopped rosemary into the onion mixture. Stuff the mixture into the cavity of the chicken, making sure not to pack too tightly. Season the chicken moderately with salt and pepper. Put the carrots and celery (if using) in a large roasting pan and place the chicken on top, or put the chicken on a roasting rack in a large roasting pan. Pile the remaining rosemary sprigs all over the chicken as if you were building a tepee. Reduce the oven temperature to 400 degrees F and roast the chicken for 50 to 60 minutes, until the chicken is golden brown and the rosemary is charred. Remove the pan from the oven, take the chicken in the roasting pan outside, and ignite the charred rosemary with a match. (An outdoor grill is a convenient place for this burning step.) Let the rosemary burn until the flames die down completely, then return the chicken to the house and let rest in a warm place for 10 to 15 minutes.

Before serving, brush the burned rosemary off the chicken and discard the stuffing. Carve the bird and serve.

Dandelion Salad with Poached Eggs, Bacon, and Garlic Croutons

SERVES 4

Although this is referred to as a breakfast salad, it also makes a great lunch. It's a French-bistro classic with lots of assertive flavors, and crowned with chapons—garlic croutons made from stale bread crust. The croutons are nice if you cut them large before dipping them into the egg yolk, but you can also break them into smaller pieces.

Using true free-range eggs raised locally on a small farm is critical for the success of this recipe. If you want to have some fun, test the difference. Break a store-bought egg from a commercial egg factory into a bowl next to one from a small free-range flock. The shell of the factory-farmed egg will break easily, and the contents will disperse into an undefined mass. By contrast, you'll have to rap hard on the side of the bowl to break the free-range egg, revealing a deep-orange yolk that stands up tall and proud.

GARLIC CROUTONS
½ loaf rustic, country-style bread
2 tablespoons extra-virgin olive oil
Kosher salt to taste
1 clove garlic, peeled

6 slices thick-cut bacon, cut crosswise into ½-inch pieces
1 small clove garlic
Kosher salt to taste
1 teaspoon Dijon mustard
1½ tablespoons red wine vinegar
¼ cup plus 1 tablespoon extra-virgin olive oil
½ pound tender, young dandelion greens or arugula leaves
½ teaspoon white wine vinegar or lemon juice
4 eggs
Freshly cracked black pepper to taste

Preheat the oven to 400 degrees F.

MAKE THE GARLIC CROUTONS USING JUST THE CRUST OF THE BREAD: With a serrated knife, carve the crust off the bread in several long, curved slabs about ¼ inch thick. (Reserve the shaved loaf for bread crumbs or another use.) Brush the crusts with the olive oil and sprinkle with salt. Spread the crusts on a baking sheet and bake until light golden brown, 5 to 7 minutes. When the croutons are cool enough to handle, lightly rub them with the clove of garlic. Set aside.

Heat a medium sauté pan over medium heat. Add the bacon and fry until golden brown, about 5 minutes. Transfer the bacon to a plate lined with paper towels and set aside.

Pound the garlic and a pinch of salt to a smooth paste with a mortar and pestle or the flat side of a chef's knife on a cutting board. In a small bowl, whisk together the garlic paste, mustard, red wine vinegar, and another pinch of salt. Let the mixture stand for 5 to 10 minutes, then whisk in the olive oil. Taste the vinaigrette with a dandelion green; you may want to add a little more olive oil or an extra drop or two of vinegar.

Fill a heavy sauté pan or a medium saucepan with 2 inches of water. Add the white wine vinegar and a pinch of salt and bring the water to a simmer. Crack the eggs one at a time into a small bowl or teacup and gently slide each egg into the water. Poach the eggs for 3 to 4 minutes, depending on personal preference for doneness, turning once or twice. Using a slotted spoon, remove the eggs from the water and gently blot dry with a paper towel. (For a neater appearance, trim the edges of the eggs with a small, sharp knife.)

Combine the dandelion greens, bacon, and croutons in a large bowl and season generously with salt and pepper. Gently toss with just enough vinaigrette to lightly coat the greens. Divide the salad among 4 individual plates, carefully arranging the croutons so they're visible but not smashing the greens. Top each salad with a poached egg. If you have any vinaigrette left over, drizzle a little around each plate. Serve immediately, passing the peppermill and a crock of salt at the table.

CHAPTER 10

NEW ROOTS

I LOVE POTATOES. I'LL EAT THEM BAKED, FRIED, MASHED, SMASHED, for breakfast, dinner, or lunch, in any form and with anything. It's one of those foods I've found everywhere I've been in the world, boiled and served with dhal high in the Himalayas, roasted on an open fire in a *rugo* hut in the mountains of Burundi, mashed and served with fried chicken in Kansas.

These ubiquitous tubers are the envy of the vegetable world, well traveled and accepted every place by every culture. On the slopes of the Andes, in a mud hut at 14,000 feet, as guinea hens raced around my feet and smoke teared my eyes, I ate them roasted on an open fire and served with garlic and chiles. They were dry and floury, so different from the moist Lasota Reds or Pontiacs I like to grow. I can live without bread, survive without a beet or carrot, eat meat or not eat meat, but potatoes I must have, and it is potatoes I'm looking forward to now.

Gene and Eileen Thiel farm at 4,600 feet in the Wallowa Mountains, near the little town of Joseph, Oregon. Known by folks in Portland and Seattle as the Potato Man, Gene was born in Idaho to five generations of root people. Gene Thiel knows potatoes. His grandfather traveled by railroad cattle car from North Dakota in the early 1900s and established the family farm in eastern Idaho.

It's Sunday afternoon as we drive up the driveway to the Thiels' current home, located above town, about a quarter mile from their farm. Gene is just waking from a nap. Eileen is standing on her front porch, looking at a cloudy sky with shafts of light spotlighting sections of the town that spreads out below their home. I introduce myself and then run for the camera, not realizing that this place has beautiful light all the time. When Gene emerges, we greet each other, and he watches as I awkwardly try to fix the camera, which has malfunctioned.

We all hop in Gene's truck, and he takes us out to his farm. The fields are a visual banquet. Big and open and full of light, they are ringed with dramatic peaks and slopes covered in golden grass. The setting is so striking that I wonder how anyone can get any work done here. For Gene and Eileen, this place was the harmonic convergence of ideal potato conditions, a perfect blend of high elevation, deep glacial soils, clean and abundant fresh water, and low humidity.

Gene launches into a potato fish story, about having hauled in a 5-pound, 12-inch russet a few days before. He walks through rows, challenged by his wife to find another big one. I've seen the painted postcards from Idaho with a single potato filling up the back of a flatbed truck, and I've always believed that everyone should have a chance to save face, so I join in the search.

He instructs me to look for a plant with a single thick stem and a slight heaving of the soil around it, telltale signs that a giant is lurking beneath. We walk the rows and find one that shows promise. As he pulls on the hardy stems, a large specimen emerges from the moist ground. It's not a 5-pounder, but it's large enough

to make me gasp. "Get the crane!" I exclaim, and ask how among thousands of plants he knew it was there.

"You develop potato hands," Gene says. "You can sense a potato in the soil." I wonder what it must be like to devote your life to an invisible crop, to grow something that lives and breathes solely in the cosmos of the soil.

I ask Gene why he and Eileen decided on this place, how they came to move to this region.

"I'd read an article in a farm magazine on the production of seed potatoes in this region," Gene responds, and I settle in for the meandering answer I can see is coming. "We were looking for something that wasn't rain forest and had a depth of soil. We made a trip here, and we saw that the land hadn't been exploited. I could see that this wasn't just one pocket of productivity—the whole landmass was productive. I think of my grandfather and father; they had an eye for soil and vegetation. In the Old Country, it was intuitive. You could look at a landscape and see many stories in the soil—you could see plant health, plant size. When you've come from that background, you have that genetic cell memory; you see stuff. When I saw this ground, I knew. You could see the landscape, this rich climate. There's a lot of growth, there's a lot of heat units, there's a lot of regeneration.

"When we first got to our farm," he adds, "I got out and dug in the ground and took a handful and tasted it. The realtor was kind of shocked, and he asked, 'What are you doing there, Gene?'"

When Jeanne Marie and I looked for land in British Columbia, we carried a shovel around with us. The real estate agent thought we were crazy. At every potential farm property, I would spend about an hour digging holes, checking soil depth and structure and life. When we landed on the place we eventually purchased, I must have dug a hundred holes.

"Why potatoes?" I ask Gene.

"Potatoes are part of my makeup," he says. "It's what we struggled to survive on. It's a universal vegetable, and it would adapt well to this climate and this type of soil."

He pulls up a plant, revealing a nest packed full of long, tan tubers with little points like ears and noses. "Here's a LaRatte potato," he says, holding it out and away from him as if he's holding a small, wild animal by its scruff. "They date back to 1700 in Switzerland. They came down into northern France, where they called them Rats, because they got points, like a rat's nose and ears. It's not a glamorous name, but they have a glamorous flavor."

He's moving through the field like he's in some sort of tuber trance, stopping to pull up individual plants, uncovering an astounding range of variety. The 10-acre field has ten main varieties, each of which Gene identifies from their leaves.

"These are true gourmet potatoes," he says, pointing to an elongated yellow potato called Yagana he has just dug. "They are absolutely beautiful. Roasted, they're excellent, with just a little olive oil." He moves on to another one. "This is a Sante potato that came from my younger brother, an Idaho potato farmer. He said, 'Gene, this is the kind of potato you need on your organic farm.' And he was right. It gets bigger than a Yukon; it sets way down. The texture is really great."

If you were watching from above, it would look as if the four of us, wandering up and down the rows with our heads down, have lost something. Eileen interrupts Gene's potato rap and shakes her head as she describes his audacity in arguing the finer points of cooking potatoes with the classically trained chefs he sells to.

Our first evening meal reveals that both Gene and Eileen can hold their own in the kitchen, turning out roasted lamb, French picnic tart, tomato salad, sweet-corn succotash, and, of course, potatoes—five varieties and colors, halved and baked. The meal is topped off with a pie made of homegrown McIntosh apples.

I am always amazed at the deep satisfaction I have after a meal prepared by the folks who have grown the ingredients. Often lacking any recipes or formal training, farmers and food gardeners are always careful not to bury their homegrown ingredients beneath an avalanche of sauce or hide them within some complex preparation.

For growers, nothing speaks more elegantly than the corn or the carrots or the lamb or the potatoes themselves, foods lovingly grown and left simple and uncluttered.

During dinner, Eileen describes her husband's habit of occasionally sleeping in the furrows of his potato field. "Women do get jealous of the farm," she says. "It's like living with a mistress. The farm always comes first. You have to get used to it."

For Gene, a potato is not just a potato. It represents a cultural and family history, a childhood memory, a web of relationships, and a whole range of culinary experiences. "The strongest memories of the land probably come from our youth," Gene tells me. "They're indelible in your mind. If you've worked with potatoes as much as I have, you find out that when they're thrown into burlap sacks, every one has a distinct sound. And you get so indelibly impressed with it that it becomes a form of music. You're tuned to nature, all the vibrations. It's really rewarding to know that you can feel those resonances, that you can totally immerse in them."

In the quiet and repetition of field work, the mind has a chance to expand, the imagination to loosen. It's in those moments when our hands are busy bunching or hoeing or pruning that the essence of our work reveals itself. It comes in small and subtle revelations, like discovering how a certain insect or wild plant has been contributing to the well-being of the farm, or finding one tomato or carrot among thousands with unique qualities worth propagating, or hearing music in the mundane and repetitious work of filling boxes or burlap bags.

In a society so disconnected from natural cycles, farmers have become the voice of the land. Along with all the amazing food we bring to the weekly farmers' market, we also bring a sense of rootedness and a natural wisdom that people seem to long for. The hysteria over arugula or white asparagus is probably just a symptom, a longing for connection to the real world. Gene Thiel and his musical potatoes connect people to that world.

When we wake at 5:30 A.M., there's a chill in the air and a major cloud cover blanketing the west—sober reminders that summer and now fall are coming to a close and winter is close behind. When I get up, it's still dark. I find Gene in the kitchen, making hash browns. He's been at it for a while, carefully moving through a self-imposed regime of grating, squeezing, and slow frying that creates a surprisingly delicate and light, crispy hash-brown cake. He cooks up some eggs and some local lamb sausage, and Aaron and I sit down with him for breakfast, watching the first light edge onto the horizon.

"It's really rewarding to go to restaurants and markets and find people who really appreciate what you're growing," Gene reflects as we finish our meal. "It's fundamental—we need that sustenance, that connection, that completion. When you produce a product and they see its value, it's like searing truth into another person. They taste that truth. It's the ultimate compliment."

Inevitably, talk turns to the world's greatest potato disaster. One million people starved in the 1800s during the Irish Potato Famine, for a tragic reason: the fields were genetically homogenous, a single variety growing on acre after acre, a single variety succumbing to disease. When I was working on my first book in Peru in the early 1980s, I saw small fields the size of a suburban front lawn that contained more than thirty varieties. That genetic diversity was not just to satisfy some aesthetic or culinary need for variety; it was a form of security. If one variety fails or succumbs to disease, others will survive.

"The potato blight we have now is 100 percent man-caused," Gene says passionately, "man-created, and man-sustained, and man-propagated. It's an aberration to grow potatoes as a monoculture—they can't defend themselves. You need to understand all the plant's culture and history; then, you can create a scenario of antagonism to disease. Some of it you have to imagine, some of it you understand, some of it you have to make up."

I am relieved to hear Gene talk about making things up. Having come to farming with no formal education, I feel like I'm making things up all the time. When I started, there was no manual to consult, no expert who could definitively provide advice on the constantly changing world we work with. Every crop, every place, every climate, every year is different. We can establish a set of principles to work by, but our specific responses require waiting and watching and responding creatively in the moment.

The agricultural industrialists have tried to boil it all down to technological and petrochemical solutions to what are essentially biological and spiritual problems. The result has been a disaster for the food system: poisoned food, depleted land, and a huge loss of wisdom and knowledge about how to live on this earth. Those of us trying to provide an alternative have discovered what an unlimited source of creativity and discovery it is each day to work with nature rather than against it. Making things up requires humility, a sense of wonder, and a willingness to pay attention—close attention.

Gene tells us that the *Oregonian* is coming out with a front-page article: "Washington, Oregon, Idaho lead the world in fungicide, herbicide, pesticides pounds per acre on potatoes—275 pounds per acre."

"And they're proud of it," he says.

Gene has seen it from both sides. He farmed conventionally for twenty years with his family near the little town of New Sweden, Idaho, growing potatoes and grain and raising cows. He tells me that although he was part of the industrial-farming scene, he always had different instincts, did things that were not typical of the way most farmers were treating their land. He describes an event that changed his life. "My father had put some triple-sixteen fertilizer out on a field next to where this old farmer lived," he says, almost apologetically. "One day, I stopped by the old farmer's cabin. He called me over and he got really stern—not just stern, but angry—and he warned me about what that fertilizer would eventually do to the land. He absolutely demanded that I sit down and think about that. I was wondering why he was so angry. It was like a sense of foreboding—something went deep into my psyche."

Gene's son Patrick tells me, "I told Dad a number of years ago that we should get into this organic thing," having just discovered the idea himself. "What I didn't realize is that, twenty years before, Dad had helped start Oregon Tilth"—one of the most prominent organic farming organizations.

"I've got brothers in Idaho that I talked to about going organic, and it's terribly frightening for them," Gene says. "There's a big waterfall on the fork of the Snake River, and it's like telling them to go over those falls in a canoe and telling them that they're going to survive. It's that threatening.

"We won a National Potato Award for the protection of the environment, and my son went to pick up the award," he continues. "When some of the other farmers found out that an organic farmer won, they got upset. They didn't get confrontational, but they felt quite threatened, and kind of went into a hushed mode.

"There's some form of entrapment in the commercial potato industry. You're entrapped by your debt. These organic potatoes are extremely more profitable for me than my last involvement with industrial potatoes.

"But it's not just that. I look at my potatoes and think, 'These will go to a certain restaurant, and these will go to certain other restaurants, and I know the chefs, but that's a ton of potatoes, and that's quite a few people in one week who will be consuming them. And I wonder who all those people are and what they'll think of that product, and if they'll feel connected to it.

"It happens every week that I'll be in a restaurant and I'll hear, 'Hey, Potato Man.' That's a very sustaining thing—you feel you have this affirmation with the people who are consuming your food and that it's an extended family.

"You can only work so much and produce so long. But the end result for me is not just succeeding and retiring. It's more a belief and a process of belonging. The practicing is more rewarding than a big blue ribbon and an accolade."

❧

"I AM THE ONLY ONE IN WASHINGTON STATE THAT GROW PENIS," Hilario Alvarez tells us in his broken English as we trail along next to him while he meanders through his fields. "We have green penis, salted penis, and roasted penis. You want to try?"

Green, salted, and roasted *what?* I look back at Aaron, who looks as baffled as I am. Hilario walks a little farther, bends over a row of plants I am not familiar with, and pulls one up. Then I get it. Peanuts!

He strips the peanuts off the roots and hands them to us. I hesitate for just a second, like all those uninitiated folks over the years who have hesitated before accepting my spontaneous offering of uncooked sweet corn or a carrot with soil still clinging to it. We peel the soft shells and savor the taste of fresh peanut for the first time in our lives. Hilario says that he starts them in the greenhouse in March and transplants in May. The customers at Seattle's Pike Place Market go crazy, paying $3.50 a pound for every peanut he grows.

In a neighborhood where many speak only Spanish, the funky plywood sign in front of the farm says, in English, "We Grow a Hundred Types of Vegetables." This diversity is a source of great pride for Hilario and his family. It's also his calling card in the marketplace.

"Eighty-five varieties of chiles, forty-five different summer squashes, fifteen different winter squashes, ten corns, eggplants . . ." Hilario had rattled off this list, unprompted, when I first called him to arrange our visit. This astounding number

of varieties would suggest that he's trialing seeds rather than growing food for the commercial marketplace. In fact, he's doing both: many of the varieties he's now growing and marketing are from his own selections.

While Hilario expounds on the remarkable scope of his operation, I am thinking how amazing it is that he is even standing here in his own fields, planted with his personal vision. In this country, almost all the hoeing and harvesting and milking and pruning are done by Hispanic people, many of whom risk their lives to travel illegally across the border, like Hilario did, to grow nourishment for a nation that will no longer work in the fields. I consider the absurdity of a policy that guards the borders to keep out the very people who produce our food. I imagine what would happen if the borders really were sealed and if all those who had crossed illegally were removed. Food would go unharvested, cows unmilked, and eggs uncollected. I imagine, instead, what would happen if these workers were welcomed and respected for their contribution, and encouraged to expand on their expertise and imagination.

Hilario tours us through Calliope, Nadia, and Orient Express eggplants, Romanette and Liana beans, and Magda, butter scallop, and costata Romanesco squashes. He is used to having visitors who are not particularly well informed, so he seems a bit puzzled when he realizes that this white guy toting a camera and speaking broken Spanish can identify the plants and understands the intricacies of how he is growing them.

The Alvarez farm is flat and ringed in the distance by an expanse of undulating low hills. The air is permeated with the smell of the feedlot across the road. Every winter, after the fields have completed their spring, summer, and fall duty, a spreader truck rolls in, filled with cow manure from the cow pens. The material is turned in and allowed to mellow over the winter months.

In most years, the early frost would have made summer vegetables a distant memory by now, but, this October, Hilario's fields are still packed with peppers, eggplants, and tomatoes, many of which are barely visible for the late-season weeds that tower over them. The pepper field is like some kind of out-of-control block party. Eighty-five varieties, most hot and many from Hilario's own seed, collide in an 8-acre burlesque of color and shape. Every few feet, the variety changes; leaves shift from large green to small gray or purple, fruit from long and hornlike to round and multicolored, like lights on a Christmas tree. The fall weeds waving in the furrows add a wild dimension to an already wild display.

There is humor in this field, a former migrant farmworker's subconscious commentary on the ultralinear, monocultural, totally predictable fields of America's industrial agriculture.

I tell Hilario he is crazy, that I've never seen anything like this before, that he should quit harvesting peppers and open the field up as a seasonal museum. I imagine docents giving tours, stopping to discuss the history and culture and use of certain varieties, the arrangement of color and shape, what the farmer was going through in his life when he planted this section or that, as if they were standing in the Metropolitan Museum of Art, analyzing a Matisse or a van Gogh. But, even as I picture this, I can't imagine how Hilario's exuberance could possibly be contained for contemplation or analysis.

Hilario's pepper field is the hub of energy here; people come and go for peppers day and night. I almost stumble over Koua Lee, originally from Laos, as he squats in one of the rows, picking hot chiles for his store in Seattle. I express my surprise that he would come this far to harvest peppers. He says that he used to farm, that "farming puts you outside the real world and shows you what you really want." I ask him whether his store focuses on organic products. "I don't care about organic—we're all going to die anyway," he responds.

Hilario says he used to show up at the farmers' market with just a few varieties of peppers and that people wouldn't buy much. As his pepper collection grew, so did his sales, and the stand evolved into a major market attraction. Now, the Alvarez stall at the Pike Place Market, with the pepper strands and wreaths and the insane diversity of color and crop, literally stops traffic.

Hilario cruises his pepper field at the end of each season, carefully looking for the unexpected—a new cross, a different color or shape. He does not sell seed, and he tells me there are varieties here that do not exist anywhere else. He corrects me when I refer to the eighty varieties. It's eighty-five, he says sternly.

The buildings and everything around them are in a state of complete chaos here, vehicles parked at every angle, tumbleweeds enveloping anything that hasn't moved for more than a couple weeks, cardboard and plastic strewn across the main area. The machinery here is old and run-down, and every vehicle seems to be on its last legs. Everything is low-tech and simple, with the emphasis on providing jobs to people rather than to machines.

In this untidy riot of color and life, the farming has a beautiful simplicity. It's useless for me to try to elicit some in-depth discourse on the technique or philosophy behind the free-form polyculture that has been established in these fields. It's not that there isn't a great deal of knowledge and thought that has gone into this; it's just that the cultural expression is different. These folks don't seem to have the same need that I do to talk and to analyze, even supposing my Spanish were more than merely serviceable. For Hilario and his family, this work is just what they do, who they are, and where they came from.

Hilario's eighty-year-old mother, Necolasa, and his eighty-five-year-old father, Antonio, sit behind the house under an umbrella with a freezer box, two barbecues, and a battery charger, carefully removing the green husks from piles of corn in preparation for a day of tamale making. His mother shows me ears that are worm damaged and only partially filled out with kernels and explains how lack of water caused both. She points to her son as he is walking away and tells me that he has successfully bridged two cultures, that his understanding of the marketplace, of what people want and how to package and present it, is precise.

Boxes are stacked everywhere, all full of a dizzying array of variously colored, shaped, and sized chiles, tomatoes, and eggplants. Behind the main refrigeration and loading area, a cluster of plum trees provides shade to a group of women and children making wreaths out of chiles. They work late into the night, using a single halogen spotlight jerry-rigged on a makeshift stand. A small electric grill sits on a nearby table, hot and active from early morning to late into the night roasting chiles, heating beans and tortillas.

A crew of young men draw from endless stacks of boxes to load a step van for the three-hour trip over the Cascade Mountains to the Pike Place Market. They tell me they will return after midnight and load up again for a three-day weekend market marathon in Pasco, Seattle, and Yakima.

I get the sense that from early spring until winter, this is a round-the-clock operation. Even darkness doesn't seem to slow things down. I see the shadows of men harvesting by moonlight, the white of their plastic buckets marking their movements in the dark.

Maybe this urgency is the work ethic of someone who once had nothing. In Mexico, Hilario made $5 a day working in a feedlot. Now, he owns his own land, he's built his own house, and he employs more than a hundred people, growing just about everything he can think of.

I think of Gene Thiel, his farming life revolving around the intimate subtleties of a single crop, his passion for farming, and his philosophy, distilled into the infinite nuance and mystery of the familiar. For Hilario, it is all irresistible, reaching out eagerly into the universe, where he can never gather enough in, never try enough experiments, never grow enough varieties and colors and shapes. I remember when I felt that way myself, when I wanted to try everything, touch everything, and express myself in vivid and unmistakable abundance.

I'm somewhere between the two farmers. Hilario's world is an immigrant's dream, where anything is possible; Gene has earned a mastery and quiet reflection I aspire to. I can see my own life and farming on a continuum now, as part of an overlapping of lives and seasons at once constant and unique.

As a full moon rises, it is finally time to eat the tamales. The process took all day, a carefully executed ritual from the harvest of the corn and the husking and grading and removal of the kernels to the grinding and filling of the husks.

Hilario and his two brothers, his grandson, and a nephew sit around the kitchen table with Aaron and me. The women either work in the kitchen or watch a Spanish soap opera that blares on the TV. Each time we finish a tamale, another mysteriously appears on our plates. There will be no refusal here. We eat them with

fresh chili salsa and a little sour cream. When I ask Hilario's mother what's in the tamales, she looks at me with surprise and says, "Puro maíz! No mas," in a tone that implies, "Why would we need to add anything else?"

Aaron and I are stuffed from the late-night tamale orgy. We exchange glances and signal each other that it's time to leave. I thank Hilario and his family for their hospitality. He offers us a stern warning: "Do not go to bed on a full stomach." We take his advice and walk the perimeter of the farm several times. As we walk, we scan the flat, sandy, moonlit fields intently, searching for glints of color or infrared heat emanating from the peppers, imagining in their unseasonal company that summer could have just begun.

♣

It's raining when we get over the pass to the west side of the Cascades. The landscape is lush and green and cool, and it finally feels like we are on our way home, back to our farm, and to the remnants of a season we left behind. The farther north we travel, the cooler the air feels, and the light takes on a winter cast. When we reach Seattle, my excitement increases. I can smell home now and am absolutely determined that, even with limited ferry schedules, we will make it there tonight.

At 4:00 p.m., we get trapped in a sea of traffic just north of the city. I am feeling crazed to be so close but so slowed down. It takes two hours to get to Bellingham, where we stop to pick up a compost-tea brewer that has been waiting for us at a friend's house for the last three months.

At the border, I watch as a customs agent pulls over several cars in front of us. I glance back into our van, now dominated by what looks like a rocket launcher (the compost-tea brewer) and an unruly pile of potatoes, watermelons, peppers, honey, poppy seeds, eggs, tamales, beans, a trumpet, two cameras, a drum, an old sewing machine, and the remains of my friend Charlie Eagle's garlic braid that we left home with almost three months ago. I am certain that when the customs official takes a good look at this rig, its contents, and its two travel-weary inhabitants, he'll want to haul us in for the thorough search.

"What's your status here?" he asks when we pull up to the booth.

"We're landed immigrants," I answer.

"Got anything?" he asks.

I start to go down the list and tell him about the compost-tea brewer, what it does, how it introduces millions of microorganisms into the soil, why that's important for the land. He stops me in midsentence, hands me back our passports, and waves us on.

The last ferry to Fulford Harbor on Salt Spring Island leaves at 9:00 P.M. We each heave a huge sigh when we board the boat. David Wood's Salt Spring Cheese delivery van is on board, along with many familiar faces. The moon reflects on the glassy surface of the water as we glide past the dark shapes of neighboring islands.

I remember our departure across this channel three months ago, how difficult it was to say goodbye, to leave at the start of the season. This year, Aaron and I have had summer in many places, with many people. Now, at last, as we coax the van to its final stop, Jeanne Marie and Benjamin are welcoming us home like ancient explorers returning with a strange harvest, and a long, scribbled to-do list for summers yet to come.

※

Gene's Breakfast Hash Browns

SERVES 2

Gene Thiel takes his hash browns pretty seriously, so much so that, one morning, I woke up at about 5:30 A.M. and found him in the kitchen, already deeply immersed in his hash-browns routine. Served with farm eggs and lamb sausage, they were light and crispy, especially satisfying eaten in front of a large window with a glorious view of the peaks and golden slopes of the Wallowa Mountains.

This recipe is only as good as the potatoes used to prepare it. Avoid using a watery potato such as the average supermarket russet. Instead, use a dry potato with high solids. (A Burbank is best, but it's hard to find; Ranger Russets or Yukon Golds are also tasty options.)

Eileen makes her own garlic powder for this recipe from homegrown garlic. She dries the cloves in a large, homemade dryer (you can do it at low heat or with only the pilot light in the oven) and grinds them in the blender. She treats wild mushrooms the same way, and, apparently, Gene's gotten into sprinkling wild-mushroom powder on his hash browns as well.

1 pound organic potatoes such as Ranger Russet or Yukon Gold, scrubbed
Kosher salt to taste
Freshly cracked black pepper to taste
Granulated garlic powder, preferably organic, to taste
1½ tablespoons olive oil
1 tablespoon unsalted butter

Place a collapsible steamer basket in a deep saucepan and add about 1 inch of water. Bring the water to a boil, put the potatoes in the steamer basket, reduce the heat to medium-low, and cover. Steam the potatoes until just done—they should offer a slight amount of resistance when pierced with a fork—10 to 15 minutes, depending on the size of the potato. Using tongs, remove from the steamer basket and let cool.

When cool enough to handle, peel the skin off the potatoes with your fingers and coarsely grate the patatoes into a large bowl. Season them generously with salt, pepper, and garlic powder.

Heat a medium nonstick frying pan over medium heat and add the olive oil and butter. When the butter is melted, spread the grated potatoes evenly in the pan and fry, turning once, until golden brown and crispy, about 5 minutes per side. Serve immediately.

Rustic Potato and Leek Tart

Eileen Thiel said a small yellow potato, such as Yellow Finn or Yukon Gold, would work well for this recipe. This tart is delicious right out of the oven. With a green salad, it makes a decadent little lunch. The key is to slice the potatoes perfectly thin so they cook at the same rate as the tart dough.

SERVES 6 TO 8

SAVORY TART DOUGH
1¼ cups all-purpose flour
½ teaspoon sugar
½ teaspoon kosher salt
½ cup cold unsalted butter, cut into small pieces
About ¼ cup ice water

1 pound leeks
1 tablespoon olive oil
2½ tablespoons unsalted butter
Kosher salt to taste
⅓ pound small, yellow potatoes such as Yellow Finn or Yukon Gold,
    cut into very thin, round slices
Freshly cracked black pepper to taste
2 ounces fresh goat cheese, chilled
1 egg, beaten
1 tablespoon thinly sliced fresh chives

TO MAKE THE SAVORY TART DOUGH: Combine the flour, sugar, and salt in a large bowl. Add half of the butter. Using your hands, gently toss the butter around to coat each piece with the flour mixture—this helps the butter to cut in evenly. Using a pastry cutter or 2 knives, cut the butter into the flour mixture until it is the texture of coarse oatmeal. Add the remaining butter, gently toss again to coat each piece with the flour mixture, and quickly cut again until the larger pieces are about the size of lima beans. Sprinkle the ice water into the bowl in 2 or 3 additions, using your hands to lightly toss the mixture between your fingers and moisten it evenly. Stop adding water when the dough looks raggedy and rough but holds together when you gently squeeze a small amount in the palm of your hand. Form the dough into a ball—be careful not to knead it, just squeeze it gently into one solid mass. Wrap the dough ball tightly in plastic and press it into a flat disk. Refrigerate for several hours to relax the gluten and chill before using.

Position a rack in the lower third of the oven and, if available, place a pizza stone on top. Preheat the oven to 400 degrees F.

continued >

On a lightly floured work surface, roll out the tart dough into a 14-inch circle. Brush off any excess flour on both sides with a dry pastry brush. Transfer the dough to a baking sheet lined with parchment paper and refrigerate while you cook the leeks.

To prepare the leeks, cut off the roots, trim the tough, dark green tops, and peel off an outer layer or two. Halve the leeks lengthwise and then cut each leek crosswise into thin half-moon slices. Wash the leeks in a large basin of cold water, agitating to remove all of the dirt. When the dirt has settled, scoop the leeks out of the water with a strainer. (It's not necessary for the leeks to drain thoroughly—the water helps prevent the leeks from drying out when sautéed.)

Heat a medium sauté pan over medium heat and add the olive oil and 1 tablespoon of the butter. When the butter has melted, add the leeks and a generous pinch of salt and sauté until the leeks are tender, about 8 minutes. (Add a splash of water if the pan goes dry before the leeks are done.) Remove from the heat and let cool.

In a small saucepan, melt the remaining 1 1/2 tablespoons of butter and set aside. Remove the dough round from the refrigerator and spread the leeks evenly over the dough, leaving a 1 1/2-inch border. Place the potato slices on top of the leeks, overlapping them here and there. Season the potatoes evenly with salt and a few twists of pepper. Drizzle the melted butter over the potatoes and crumble the goat cheese on top. Fold the exposed border over the potatoes, making pleats about every 3 inches, and lightly brush the dough with the egg.

Bake for 15 minutes. Rotate the tart and bake for about 15 more minutes, until the crust is golden. Transfer to a wire rack. Let the tart cool for a few minutes, then sprinkle the chives on top. Serve warm or at room temperature.

Hot Peppers Preserved in Vinegar

This is an easy way to preserve fresh, hot chiles. We can them every fall and eat them right up until the next summer's pepper crop starts to ripen. You can use them in place of dried hot-pepper flakes in most recipes, or pass them around at the table so everyone can add as much spice as they like. We eat them with just about everything: pasta, sautéed greens, beans, and eggs.

MAKES TWO
8-OUNCE JARS

6 ounces small, fresh hot red chiles such as cayenne
(about 2½ dozen peppers)
About 1 cup Champagne vinegar
About ¼ cup olive oil

Halve the peppers lengthwise and then cut them crosswise into thin, half-moon slices. Put the peppers and ³/₄ cup of the vinegar in a medium bowl and stir to combine. Transfer the mixture into two 8-ounce jars with tight-fitting lids. There should be enough vinegar to comfortably cover the peppers; if not, add more as needed. Cover the peppers in each jar with about 2 tablespoons of olive oil and seal the jars. Let the peppers stand at room temperature for 2 days before using. The peppers will keep well for several months stored in the refrigerator.

Char-Grilled Red Peppers with Garlic, Parsley, and Oregano

SERVES 4 TO 6

There's nothing fancy about this recipe, but grilled peppers with garlic and herbs are always delicious. I just wish that everyone had a pepper field like Hilario Alvarez's in their neighborhood. Having access to the astounding range of pepper varieties makes the preparation of this dish so much more interesting; each variety provides a completely different experience. Some of my favorite sweet-pepper varieties are the deep-orange Ariane, the red Lipstick, and Corno di Toro.

10 medium red bell peppers

2 cloves garlic, very thinly sliced

3 tablespoons roughly chopped fresh flat-leaf parsley

2 tablespoons roughly chopped fresh oregano or marjoram

¼ cup extra-virgin olive oil

Kosher salt to taste

Cayenne pepper to taste

Red wine vinegar to taste

Prepare a fire in a charcoal grill or preheat a gas grill.

Place the peppers over high heat and grill, turning as needed, until charred on all sides. If the peppers still feel a bit firm, put them in a bowl and cover the bowl tightly with plastic wrap—the residual heat will finish cooking them. If the peppers are already tender, set aside to cool at room temperature.

When the peppers are cool enough to handle, peel back the blackened skins with your fingers. Discard the skin, core, and seeds. Cut or tear the peppers into strips about ½ inch wide and place them in a medium bowl. Add the garlic, parsley, oregano, and olive oil. Season the peppers with the salt, cayenne, and red wine vinegar and toss to combine.

Serve the peppers as an hors d'oeuvre on freshly grilled bread rubbed with a clove of garlic, or pass at the table as an appetizer with olives, cured meats, and crusty bread.

Fresh Corn Tamales

MAKES ABOUT
12 TAMALES;
SERVES 6 AS AN
APPETIZER

Our tamale experience at the Alvarez farm was organized by Hilario's eighty-year-old mother, Necolasa, and his eighty-five-year-old father, Antonio, who followed a well-prescribed practice that started with harvesting the corn and ended with puro maíz: *fresh tamales served with salsa made of vine-ripe tomatoes and sour cream.*

This recipe was adapted from Authentic Mexican, *by Rick Bayless. It has some extra corn kernels added to the masa dough for texture. The fresh corn makes the tamales sweeter than classic tamales, and they're much easier to make. Try them with grilled skirt steak, sliced avocado, and salsa fresca.*

3 large ears fresh corn, in their husks
½ cup finely chopped scallion
1 pound store-bought fresh masa for tamales
¼ cup unsalted butter, at room temperature, cut into small pieces
¼ cup good-quality fresh lard
1½ tablespoons sugar
½ teaspoon salt
1½ teaspoons baking powder

Using a large knife, cut through the ears of corn just above the base of the cobs. Carefully remove the husks without tearing. Put the husks in a plastic bag and set aside. Remove the corn silk and discard. With a serrated knife, slice the corn kernels off the cobs onto a piece of parchment paper, using the back of the knife to scrape the remaining little bits of corn off the cobs. Transfer two-thirds of the corn kernels into the bowl of a food processor and set the remaining corn kernels aside. Pulse the corn in the processor to a medium-coarse puree.

Add the scallion, fresh masa, and the butter to the bowl of the food processor. Using a teaspoon, add the lard in small chunks to the bowl. Add the sugar, salt, and baking powder. Pulse the mixture several times until the ingredients begin to blend together, then process until the mixture is light and smooth, about 1 minute. Transfer the filling to a medium bowl and fold in the reserved corn kernels.

Place a collapsible steamer basket in a deep saucepan, and add 1 inch of water. Line the steamer with the smallest reserved corn husks—this protects the tamales from direct steam contact.

Using the largest husks (or two overlapping small husks), place about ¼ cup filling just above the base of each husk—the husks will naturally begin to curl around the filling. Fold the top of the husks over the filling to form little packages (it's not necessary to tie the husks closed). Stand the tamales upright in the husk-lined steamer, with the open ends of the husks up. Place a few additional corn husks on top of the tamales and cover. Bring the water to a boil and reduce the heat to a simmer. Steam the tamales until the filling begins to separate from the husks, adding more water if needed, 1 to 1½ hours. Serve warm.

NOTE: Fresh masa is generally available at Mexican grocery stores. To easily monitor the water level when steaming the tamales, place a penny in the bottom of the saucepan. The penny will rattle in the pan as the water simmers. If the penny stops rattling, add more water.

Aaron Ableman

Acknowledgments

Like most books, this one was a collaboration, involving many individuals. I'd like to thank the following people:

Leslie Jonath, who directed her infectious enthusiasm toward this project, both in its inception and in bringing it to publication with Chronicle Books; my agent, Jane Dystel, who, even when the project seemed to be dead, didn't give up until she found it a home; Cynthia Wisehart, who has worked with me on all my books, helped me find my voice, and who brings incredible insight, intelligence, and skill to my work—this book would not have been possible without her. Dona Haber for her help and support in the early stages of the project. John Bergez, who arrived on the scene at a critical juncture and provided important editorial input and valuable support in completing the manuscript. Gretchen Scoble for designing the book with the right balance of visuals and content. Ann Vilesis, who did the research for our journey and created an itinerary out of the confusion of conflicting schedules and locations scattered across the United States and Canada. Zenobia Barlow, of the Center for Ecoliteracy, for her unswerving belief in my work and her moral and financial support toward getting it out there. Alice Waters and the Chez Panisse Foundation, for their very generous financial support. Randy Wright and Color Services for donating all of the processing of the film, and for their great service and technical mastery. Tasha DeSerio, who extracted the recipes from each of the farmers and the chefs they work with, and converted them into a wonderful and practical addition to the book. Elias and Donna Chiacos, Sean Hutchinson, Ann Wisehart, Steve Beck, and Fred Brossy, all of whom took valuable time to read the manuscript and provide me with excellent comments and suggestions for improving it. Anthony Matthews, for his help on the farm during my absence. The board and staff at the Center for Urban Agriculture at Fairview Gardens, for letting me drift away during this long process. Our dear friend Sydney Ocean, for her help and support to our family during my travels, and her partner, Steve, for sharing her with us. My eldest son, Aaron, who not only helped get us 12,000 miles around the country but also provided a quality of companionship that can come only from such a wonderful son. Aaron's personal vision, creative insight, and youthful optimism color every part of this book. My wife, Jeanne Marie, who once again acted as unsung hero, keeping the farm going during our long journey, looking after our two-year-old son, Benjamin, and holding all the pieces of our lives together while I immersed myself in writing the manuscript and editing the photographs. My mother for her love and encouragement. My father, who turned our journey into a personal revelation by bringing to life a piece of my history I didn't know, and who imparted the spirit of rural community to me. Finally, all the farmers we visited and those whom we could not visit, you are the future, your work is the inspiration from which our society must draw, you are the true patriots, and your love of land and good food is a powerful force for change. Thank you all so very much.

Index

table of equivalents

The exact equivalents in the following tables have been rounded for convenience.

LIQUID/DRY MEASURES

U.S.	METRIC
¼ teaspoon	1.25 milliliters
½ teaspoon	2.5 milliliters
1 teaspoon	5 milliliters
1 tablespoon (3 teaspoons)	15 milliliters
1 fluid ounce (2 tablespoons)	30 milliliters
¼ cup	60 milliliters
⅓ cup	80 milliliters
½ cup	120 milliliters
1 cup	240 milliliters
1 pint (2 cups)	480 milliliters
1 quart (4 cups, 32 ounces)	960 milliliters
1 gallon (4 quarts)	3.84 liters
1 ounce (by weight)	28 grams
1 pound	454 grams
2.2 pounds	1 kilogram

LENGTH

U.S.	METRIC
⅛ inch	3 millimeters
¼ inch	6 millimeters
½ inch	12 millimeters
1 inch	2.5 centimeters

OVEN TEMPERATURE

FAHRENHEIT	CELSIUS	GAS
250	120	½
275	140	1
300	150	2
325	160	3
350	180	4
375	190	5
400	200	6
425	220	7
450	230	8
475	240	9
500	260	10